ON THE RECORDs

Also by Graham Sharpe

PROSTrATE Cancer – The Misunderstood Male Killer

Vinyl Countdown

A Gentleman's Guide to Calculating Winning Bets

1001 Great Gambling Tips

Dorothy Paget – The Eccentric Queen of the Sport of Kings
(with Declan Colley)

William Hill – The Man & The Business (with Mihir Bose)

The Man Who Was Screaming Lord Sutch

Free the Manchester United One – The Inside Story of Football's
Greatest Scam

The Magnificent Seven – How Frankie Dettori Achieved the Impossible

ON THE RECORDS

NOTES FROM THE VINYL REVIVAL

Graham Sharpe

Oldcastle Books

First published in 2024
by Oldcastle Books Ltd,
Harpenden, UK

oldcastlebooks.co.uk
@OldcastleBooks

ISBN
978-0-85730-587-9 (Paperback)
978-0-85730-588-6 (Ebook)

2 4 6 8 10 9 7 5 3 1

Typeset in 11.75 on 14.4pt Goudy Old Style
by Avocet Typeset, Bideford, Devon, EX39 2BP
Printed and bound by TJ Books, Padstow, Cornwall

Dedicated to everyone who believes that anyone using the word 'VINYLS' should immediately be banned from ever again purchasing anything from a record shop.

CONUNDRUM

Every time I buy another LP, I believe at that moment that I am enhancing my collection. However, I have to accept that I'm also diminishing the time remaining available to me to listen to the ones I already own. How to square this circle?

IN WHICH...

FOREWORD

All of a sudden, as the end of 2023 came into sight, we seemed to be dragged back to the 60s and the beginning of the long-lasting 'rivalry' between the Beatles and the Rolling Stones.

That 'rivalry' was always something of a media hype – as, don't forget, the Beatles handed the Stones their song, 'I Wanna Be Your Man' to put out as a hit single as early as 1963.

Now, 60 years on, no sooner had the London boys, the Stones, enjoyed a huge hit with the single, 'Angry', and the LP on which it was featured, *Hackney Diamonds* (on which the track, 'Bite My Head Off' features a guesting Paul McCartney) than their Liverpool equivalents issued what was claimed to be 'the very last Beatles' single'.

It was called 'Now And Then', originally penned by Lennon, but which had resisted all completion efforts since the former's death. It had now been brought to a conclusion by McCartney and enhanced by contributions from both Ringo and George. Reaction to 'Now And Then' was mixed, but I absolutely loved its melancholic feel. I found it a very emotional listen and began playing it at least three times a day. Not everyone agreed, and a number of friends whose opinions I respect did not seem to welcome the song, despite the input of all four group members. For me, the accompanying video was the clincher. Tears were blinked away on seeing and hearing the Fab Four back together. Like so many others, I snapped up what could well be both the Stones and the Beatles' final musical contributions, as soon as they appeared.

Surely, with this latest cooperation, and these two singles both topping the charts, the whole pop-rock music and record industry had gone full circle. Likewise our own record-buying lives – for us children of the late 40s/early 50s what in the future could ever top these two momentous, musical miracles appearing virtually simultaneously, just as six decades earlier the two groups had burst into our consciousness, sparking the whole, phenomenal 60s scene and its musical revolution?

INTRODUCTION

Following the publication of *Vinyl Countdown* in late 2019, I had to endure – as have, and will, an uncomfortably large percentage of men of a certain age – various indignities and unpleasantries, imposed entirely – but ultimately very successfully – by overwhelmingly caring and super-competent employees of the NHS.

Their skills and attention proved to be the major factor in enabling me to survive and progress, thus far, beyond most of the efforts of prostate cancer to ensure the opposite outcome.

But I must also record the astonishing ability of music – via both vinyl and CD, which I, of course, listened to regularly at home – to help me maintain a positive outlook whilst undergoing treatment. Such as when the brilliant radiotherapy team found machines to enable me to listen to my calming and involving favourite artistes, such as Melissa Etheridge, Eddy Grant, Roxy Music – who came with me for my sessions.

Thanks, also, to the specialist who offered me the chance to take a look at some of my most intimate organs on a screen with her, while we both happily listened to The Who. This was confirmation for me that my own obsession with music is an ultimately reassuring, and rewarding, trait. However, it appears that my long-suffering wife does not exactly agree with me – when I asked Sheila if she fancied writing something for this book, this is what she came up with:

'Although I have always liked music, Graham's obsession is, for me, too much. Our home is dominated by his collection. As soon as a space is made, he fills it – which makes it nigh on impossible for me to clean properly. This is most frustrating at times – as I like things neat and tidy. But I am no music hater. From about the age of 10 I was interested in music – firstly, the Beatles, then the Small

Faces becoming all-time favourites. I would go to the *New Musical Express* poll winners' concert annually with school friends – and saw the Rolling Stones with Brian Jones, Fleetwood Mac with Peter Green and Jeremy Spencer. Aged 14, and during school term-time, I also went with Susan Brooks to the Valentine's Ball held in a Tottenham Court Road venue. Her dad was an RAF officer, and he took us there. We went inside, and saw Status Quo, with Alan Lancaster. The Herd were also playing, and Procol Harum were there to pick up an award. Rick Parfitt was signing autographs – unfortunately when it came to my and Susan's turn he just said, 'that's it – no more!', got up and went. We were gutted. At the end of the evening, Susan's dad was waiting outside to take us home. I've no idea where he'd been while we were enjoying ourselves, but all he wanted to know was whether we'd had a lovely evening.

The first record I bought was 'A Hard Day's Night', and I also went to the cinema to see the film. I bought most of the Beatles' singles. My first LP was *Beatles for Sale*. My favourite, *Revolver*. I never bought Rolling Stones singles but did purchase *Sticky Fingers*. Small Faces singles were always purchased – and an LP which Graham says would be quite valuable... if it didn't have the scratches! I loved Free and have their *Fire and Water* album. Also liked Bad Company records and, when he is on tour, I will always see Paul Rodgers. I like Vinegar Joe's *Six Star General* LP – Elkie Brooks and Robert Palmer were great to see together. Although I like Brian Johnson, Bon Scott's vocals were better for AC/DC – and I enjoy them having no ballads!'

Hm. Not quite what I was expecting when I asked! So I asked Jan, wife of my fellow prostate cancer survivor pal, Ron Arnold – with whom I bonded while we were both receiving treatment for the condition – how she felt about his vinyl vagaries:

'Ron's hobby of collecting vinyl was okay to start with, but, to my mind, it's now getting out of hand. Not only has he built a large chest of drawers in the spare bedroom (daughter Penny's room), but also a set of shelves in the corner. He now says he needs another set of drawers for more records. He loves vinyl, and it gives him something to do. It gets him out and about on his own, with Penny and Graham, while I get a bit of peace and quiet, and a couple of hours on my own to get housework and washing done. I read and do my puzzle books without interruptions.

Ron is very excited when he brings records home. Some are very old songs from the War, big bands, which I quite like. It makes me feel older when I recognise the songs from the War and remember most of the words. I did tell Ron that, if something happens to him before me, everything goes in a big skip. Of course, I won't do that... well, not before Graham or Penny's friend has seen them! I know, nearly every time he goes to town, he will have a full carrier bag of vinyl, and, of course... some lovely cakes for us – so maybe it's not so bad a hobby after all! Of course, the cakes are a bribe – I don't know whether that helps me forgive him for the vinyl cluttering the house up.'

A theme may be developing here. Still, I very much hope you'll enjoy my latest record ramblings – along with a few from fellow vinylholics.

IN WHICH I WONDER: MORE OF THE SAME, OR SOMETHING DIFFERENT?

The Kinks with 'You Really Got Me', The Troggs with 'Wild Thing', The Four Tops with 'Reach Out I'll Be There', Sandie Shaw with 'Always Something There To Remind Me', The Byrds with 'Mr Tambourine Man' – they all enjoyed huge hits early in their careers, and followed them up with very similar tracks – 'All Day and All of the Night', 'With a Girl Like You', 'Standing in the Shadows of Love', 'Girl Don't Come' and 'All I Really Want to Do' – which duly charged up the chart, almost emulating their predecessors.

On that basis, I wondered when I started to write this book whether to do likewise and concentrate on making the follow-up more of the same?

But then I realised that the Beatles, the Rolling Stones, Manfred Mann, the Hollies, Kate Bush adopted no such tactic when following up their initial hits, just coming up with something different, yet equally attractive to potential purchasers.

This left me considering how, precisely, to follow up *Vinyl Countdown*. My first tribute to the musical format with which I grew up, and to which I've remained stubbornly committed, despite being continuously abused, pitied, vilified, scoffed-at and scorned, for such misplaced loyalty.

I hope you'll agree I've managed to produce a combination of similar-but-different in terms of the content on offer. After all, the subject matter is the same – the wonder of vinyl and how it has survived having the last rites read over it some years ago before slowly but surely reasserting its hold over a significantly large number of long-serving music enthusiasts – and many recent converts. Of course, the genie can't be forced back into the bottle, and streaming, or whatever it is that youngsters do to listen to tunes they like, will remain the dominant musical format du jour. But stats show that the vinyl revival achieved a significant milestone as 2022 became 2023, followed by 2024, and it was revealed that more money had been spent on buying records than CDs by the British public during these years.

This appeared to me to be confirmed by a stunning decline in the cost of second-hand CDs which, in local charity shops, collapsed to as little as 10 for £1 – an ultra-attractive price-point which I was keen to exploit, reaching what was surely a high-water mark in my collecting career when I was able to buy a brand new triple CD of Beach Boys music – 78 tracks in total – for a mere four bob, four of your English shillings, twenty of these new-fangled pence, forty-eight of the proper ones. Ludicrous value whatever the currency.

There are many others, of similar age and vinyly-inclined, who are quite happy ignoring all of the many modern ways of listening to and compiling on some incomprehensible, tiny machine, music they enjoy. They will understand the absolute satisfaction experienced by the three contentedly ageing men seated happily in the reception area at Harpenden's Eric Morecambe Centre, clutching the very different vinyl purchases they had made in the past hour or so from the regular Record Fair being staged in the building.

It is probably not inaccurate to refer to the three tea-sippers as an Unholy Trinity – despite one of their number being a genuine Methodist Church minister. The other two – one of which was my own 71-year-old self – could perhaps also be described as rather ungodly – despite the fact that both of us had probably played the odds by praying once or twice as we each underwent treatment for prostate cancer.

It was undergoing this experience which introduced your author to his now very good, and slightly older, pal, Ron Arnold, as they both received radiotherapy treatment at Mount Vernon Hospital.

The youngest member of the trio, Gordon Lane, is my near neighbour. When we first spoke to each other, we became aware of a shared vinyl addiction. Gordon's musical interests began with

Marc Bolan, mine with Duane Eddy, and Ron's with a variety of late 50s/early 60s acts, but particularly the Shadows.

We have all happily accepted that we are vinyl victims, unlikely ever to be cured. On this day, as we variously drank tea or coffee with, or without, an accompanying biscuit, one of us was content to have spent a mere fiver on acquiring several LPs and singles of enviable vintage; another paid twice as much to acquire just one double ten-inch compilation. And the third, with a pair of records to show for his work, was now three figures worse off.

But all three of us were beaming beatifically inside, despite knowing full well that our better halves would have our guts for garters if they ever found out.

Now, before going any further, how well do you remember the terrible consequence of Covid... the vinyl lockdown?

IN WHICH VINYL IS LOCKED DOWN

Records were an important comfort blanket for many of us during the Covid catastrophe. When it struck, it was concerning for everyone, particularly so for those of a certain age.

In late January 2020, I wrote in my diary: 'Coronavirus is about to kill us all, apparently.' Ultimately it didn't, but it did mean the Robert Cray concert I'd been looking forward to attending was cancelled.

On 3 March 2020, then PM, Boris Johnson, warned that up to 80% of the population could expect to get Covid.

Eight days later, Sheila and I attended what would be our final concert for many months – Bryan Ferry, at the Royal Albert Hall. The gig didn't appear to be sold out – or, perhaps more accurately, a large number of people had declined to attend. After a slightly rusty start, Ferry found his groove and cruised into excellence as the gig proceeded. I also had a rusty start as the woman sitting next to me decided that she wanted to sing along with Bryan, and had to be prompted to desist, unless she could show me her name on the programme.

My diary entry for 14 March 2020 suggests I was feeling less than confident that record shops were going to remain visitable for long, courtesy of Covid. I wrote: 'It is rapidly becoming like living in a disaster movie.' The next day brought rumours that over-70-year-olds – which I wasn't at that point – would soon be facing 'compulsory quarantine'. The record collection was becoming my go-to retreat to try to forget what was happening around us.

On 16 March, Boris Johnson warned everyone to stay away from pubs, bars, theatres and restaurants. He didn't mention record shops... but there weren't many open.

We're booked for lunch in a local pub tomorrow – and intend to go. But will the pub even be open? The threat was moving closer as, on 17 March 2020, Sheila and I attended a 'defy Boris' lunch, to enjoy which, eight of us congregated at The Castle pub on Harrow-on-the-Hill – open, if somewhat – indeed, extremely – quiet, apart from our raucous octet. We have a great time, tinged ever so slightly by a low profile sense of unease. Defiantly, as we departed, we all agreed we'd regroup at a local restaurant in a week if feasible. It wasn't.

However, on 18 March, as the death toll passed 100, there were still CDs to be bought in charity shops, and I snapped up a 5 CD singles 'Definitely Maybe' Oasis 'cigarette box' set for £8.90, which seemed usually to sell for £20 at least. The Covid threat was soon affecting every bricks and mortar record shop, all of which were forced to close on and off, leaving collectors reliant on online and postal dealers. On 20 March, an announcement came that all cafes, bars, restaurants, gyms, leisure centres must close immediately. With most record shops preparing to, or already, shut, and wondering when they might reopen, some feared that they never would. Some didn't.

On the evening of 23 March, we were put into something very close to lockdown. Only permitted to leave home for shopping purposes. One exercise walk a day permitted, and that's about it. I immediately withdrew everything I had been offering for sale online which couldn't be put into a postbox for sending.

Earlier in the day, Wolverhampton's 'Vinyl & Vintage' record shop, run by Claire Howell, began posting information online and, with the lockdown scheduled to begin on 26 March, she advised customers of the 'temporary closure' of her shop under this heading:

VINYL & VINTAGE PHYSICAL SHOP TEMPORARY CLOSURE

Vinyl & Vintage regret that we are temporarily closing our doors due to the outbreak of Covid-19. We feel that it is the responsible thing to do to protect you, us and loved ones.

We will still be offering an online service and you can find some of our listings by visiting our web page www.vinylandvintage.net and click the Discogs link.

Customers who wish to order via our Discogs page should email or text me the order with a possible curb (*sic*) side collection at allocated times and days of the week. We will, of course, also post, in the event you are unable to collect. We will be using Royal Mail only whilst they still operate. Those of you that have items reserved, they will be held for you. We can arrange a curb (*sic*) side collection. This is likely to be on a Tuesday and Saturday.

We will regularly be at the shop organising and pricing and getting stock ready for when we reopen. We shall also be listing new items on our Discogs page. We will not open the door to you if you see us inside!

We are here to help whatever it may be and you can email us direct on its.foryou@hotmail.co.uk or by calling 07760 168972. Claire & Sarah

Reading this, one recalls the sense of uncertainty and concern being felt by virtually the entire population – let alone we record collectors who, at least, had our collections to escape into for temporary respite from the near-panic gradually gripping, well, frankly, all of us. As lockdown continued, there were warnings from UK Music chairman, Tom Watson, that many independent stores could go under if not allowed to meet the demand for vinyl. On 26 March, I must have been getting bored with being confined to barracks courtesy of Covid restrictions – so I started shuffling around my double LP sets to tweak my storage system.

Some six weeks later, on 8 May 2020, Claire was posting:

'Vinyl and Vintage are starting a click and collect service ONLY Monday 11th between 11am and 2pm, AND Saturday 16th, 11am to 2pm. You can call to reserve items to pick up and collect from outside the store. You will not be allowed to enter the store. If you have reserved items already you MUST call for a time slot to collect. We will give you details on how to pay and where to go if you are coming via car or on foot. If you would like to have a look at our Discogs page to see what we have please go to www.vinylandvintage.net and click the Discogs link. Sorry not all our stock is on there but there may be something you'd like, over 3,500 items listed. This is a trial so we will see what happens. And Jamie who reserved some items just prior to lockdown please get in touch.'

This was, at least, an indication that things were, we desperately hoped, beginning to improve and that here was one way to reconnect with vinyl. However, the day before Claire posted this, I had received a surprise text from the NHS telling me that I was considered to be 'at risk of severe symptoms' if catching Covid, and that I should isolate until 30 June. I felt this text was a huge overreaction, probably related to my age, 69, and a recent run-in with prostate cancer. I immediately contacted my GP – this was in the days when one could do such a thing and expect a response before several months had passed. On 11 May, I spoke directly to her, to be reassured that the NHS text was 'somewhat over the top'.

Other record shops were, of course, also struggling to stay afloat and thinking laterally in order to do so – such as Vinyl Vanguard (motto 'stylus over substance') based in St James Street, Walthamstow, which, in a 23 May post, apologised that 'we're not down, just shut down', but offered potential customers home deliveries by bike or on foot.

They came through the crisis, and are fully back up and

running, with Mike and Simon happily 'waiting to engage you in a discussion' (pun probably intended).

Now, on 2 June 2020, back at V&V, Claire had promising news:

SHOP OPENING

'Hello, everyone. We hope you are all doing well in these difficult times, but we hope the worst is behind us now as we look forward to opening on the 16th June at 10am. There will be a few changes. The door will operate on a buzzer system and you will be let in by us. You may be asked to wait in an area just outside the shop as there will be a limited number of people allowed in at any one time. There will be hand sanitiser on the wall that must be used on entering. The counter will have a screen around it and you will not be allowed to enter the office area. We suggest initially that a mask is worn in the shop and perhaps gloves. Social distancing will be required at all times.

We are looking forward to seeing you all. New stock has been ordered and we have the new Lady Gaga exclusive colour and clear vinyl LPs available. The new Rolling Stones colour exclusive and the David Bowie releases will also be in store along with lots of new used stock – 1,000s of 12″ and CD singles in the bargain bins and tons more interesting stock.

During this time, for those who don't wish to come into the store, we will offer a click and collect service at the back of the store for orders via Discogs or by phone.

Record cleaning machines are available for purchase, by delivery by post or collection.

Until the 16th! Stay Safe!'

As a result of Covid, Julian Smith was restricting customers to two at a time in Second Scene, near Watford. As I was rootling amongst records displayed outside, while waiting for a chance to get inside on 17 July, Julian nipped out to see me – I told him he was putting on weight, and we both accepted we were too hairy due to lack of hairdresser visits, courtesy of Covid, while he also warned me he hadn't had a chance to shower that morning – I didn't bother telling him 'me, neither'!

When I was permitted to cross the interior threshold, I bought another Barclay James Harvest LP, and Julian introduced me to a chap who had clearly read *Vinyl Countdown*, accusing me of being 'the bloke who eavesdrops at the Bushey Record Fair'. He's right, mind you.

In September, 2020, I went for my first haircut since lockdown, and when I went to the post office with the Oasis CDs I'd sold the day before, I was quizzed about where my hair had gone! Then, outside, two teenage girls asked if I could help them save a dying baby mouse/rat/squirrel – couldn't really tell what it was – I had to confess my lack of veterinary skills and leave them to it.

My pal Les had told me about a new 'shop', just around the corner from him, opened by an old boy who seemed to be selling off unwanted stuff from his house – including records and CDs. I thought it would be poor manners not to assist him in that endeavour. He also had books, record players and other random stuff but I made a beeline for the records, finding an old favourite from my disco days – the single 'Moon Hop' by Derrick Morgan, on the Crab label, which cost me a quid.

I looked it up in the *Rare Record Price Guide* after playing it and ascertaining it was – unusually for a reggae single – in excellent nick. Just as well, as the RRPG reckoned it a 40-pound 45 – well, that's some sort of reparation for the number of times myself and my fellow long-hairs from those days had to take evasive action to avoid attacks by skinheads (one of whom could well have been the old boy)!

There was now another significant blow to record shops, when the second national lockdown began at midnight on 5 November.

Claire's shop also had to close again but, on 28 November 2020, there was positive news from her:

'Looking forward to seeing you all again at Vinyl and Vintage. We reopen on Wednesday 2nd at 10am – 4.30pm. We have been working hard, pricing and cleaning used stock ready to sell – loads listed on Discogs, but so much more in store. From tapes and magazines and books, to soul 45s and LPs – rock – indie – prog and folk vinyl. Some new releases too – and gift ideas like record bowls with download codes – guitar picks and gift vouchers from £10. Lots more LPs in the 5 for £10 and bargain pick 'n' mix 15 items for £10.'

I really didn't know whether to feel complimented or offended when I walked into the Oxfam charity shop in Pinner, on 1 December 2020, to be confronted by a copy of my own *Vinyl Countdown* book. No, I didn't buy it for myself. However, I did go over the road to St Luke's charity shop, where I had to wait until someone came out before I went in – that's how shop numbers were being restricted. I bought a 12" Wishbone Ash single.

The second lockdown ended on 2 December 2020. On 4 January 2021, a third lockdown was announced by the Government, from 6 January:

'People will only be allowed to leave their homes for the following reasons:
• to shop for basic necessities, for you or a vulnerable person
• go to work, or provide voluntary or charitable services, if you cannot reasonably do so from home
• exercise with your household (or support bubble) or one other person, limited to once per day, and you should not travel outside your local area
• to meet your support or childcare bubble where necessary
• to seek medical assistance or avoid injury, illness or risk of harm (including domestic abuse)
• to attend education or childcare'

It wasn't the end, but maybe the end of the beginning. On 10 February 2021, Claire declared:

'Hi all, hope you're doing well and keeping safe. We are waiting to reopen and in the meantime are ordering new releases and any you want putting aside or posting out just contact us via email: its.foryou@hotmail.co.uk or text on 07760 168 972. You can call too.

New releases: triple Dio colour vinyls with lenticular sleeves – Whitesnake colour – Emmylou colour – David Bowie and Morrissey single – Neil Young – all out this week. Hit the link here on our webpage (or menu button) and go straight to our 'itsforyoumusic' site on Discogs.

Over 6,000 items listed and more being added. Happy to reserve or post out. Thanks for your time and continued support and see you when we are able to reopen or legally do click and collect. Stay Safe and Keep Warm. Claire.'

On 17 March, my sister Lesley – four years younger – sent me a text saying, 'I've run out of oomph. Having Covid has definitely taken my enthusiasm away.'

Her words resonated with me. But it wasn't over yet, and on 2 April 2021, Claire was explaining:

'Hi all! We hope you are all doing well and have kept safe over the last 4 months – we are looking forward to reopening with loads of new and used stock. We shall be opening at 10am on the 12th April until 4pm. May be the only time we open on a MONDAY!!

Lots of in-store offers. For the month of April:

1. For a cash spend of £20 or over a free black record bowl.
2. Loads of Mix 'n' Match CDs/7 inch/12 inch/mags etc., usually 15 items for £10 will now be 20 items for £10.
3. Spend £100 – a free black record bowl and a FREE ROCK PEN – artists from The Beatles to The Clash and Iron Maiden.
4. Lots of new rock / pop t-shirts at £10 each 2 for £18 plus official merch at reduced prices.
5. Official Rock Band Record Deck slip mats £10 each or twin packs for £18 artists The Beatles / Motorhead / Pink Floyd / Queen / AC/DC.'

It was good to hear, on 8 April 2021, that one of the few pleasures still sustaining the nation was... listening to music. This would have been obvious to those of us already of a mind to listen regularly to our record collections – but a survey by the BPI record labels association (no, me neither!) revealed that 'over a quarter of us have increased how much (music) we listen to, compared to before the lockdowns started'. I listened to Capability Brown's 1973 *Voice* LP this evening. It has a quite startling 'zipped mouth' cover.

The pressure of living with lockdowns and Covid was clearly taking its toll by 19 April, as my diary reported that I was 'creating a list of records I'm prepared to sell'. On it were all three Big Star LPs I owned, Graham Bond's *Holy Magick* (these days a £150 record, although mine was not in top condition), a Chapter Three LP, not so sought-after, I fear, and a Syd Barrett, which probably would be.

I must have changed my mind as they all still appear to be in the collection. Phew.

On 2 May 2021, the Entertainment Retailers Association reported: 'Record shops have made a triumphant return to business after the lockdown, with aggregate sales of physical albums – CD and vinyl combined – up 70.7% across the two weeks compared with the same period last year.' The percentage for vinyl was 91%, CD 64.6%.

Perhaps the latest 'end' was in sight by 5 August 2021, when Claire declared to customers new, old and potential:

'Thanks again for your support of Vinyl and Vintage. Just a quick note to say we are open as usual today / tomorrow and Saturday but closed on Tuesday 10 August 2021 and Wednesday 11 August 2021. The dreaded stock-check I'm afraid, but, excitingly, lots of collections to sort and get in the shop. This week we have a small rock collection going out on Friday 6 August and some African and old RSD collectables that were traded in this week. A great Kiss collection of old fan club mags to CDs and DVDs and books and tour programmes.

As always we are happy to buy or exchange (trade) unwanted vinyl and memorabilia and old rock t-shirts posters and CDs. feel free to WhatsApp or call me. So, wrapping up – get yourselves down to V&V!!!'

As Neil Young and Joni Mitchell had already done, Nils Lofgren was reported to have removed his music from Spotify on 29 January 2022. He did so for the same reason as Young and Mitchell, because they believed that Covid misinformation was being spread by the streaming service's 'The Joe Rogan Experience' podcast. Rogan is a 'comedian, presenter, and UFC color (*sic*) commenter'.

I read a fascinating article in an edition of the regular newsletter I receive from Prostate Cancer Research (pcr.org.uk) in which fellow sufferer, 'Jamie', explained how he was inspired by his diagnosis to start fundraising for PCR - which he achieved successfully by approaching rock stars and their representatives, such as Genesis, the Killers, Kate Bush, Coldplay: 'During the first Covid lockdowns I collected signed items that were put up for auction in 2021 - raising £4,000.' Really well done, him.

By 20 February 2022, Claire was at last able to post without mention of lockdowns, closures and problems of that nature:

'SATURDAY 23 April 2022 will see our 10th participation in RSD! Check out www.recordstoreday.co.uk for all the releases. We will be stocking a good selection of these titles listed so please follow us on Facebook for all the details and buying regs! We are still open Tuesday to Saturday 10am to 4.30pm and have been buying lots of excellent collections from Rock to Soul - Reggae and Hip Hop to Jazz and Blues. Including Vinyl and CD and some great magazines and books. Plus some amazing vintage posters from the late 70s onwards.'

Let's hope fervently that we will never be forced back into the frankly fraught and not a little frightening world of lockdowns. Claire wasn't forced to close her shop again... until 9 March 2023 when it happened again, but this time because of a heavy fall of snow. Whilst researching this piece I asked Luke Gifford of The Record Deck, who sells from the rivers he floats along on his barge, whether he had been able to continue doing business during lockdown. He told me: 'No, we were shut, many of the canal traders were closed too, but, actually, not all of them, the fuel boats etc. were still okay to trade, very essential.'

IN WHICH I EXPLAIN FAMILIAR
FAMILIAL STAND-OFF

Please allow me to explain in a little more depth at this point just how Sheila and I reached our present stand-off.

Why, you might wonder, would I be remotely interested in buying a record which only contained tracks I already had on other albums, and looked as though it had seen better days – sporting a cover literally coming apart at the seams? Well, I liked the group, and, yes, I had all the tracks, but not with the same cover design, and I'd had a look at the surface of the record and it looked very little played. But, no, I was well aware that to buy it would certainly mark me out as a helpless vinyl addict. So I slotted it back in amongst the uninspiring selection of other records in the box – classical music, long-gone ballad crooners, forgotten comedians, middle-of-the-road cabaret fodder... NO, sorry, that way lies financial folly, I told myself.

I walked out of the shop, heading back home, clutching the newspaper I'd come out to buy. I got halfway up the railway bridge before I turned round, went back to the shop and bought the record – along with ten CDs.

Yes, I am indeed a helpless, if not hopeless, vinyl addict. But I felt good about changing my mind and making the right decision. I'd liberated the record from its otherwise probable final resting place, and given it a new lease of life.

When I got home, though, I realised I might have trouble smuggling this booty past the ever-vigilant Sheila – always on the look-out for this kind of incomprehensible behaviour, which she believes has a significant adverse effect on her much-prized ability to keep the house clean and tidy. So, I hid the record and CDs in the back of the car, before going in.

If you are sympathising with me at this point, I suspect you're going to enjoy the contents of this book. But should you – totally understandably – side with the logical conclusion that my wife is clearly in the right, we may as well part company here, before we go inside and things become even more difficult to explain.

I also need to confront the ageing pachyderm in the inner sanctum.

What should I do to ensure my record collection goes to a good home/is sold to a trustworthy collector or dealer should I expire in the rather more imminent future than would be my own choice?

I was seventy two years and a couple of months old when I began seriously writing this book. Mind you, the physiotherapist I visited earlier that day had asked me whether my medical records were erroneous in suggesting that I had progressed beyond three score years and ten, when I looked not much older than, oh... sixty-eightish?

It would, though, seem likely that within ten years or so I won't be giving much of a damn about playing any of my psychedelic records, even in the unlikely event I still recognise what they are. Perhaps, then, I ought to begin thinning the collection down to a level which Sheila – certain to be around for many years after I depart – will be able to cope with. If I ask her about that, though, I'm sure she'll just tell me, 'Keep the Small Faces, Free, Bad Company, AC/DC, Vinegar Joe stuff, maybe a few Beatles and Stones albums... bin the rest.' Which is fair enough. She'd still have some 50 LPs and a couple of dozen singles to keep her going. More importantly, she'll still have Julian Smith's telephone number, so that she can ring and tell him I've gone, and ask if he could pop round to see her asap.

I have every confidence that Julian, owner of nearby Second Scene record shop, will be more than happy to drop everything and head round to our house – even though I also have to accept that, as a result, a Watford supporter will thus become owner of a Luton Town fan's vinyl – which is tough for me to come to terms with.

What's the alternative?

Disposing of as many as possible of the ones I can happily live – sorry, die – without, by whatever means I can before the stylus finally reaches the final groove?

Given that I have tried to do this on numerous occasions before and still have 3500+ LPs in the house, this is likely to prove easier in theory than practice.

IN WHICH DICK HELPS LIFT THE FOG

Before we go much further, old friend Richard (Dick) Sear helps me clear away the sweet fog covering some elements of my memory of mid-to-late teenage times listening to sounds, turning on, chilling out and tuning in. I asked Richard for his own memories of blissed-out record listening in the smoky internal environment on way-out 60s Herga Road, Wealdstone.

'Blimey, that's really testing my memory. It was Steve Searle's house, near the Pickford warehouse. He had quite a collection – also, he had coupled together two decks, and an amp which he rigged up in the alcove in his bedroom.

'We would listen to loads of stuff like Pink Floyd – nearly wore out the album *The Piper at the Gates of Dawn* – Bob Dylan, Leonard Cohen, Jefferson Airplane, the album with 'White Rabbit' on it.

'Steve was also a big Gustav Mahler fan... and Beethoven, too.

'I do remember saving up my money and buying an American import *Mellow Yellow* album by Donovan.

'I surprise myself with how much I remember, as it used to get a little 'smoky', if you get my meaning!

'I think the guys who went around to his house included myself, Ian French, his brother John, Ian Wright (Wally), John Kayton (Big Johnson). I'm sure there were loads of others, too?

'We used to buy our records from the shop opposite Sopers in Harrow, I think it was called Stricklands?'

Indeed, it was, Dick!

IN WHICH I FINALLY SELL OUT

Still under constant domestic pressure, in June 2022 I began seriously trying to sort out a stash of records which I'd be prepared to part with. But how to do so?

Selling them is obviously one option.

If one takes them to a record shop, the amount paid is going to have to allow the potential purchaser to make a profit when they sell them on, as most shops are in business not so that the boss can enhance their own collection but so that the shop can remain profitable.

Haven't you noticed what glowing recommendations records that you pick up and ponder over when you're in a shop always get – but should you bring the identical record in to offer to the proprietor (s)he will insist that 'hmm, we see a lot of these, not sure we need any more', or, 'yeah, this was popular only a while ago but I've noticed they don't move as quickly these days', or, 'crikey, you should have brought these in before, they were going for 30 quid a throw, but now the market is flooded and I'd be lucky to get a tenner.'

But if one then decides to sell via eBay, Discogs, Amazon, elvinyl, etc., there is all the hassle of having to catalogue them, and then to transfer that information to the site's chosen way of listing the records. Then, of course, there are usually fees involved for utilising someone else's site from which to get rid of your own items, which can cut down on potential profits as you either pay for advertising the records and/or more when you sell them.

If you do finally manage to overcome the obstacles and eventually secure a few sales, and begin to think that maybe this isn't too bad a way to do business, it is only a matter of time before your purchasers begin to send notes telling you that: when their record arrived the cover was creased; the record was scratched;

it wasn't the edition they were expecting; they'd made a mistake; you sent the wrong pressing; it never arrived, can they have their money back?

I've tried most of these selling options and methods, and they have never seemed to result in a satisfactory feeling once I have undergone the relevant processes. To be honest, I much prefer being a buyer rather than a seller, although I had always quite fancied trying out selling at a record fair, which, as you'll discover, I got the chance to do before I finished this tome... and, to be fair, as I finished writing this very item, a Terry Reid LP I'd ordered recently turned up unscratched, in a perfectly acceptable, undamaged cover, and on time, as per advertised.

IN WHICH THE REAL WORLD KICKS IN

I'd wandered into the shop for a browse. I'd been before and usually found something I hadn't realised I was looking for, so I was optimistic the same would happen. The shop wasn't particularly busy. One or two people popping in and out. I'd identified one record I was particularly interested in, but was still flipping through the stock. A man walked in. Probably a little younger than me, but maybe looking a little older. When he spoke to the shop owner, his voice sounded overloud. He was after a copy of a record he'd heard and fancied buying. It was by Solomon Burke, and called 'Cry to Me'. He wanted a copy on the London label. I knew the song. I told him I'd bought the Pretty Things' version many years ago when they'd recorded it. 'Rubbish version,' he opined. I kept my counsel. Then he mentioned another record he was looking for, Mel Tormé's 'Comin' Home, Baby'. I knew this one, too, but said nothing – my mum liked it.

The shop assistant had done a little googling and discovered that, obviously coincidentally, there was a single out there which coupled both of these tracks together, and was not expensive,

unlike the individual originals, which the RRPG rated at about
£100 for the pair.

By now, though, the man had launched into another, equally
loud, story about something he called 'a capacitator', apparently
part of his hi-fi equipment, which had 'exploded' very loudly
recently. I told him there was a local hi-fi repair shop, Harrow
Audio, which could probably help him in that respect. He carried
on talking, without ever really listening, and without threatening
actually to buy anything. I'd now found another record to buy,
so paid and departed. Once home, I suddenly suspected I may
already own one of them. I checked my lists, and I did.

Next day, I returned to exchange the record for another I'd
decided against buying yesterday as I'd already spent my ration for
the visit.

The shop owner was more than happy to swap the records, and
asked whether I remembered the loud bloke from yesterday.

'Yes, a bit obnoxious. How much did he spend?'

'Do you know, he spent the best part of another two or three
hours in here after you'd gone!'

'Really?'

'Yes, and he got a friend to come down, as well. He spent hours
looking through singles, and came up with about four which he
tried to get for much less than they were worth. At one point, he'd
left a bag on the floor, which I noticed had a load of handwritten
lists of singles in it. I am convinced he and his mate are dealers, and
that they were looking to get records cheap by pleading ignorance.
I'm not sure they didn't help themselves to a few singles while they
were at it, as well. The Solomon Burke stuff was just an excuse to
look around the whole shop and try to rip us off.'

The owner of another shop confided to me that he firmly
believed a 'new regular' had been responsible for departing with a
valuable record secreted about his person, having come in, looked
around, even at stock not yet put on general display, but declined
to remove his overcoat, despite being offered a safe place to hang
it whilst he was crate-digging.

The offer was made as an attempt to prevent the whiff of
BO which was following him around the premises. Eventually,

the non-fragrant gent departed without making a purchase. The owner was pleased to see him leave. However, a few days later, the owner noticed a rarely seen record, of which he knew he had a copy, up for sale on eBay amongst others of completely different genres, being sold in the name of the smelly man.

The owner thought he'd check on his own copy, which he then discovered was missing. Being a generous-hearted gent, the shop owner felt this was probably just a coincidence. However, when later discussing this coincidence in a phone call with the man and making him aware of his misgivings, he felt that the man virtually admitted that he had, in fact, been the culprit. When the shop owner then heard about a record fair incident involving his recently acquired unfragrant acquaintance, the chances of this being another unfortunate coincidence seemed to lengthen. It transpired that a new seller's 'star' valuable record had suddenly disappeared while the stall owner's back was turned. A search, organised by sympathetic neighbouring stallholders, who began asking whether anyone had spotted anything suspicious going on, eventually resulted in the suspected miscreant coming over to the extremely upset stall owner and declaring that he had just 'found' the missing disc amongst a pile of other records he'd been holding and could only assume he'd mistakenly kept it amongst his legitimate purchases.

IN WHICH THEY'RE GOING. GOING. GONE

The auction was scheduled for 18 October 2023.

I had finally and somewhat reluctantly accepted Sheila's urgings that there MAY just be the odd record and/or pieces of record-collecting memorabilia which I might feasibly, possibly, be prepared or persuaded that I might be able to live without. Given that an auction house handling and selling some of my betting and racing ephemera also just happened to organise auctions of vinyl and music-related material, I asked whether they might be able to assess and possibly sell a few exploratory lots for me. It would be intriguing to see what they were prepared to take and prepare for sale and what they would tell me brutally had no value at all and might as well be dumped.

I reluctantly realised that my original, complete editions of the first five copies of the monthly magazine, *The Rolling Stones Book* – number one of which was initially published on 1 June 1964 – may be worth a collective three-figure sum. A little online checking revealed maybe two or three other complete copies of these five together, with recent sales having made a couple of hundred quid. The reason these five are particularly sought-after and scarce, apart from the obvious one that they were the earliest of their type, is that they each contained, as a centrefold, a sketched drawing of the face of a member of the group – making up into a unique portrait of the group when put together. Mine were all in great condition, apart from a very slight discolouration blemish in the top, right-hand corner of number four, published on 10 September 1964.

Whilst working as a record reviewer for the local paper on which I was a rookie reporter in the late 60s, and carrying on doing so for various publications subsequent to that for some years, I also collected a host of publicity photos for all kinds of groups, solo artist(e)s and performers which now represent an absolute gallery of those who were nobodies but became somebodies, and vice versa, together with nobodies who remained nobodies. It is fascinating to look through them, though. Frozen in time, many of these faces ring a bell in the back of the brain but don't quite trigger recognition, but when you admit defeat and look down to see the name there, you often mutter, 'Oh, yes – don't look like that now, do you?' – in much the same way as we all do when we get out the old family photos and later look in the mirror. I've also finally decided to part with some of the material connected with my old friend Screaming Lord Sutch, which I collected whilst researching the biography I wrote about him, *The Man Who Was Screaming Lord Sutch*. These items include one of his famous leopard-skin print jackets, a personal diary, some recorded interviews, and personal items such as his Barclaycard, acquired in the 60s.

At the moment, I am not including any records in this inaugural (for me) auction, but if this goes well that is the obvious next step.

In the event, I was not upset that the Stones mags did not sell, nor did Sutch's jacket, but other stuff did, and I may well relist the other items.

IN WHICH I SENSE CENSORSHIP

Out record shopping at a local street market, I overheard one gentleman, who had spotted a pal and begun talking to him, mentioning that 'there's a new record shop in Hemel Hempstead' – which was news to me.

His friend, definitely not speaking about this new shop in Hemel, just for clarity, told his mate of another shop he knows of 'which has a paedo section – Glitter, Harris, King, etcetera'.

Coincidentally, shortly after this happened, I noticed a post on X/Twitter from @52Vinyl:

'Does anyone think that charity shops shoud (*sic*) have some kind of code for very dubious artists? Thinking of: R Kelly, Jimmy Saville (*sic*) Lost Prophets, Gary Glitter, The f***ing black and white minstrels (*sic*)!

'I see way too much of this crap still on the shelves. They have to do much better.'

This is a difficult issue, to be sure – for example, it could be argued that banning music by now disgraced figures is also punishing others associated with that music, who had no input to, or knowledge of, what the artist was up to away from the recording studio. If Gary Glitter is unacceptable, where do the Glitter Band stand – other than well away from their previous 'Leader'? If the 'dubious artist' was the producer of records for other groups or singers, should that music also be disbarred? Who decides which transgressions should incur this punishment?

Another poster, @CharityVinyl asked: 'I am forever struggling with my 1st pressing of Kate Bush's *Aerial* that has Rolf Harris on it. Do I keep it? Sell it? Listen to it? Ask for my money back?'

'Tough one to answer,' began another responder. 'I dunno... how far do we go... Phil Spector... Ike Turner... Art Pepper... James Brown... Chuck Berry... Jerry Lee...'

Another poster made the point: 'Not disagreeing, but where does the line get drawn between dubious and very dubious? Michael Jackson?'

Posted @thebellow: 'I've know (*sic*) a second-hand record shop that has a 'paedo-box' where they stick all that stuff and give it away.' Does the shop stage a ritual abusing of any customer indiscreet enough to help themselves from the 'paedo-box' would you think?

'Don' offered a solution: 'I volunteer for a charity and run the vinyl – Gary Glitter et al – straight into the recycling, and don't pass go!!'

Where does this end, though? And who decides what is heinous enough to deserve permanent banishment? What if the person is subsequently shown to have been mistakenly accused or convicted? Do we then have to rush out and rebuy everything they ever recorded?

I think it is safer to stick to one's own moral compass and play or ban depending on our own judgement, not the court of public opinion.

Bizarrely enough, browsing through records shortly after writing this piece, I came across a record in my collection, released some 50+ years earlier – which fits neatly into this debate. It purported to be by a group called Sakkarin on the RCA label, marked as being released on 19 March 1971, and bearing the number RCA 2064.

It has a large 'A' in the centre of the label, indicating that it is a 'promo'(tional) copy, sent to journalists in an effort to gain publicity. And the way they were trying to do that with this disc was not to tell anyone what the A and B sides were called. Instead, the A-side label message read: 'For further information please call RCA at 499 3901 EXT 31'. The only clue was the names of the writers of whichever song it actually was – who were 'Barry/Kim'. Now that was a real clue – I thought 'that probably means Len Barry and Andy Kim were the composers'. I was almost right – the Barry was actually Jeff Barry, but I was correct with Andy Kim – and these two actually wrote the massive hit of its day, 'Sugar, Sugar', for cartoon group The Archies.

In autumn 1969, the single topped both Billboard's (for four weeks), and the UK singles chart (for eight weeks), ranking as number one single for the year in both America and Britain. So, was this 1971 composition the same song or a different track, and who were or was Sakkarin? Well the 'who?' is easy. It turns out that it was Jonathan King – yes, him – who had invented the studio group called Sakkarin and rerecorded 'Sugar, Sugar' under that name. It was a rocked-up, anonymously sung version with heavy fuzz-style guitar backing, which reportedly sold over four million copies and charted in several countries.

As for the B side of this record – well, it had absolutely no information on the label, nothing even to hazard a guess with, but a little research revealed that it was a Jonathan King composition, 'Mainline Woman'.

All of which now sets up the morally intriguing question of 'is it acceptable to enjoy music made by someone who has been "cancelled" or written out of history for some kind of moral transgression IF you have no idea that the music was made by such a person, or people?'

I'd say, yes, perfectly acceptable.

Active musician and author – and long-time friend of the late Screaming Lord Sutch, which is how I first made his acquaintance – Alan Clayson also has a view on these moral questions:

'On hearing of Gary Glitter's release from gaol, did a fragment of one of his hits embed itself in your skull for maddening hours on end? In my case, it was the chorus of 'Oh Yes! You're Beautiful'. Is there a moral dimension to the appreciation of artistic achievement?

What about Hitler's paintings, for example – or Wagner's Götterdämmerung?

Certainly, it brings to mind the following statement by Frank Zappa: "All I hear is the music. I don't know anything about the lives of these guys. They may have all been absolute bastards. I probably don't want to know what kind of a guy (Austrian composer, 1883–1945) Webern was, but I like the music. I'm not thinking about who wrote it, or why he wrote it. I'm only listening to the results.'"

I must admit I also own a number of records which it is probably only acceptable to play when one is alone and wearing headphones, just in case anyone else happens to overhear what I'm playing. Not that such a thing would upset or embarrass me, but I wouldn't wish to subject them to something which may cause them angst.

Not that I would ever don the headphones to hear the likes of Rolf Harris' 'Two Little Boys', while I suppose his 'Sun Arise' would be deemed guilty of cultural misappropriation. Come to think of it, maybe 'Jake the Peg' was in dubious taste too.

But I have to admit that I struggle to accept the idea that just because one particular person deems a record and/or its lyrics unacceptable everyone else automatically must go along with their reasoning.

I read an undated article on the 'USA Today' website which damned a string of songs, naming '20 politically incorrect songs that'd be wildly controversial today'.

I tried hard to be offended by all of them, but was a little baffled why I should be, by some amongst them, particularly, Band Aid's 1984's 'Do They Know It's Christmas?' and 'Ebony and Ivory' by Paul McCartney and Stevie Wonder. It is certainly the case that some people are anxious to be offended and will make it their business to be so, or to claim to be so, in order to be able to criticise others, regardless that the motives of those involved were purely altruistic.

It is far too easy now to claim offence has been taken by criticising the past for its failure to live up to someone else's opinion of what today's standards are deemed ideally to be.

IN WHICH FIVE BECOME TWO

News broke of the death of Charlie Watts at the age of 80 on 24 August 2021. A decent age, but still a great shame to hear. I immediately began thinking: 'Can/should they still call themselves the Rolling Stones?'

Of course, I knew Mick and Keith would continue to play under that banner, and, of course, can claim that, because they wrote most of the songs after the early days, it is their band and they can do what they want.

Which begs the question, when one of these two finally goes, will the other carry on with a replacement singer/guitarist?

Somehow, I really doubt it. But, no Brian, no Bill, now no Charlie – for me, no Stones.

Yes, I get that your favourite football team frequently changes players yet remains your favourite football team, but you only watch them, rather than listening.

No one suggests that the Beatles still exist because Paul and Ringo are still around, do they?

I well remember seeing 'Herman's Hermits' perform on one occasion. Peter Noone was long departed. After their very modest act had finished, the drummer came to the front of the stage, informing us that he was the only original member of the band and announcing that 'WE' had sold many millions of records. When precisely does a band become no longer the 'authentic' band and begin tipping over into tribute-band territory?

It clearly isn't an exact science but I was watching television relatively recently when an interview with the Kinks was announced by the presenter. I sat and watched Dave Davies and Mick Avory come on, and begin chatting about upcoming appearances the Kinks were to be making.

Certainly while I was listening, no one mentioned Ray Davies. Could there ever be a 'Kinks' without Ray? Of course not. Without him they could only be described as a tribute/copycat group.

Yet, when AC/DC's Bon Scott died and Brian Johnson joined, there were few dissenting voices claiming that the band were no longer an authentic group.

Could there ever have been life after Phil Lynott for Thin Lizzy? There was – of a sort – but many, probably a majority, would not accept them without their iconic front man. Was Black Sabbath ever truly the 'real' group when Ozzie was on one of his absences/ sabbaticals/sackings?

Back to the Stones, though, and I had recently read a piece by Dylan Jones in London's *Evening Standard*, in which he declared about the Stones – 'who, it has to be said, are better now than they've ever been – and no doubt Keith Richards will outlive us all'. Really?

Who, I thought, are the 'us all' that Keef is tipped to see off?

More importantly, has this bloke not noticed that the Rolling Stones are in fact now just two-fifths of who they used to be? Yes, yes, Ronnie Wood seems to have been granted retrospective 'original Stone' status now. But I'm not falling for that. Was Dylan Jones seriously suggesting that without Brian, Bill and Charlie they are even STILL the Stones? Surely not. As for what they sound like, certainly their LPs over the past many years had been a novelty for a while, then rarely played, eventually just filed away alongside the proper Stones stuff from back in the day.

And then, a teaser campaign for the release of a new LP appeared within the pages of a little known local paper covering the Hackney area of London, in early September 2023.

The record is called *Hackney Diamonds* and, as you will almost certainly now know, it was the latest release by the Rolling Stones.

Quoted in *Metro* newspaper, Keith Richards explained the album title: 'We were flinging ideas around, from "Hit And Run" to "Smash And Grab" – "Hackney Diamonds" is a variation of them both, and we are a London band.'

Seriously!? If the Stones are from anywhere in London, it is surely Dartford, certainly not Hackney – probably better known, to me and other punters, anyway – for its greyhound track of years gone by. And I, for one, had never heard the phrase 'Hackney Diamonds' before.

So, why the new LP wasn't called 'Dartford Diamonds' I have no idea. After all, most of us know it to be the case that both Mick and Keef are from there, having first met each other back in 1961 – and we were recently informed, at the beginning of August, by the *Guardian* (and other media) that: 'Bronze figures of two of the world's greatest rock 'n' roll stars, Mick Jagger and Keith Richards, have been unveiled in their home town of Dartford, Kent, known mainly for its tunnel and bridge across the River Thames.'

This somewhat embarrassing launch method rather turned me against the new album from the start. When the music finally began to make itself known, I saw a rave review of the first single from the album, 'Angry'.

'Angry' was not a terrible single, although highly reminiscent of 'Start Me Up'. It has a decent chorus, but the over-glossy production is not to my tastes – it smacks of style over substance, and of being a song which will diminish at each hearing rather than growing gradually on the listener as used to be the way.

Once again, there seemed to be no consideration for longstanding fans who had been buying Stones' records for some 60 years, and there were echoes here of when loyal fans had to shell out for a double CD of 'greatest hits' tracks they already owned, just to acquire a couple of new ones, a few years ago.

And when all is said and done, for me this new release could in no way be considered a 'real' Rolling Stones record. Only Mick and Keith – ok, the main writers of their material – remain in situ in the band. Long gone are Brian, Bill and Charlie although the middle-named is at least still alive at the time of writing and both he and Charlie (posthumously, of course) do at least feature somewhere or other on a couple of tracks of the new record.

Are the dynamic duo fully entitled to carry the Rolling Stones' moniker on their own?

Mick was quoted by *Metro* newspaper as saying that for one track: 'We asked Bill (Wyman) to come in so we have the original line-up on one track.' Really? I rather doubt there was any Brian

Jones input. Perhaps they were misquoted – another source included 'rhythm section' after the word 'original'.

I'm pretty sure that, if you added together the total sales of every other solo record project by genuine Rolling Stones members – Brian, Bill, Charlie, Keef, Mick, even adding Mick Taylor – the total would be nowhere near that of those issued under the Rolling Stones umbrella.

Reporting on the launch of their new music, *Daily Mail* writer Jan Moir observed of Messrs Jagger, Richards and Wood, somewhat damning them with faint praise in the process, that: 'They are more on the ball than 80-year-old President Biden.' She also offered another reason for the album title: 'The trio explained that (it) is a slang term that refers to the smashed windscreen of a burgled car in Hackney.' Of the claim that 'We're a London band' she also reminded readers that they have been 'tax exiles for the past 50 years or so'.

In my opinion, I'm afraid, like most of us now of a certain age, they are nothing like as good as they were in the 60s, when they were fresh, genuinely exciting and vigorous, and some of the 70s, probably not far past *Exile On Main Street*, after which time they were already beginning to live on past glories.

Nothing much happened to change my opinion from the above, but I did love the response of always outspoken *Spectator* writer Rod Liddle to the new 45, declaring: 'What the new single lacks utterly is that beguiling swing the Stones had when playing smacked out of their heads.' Absolutely. When the new LP landed late in October 2023, I had a decision to make. Which version to buy? On release day, I received several emails offering me the chance to buy a version, of which there were various vinyl formats – Vinilo were first up, asking £45; Pie & Vinyl came up at £31.99, the same price being asked by Sister Ray; Burning Shed appeared to have no copies; Record Corner were asking £29.99; while Amazon were the cheapest at £27.97.

I splashed out £11.99 including p&p for the CD version, from a company called Chalky's UK, from which I'd never purchased before. It arrived early and entirely as advertised.

I listened to the new album four times in quick succession in an effort to familiarise myself with it. But it remains a little too early to say yet whether any of the tracks will lodge themselves in my brain, or whether I will just stash it alongside the other recent(ish) ones, and not make any particular effort to listen to it that many times.

IN WHICH THERE'S A VI-NANCIAL THREAT

Covid was bad enough in terms of directly affecting everyone's record collecting pursuits, but in late 2023 another threat, this one driven purely by one arrogant person, emerged to heap a financial penalty on me, and others like me, and to threaten the turnover of many record shops.

On Friday 15 September 2023 I had my six-monthly dental check-up – not something I traditionally look forward to that much at all, but this time it also meant that I had no option but to pay an outrageous £12.50 ULEZ (Ultra Low Emission Zone) charge imposed by the Mayor of London, for driving my veteran diesel car in the capital. I was originally told that this type of car was a benefit to the planet but, it transpires, it is now apparently capable of killing untold numbers of people the moment the engine is switched on – UNLESS, that is, I pay to do so – in which case, presumably that doesn't happen, or won't matter if it does.

Anyway, once paid, that fee allows me to visit other places I ordinarily wouldn't pay to visit – one of them being Alan's record shop in East Finchley, a very pleasant milieu in which to delve for discs. Alan's opening times can be erratic and it appeared that he wouldn't be open before midday, although *Record Collector* suggested 11.30 is opening time.

I arrived in Alan's environs, and had to drive – at a mere 20mph – some way down the road at the side of his establishment. By the time I park and walk up it is, give or take, noon, and Alan

is demonstrably open, albeit I appear to be his first/only customer
– a state of affairs which doesn't hold sway for long.

The shop was in a tidier state than I remembered seeing it.
I began by flipping through his 'Fiver Sale' which contained a
number of genuine bargains, albeit of records I already owned. So,
over to my default section, where lurk his psych/garage goodies –
many of them obscure in the extreme.

The problem here is having to guess at the desirability of
certain items purely via the info imparted on the cover, or by the
in-record booklet.

The first record I picked out was a, er, copy – I use the word
advisedly – of Art's *Supernatural Fairy Tales* of which I own a CD copy
and know that a pukka original would go for a number of hundreds
of pounds. This one was on offer for £25, was in very decent nick
and I fancied a vinyl copy, so put this one on my 'to have' list.

A steady ingress of people was entering the shop – a middle-
aged couple appeared, one half eager to get stuck in, the other 50
per cent just wanting the other to hurry up. Alan immediately
fussed around, making space for the lady to sit in comfort, which
she did with a stolid, stoic even, air suggesting this was not a new
experience for her.

I spotted a much younger couple chatting outside the shop
window, gesturing happily enough to each other as he came in
and she wandered off.

Alan had been treating us to some Neil Young, but mindful of
the new customer, declared, 'Much though I like Neil, maybe we
should have something a little less gloomy.'

The newbie indicated that he had no problem with the
occasional additional initial to CSN, but Alan was adamant and
on came some fresher sounds – can't now remember what – as
the man engaged Alan in conversation, asking him if he'd be
interested in a few records he'd brought with him – which he was,
a deal duly done to the financial satisfaction of each.

I'd now found a hybrid 12″ by one of my favourites – The Bevis
Frond – 'Ear Song' being the name of one of the six tracks on offer
on this two track, 45rpm A side, with a 4 track, 33rpm B side. No,
I had no recognition of it so that was my second must-have banker.

Sadly, despite looking in absolutely pristine condition, it turned out to have crackles galore when I got it home, but at eight quid I decided to stick with it as it would cost me £12.50 to take it back! Maybe on my next visit to the dentist...

In came another customer – this gent, I would later deduce from their conversation, had some connection to 'David's' in Letchworth – a fine establishment in its own right.

The pair began chatting about the upsurge in record shop numbers, with Alan adamant that, 'There are now 100 record shops in London.' I'm pretty sure Alan is very well informed and quite capable of counting beyond 99, but my first question would have been, 'And what geographical area precisely represents London?' I restrained myself, though, as Alan's subsequent remarks hinted that, if he'd included his own shop in the 100 count, it might soon be coming down to 99.

Because he suddenly, and not sounding over-disconsolate at the thought, revealed that: 'My lease here runs out within a week – I've been here for many years and the landlord has never put up what I pay.'

He didn't seem over-concerned at the thought of possibly having to close down, indicating he'd quite fancy the excuse to do some travelling – he mentioned New Zealand as a possible port of call. But I immediately wondered what he would do with the stock in the shop – maybe a stand-in proprietor while he was away. Seems inconceivable to me that he'd be happy to give up the whole kit and caboodle, but who can say – not me! Subsequent conversations with people better acquainted with Alan than myself produced overwhelming confidence that he would be going nowhere any time soon.

Having gathered up a couple of expanded singles which didn't quite make for full albums, but which were by two groups I have plenty of interest in, The Misunderstood and Elmer Gantry's Velvet Opera – the latter of which features a recorded interview from the time when most of the tracks were recorded live on DJ Brian Matthew's radio show in which 'Elmer' explains where he misappropriated that name from. It also boasts no fewer than three different versions of the only track most people could name by them – 'Flames'. Two members of the Gantry band would go on to greater glories in the Strawbs, before forming (Richard) Hudson (John) Ford.

Alan tots up my bill to 65 quid, but knocks off the fiver, for which I am grateful. I am not a huge bargainer but would have asked for a discount had Alan not pre-empted me. It does irritate me when, in certain shops, no discount is offered even when a significant sum is being handed over.

Alan was also very keen to ensure that I was aware the Art LP I was buying was perhaps not a genuine original version. We parted on convivial terms, with me very much hoping his shop will still be in operation next time I have to visit my dentist – and that Alan will still be in residence.

A couple of days later, I risked another £12.50 charge as I drove over to St Albans to meet up with cancer-mate Ron and his delightful daughter Penny, as we strolled around the regular Sunday market. Ron was looking to have been more successful than I was as he gathered up several records while I had none.

We finally decided it was time to adjourn to a nearby hostelry for refreshment, when, out of the corner of my eye, I spotted a copy of the 'Magical Mystery Tour' double single package, which I'd bought in mono not that long ago in Jersey. This one was in much better condition – and was a stereo version. It was marked at £30. I asked the dealer 'Do you take card payments?' 'Yes.' 'Do you offer a discount for cash?' 'Yes.'

How much for the Magical Mystery Tour – '£30 on the card, £25 cash.'

Money was quickly handed over.

IN WHICH, WHEN IS ENOUGH, ENOUGH?

How many records is (are?) enough records? I've been asking myself this question for so long – the best part of 50 years – yet I've never really come up with the answer.

I'm not the only one... here's what vinyl accumulator Gareth James, who writes for *Clash* magazine, and describes himself on his @justplayed X/Twitter feed as 'Music obsessive. Record shop frequenter', wrote in his excellent 'Just Played – On The Record#6' column in February 2023: 'As somebody who had to engineer a dedicated record room, I can definitely relate to this. How many times have you found yourself wondering if there's still space for one more unit in the area where your beloved tunes reside? Eyeing up a corner... or contemplating how essential that chair really is?' My records live in several rooms, to the despair of long-suffering Sheila.

But, whilst accepting what Gareth says about 'managing' the space available for stashing records, is there any chance that I will one day decide I now have as many records as I could possibly need – and immediately refuse to buy anything new unless I immediately get rid of an equivalent amount of older vinyl?

How, indeed, should the decision to part with a record be made? Okay, you may believe you no longer like the record – but unless you listen to it again at that point, how can you be sure? And to do that takes time. Multiply that time by however many records you secretly believe you might need to lose and you'll find that it represents an unfeasible amount of time, which could better be filled by listening to music you've never heard before on records you've yet to buy.

Gareth also notes: 'There's undeniably something about these magical, physical entities that makes them hard to abandon.' If we were talking here about, say, babies or children, everyone would immediately make that sympathetic sound, and agree that even to think such a thing was scandalous.

Would moving to a bigger house, or building an extension, solve the problem? Well, maybe, but both involve time and expense which could be better utilised listening to, or acquiring, more vinyl. Others have pondered this vital question – including, one imagines, the owners of the Portland, Oregon record shop named 'Too Many Records', which sounds like my kind of shop – or store, as they would probably describe themselves:

'Too Many Records doesn't stock all of the latest and newest album releases, there are plenty of places in town and online to get those. Instead, there's a focus on curated essential records for people building their collection, and rare/out-of-print/unusual records for the deeper collector to sink their teeth into.'

There's an online blogger, who also writes under the heading 'Too Many Records'. He's worth checking out. He's from a younger generation than me, and admits, 'I don't create. I only consume.' He loves vinyl because it is 'expensive, fragile and finicky'. He has 1500 records. So, obviously, he clearly does NOT have too many records. His name is Matt, and his email address is toomanyrecordsmusic@gmail.com should you wish to contact him.

IN WHICH RECORD COLLECTING IS CHANGING

Record collecting is changing. No doubt about it. Not for me personally, or for the majority of people circa my age. We're too long in the stylus for that – we know what we like and that's what we like to buy – and also know how we like to listen to it.

We're also the ones, by and large, who have been thrifty over the years but are now prepared to spend if necessary on acquiring stuff we've never been able to afford, let alone find, to buy. And we are conscious that the number of years left to us for these pleasurable pursuits is dwindling. If you've loved certain types of music for getting on for 60 years, what's the point of waiting until you can 'afford' it? You need to get it now or you never will.

But the music I love and covet comes from between the late 60s and mid-70s, by and large. And the stuff I'd most like to have is stuff that, until I stumble across it, I didn't even know existed – like the LP by Quatrain I have just ordered from mail order dealer Colin Wilkinson, which I only became aware of by reading the list he sends out regularly – written by his good lady wife, Jenny, to regular clients, and those specifically requesting it.

When I saw the description – 'Four piece band based in LA in 1969. Sole psych/prog rock LP produced by future Neil Yong producer David Briggs. Released in UK on Polydor' – my reaction was, 'sounds like my kind of thing'. A little digging on YouTube, Discogs, etc. produced a short burst of their music which I liked. That was enough. I didn't want to hear any more – I want to save it until the record arrives. Yes, I know, I might then hate it, but don't we all like a little anticipation and uncertainty in our lives?

After Quatrain on the list came Quicksand and their LP *Home Is Where I Belong*, which, revealed Colin, was 'originally released on the Dawn label in 1973'. The music is 'progressive pop rock. Includes insert'.

Anyway, this spin away from the original theme of my piece just confirms the thought with which I began it – that fewer and fewer people are now aware of these types of music, which by and large were made for the likes of me and my contemporaries – but clearly not for today's younger potential record buyers.

And the likes of me and my contemporaries are already beginning to die out – I mean, as I write, the current edition of *Record Collector* has a strap line at the top of the front cover – 'Jeff Beck, David Crosby & Tom Verlaine R.I.P.'

There will only be ever more such departures to report.

Fortunately, though, I do now see other, slightly younger, somewhat younger and ridiculously younger people in record shops I am visiting – and in which THEIR music is beginning to be given greater prominence and promotion than mine – which is being nudged off-centre towards the edges of racks and takes a little more looking for than has traditionally been the case as long as I've been, er, crate-digging, for want of a better description.

And whether this changing of the guard is going to result in a rapid diminution of value of the traditionally big-hitting second-hand records is now a matter of conjecture.

Will my *A Saucerful of Secrets, S F Sorrow, We Are Ever So Clean, When You're Dead, Velvet Underground & Nico* (non-banana) LPs remain in the high three-figure valuations, or will they gradually drift ever lower. All of them remain at the same valuation in the

2024 RRPG as they were in 2022, but I'll wager they are likelier to drop than rise in value.

Should I consider revaluing them to reduce my insurance payments?

I don't personally care much whether their worth reduces, as I have kept them because I love the music and enjoy being able to hold and look at them when it suits me, but as a legacy for my kids I'm sure they are certainly fated to be on the way down before long – not that they'd know, anyway!

IN WHICH WRIGHT IS
SPOOKILY WRONG

I heard of the death of former Spooky Tooth lead singer Gary Wright, at the age of 80, in early September 2023, and immediately thought of the now obscure record which forever haunted his career.

A grand-sounding 'World Premiere' took place at Olympia in Paris of this 1969 LP by the mainly UK rock band (although Wright was American) Spooky Tooth, created in collaboration with French experimental composer Pierre Henry. The album was apparently dedicated to 'Béatrice', although I can find no mention of such a person on the record's cover.

Working at the *Weekly Post* newspaper, where one of my many tasks was to write a record review column, I received an out-of-the-ordinary-looking LP towards the end of 1969.

I knew and liked the band involved, but the foldout cover of the record was the most startling and, yes, somewhat disturbing I'd seen up until that point, portraying a man's head, into which was being driven – THROUGH a hand being held against the head – by hammer, a large nail, and as a result blood was trickling down the man's neck.

On the top right corner of the front cover was the album title: 'CEREMONY: An Electronic Mass. Written by Pierre Henry and Gary Wright. Performed by SPOOKY TOOTH/PIERRE HENRY.'

Inside the cover was an equally bizarre illustration, of a presumably female body viewed side-on and being stretched out, with flung-back arms hiding any view of a head. The image hovering above the torso defies description but involves a red-lipped mouth or orifice poised above one of the body's nipples.

These illustrations were by one John Holmes, whose name was recorded under the track listings – six of them, all crediting Spooky's own vocalist/organist Wright.

Wright also topped the names of the group, above Mike Harrison, lead vocals, Andy Leigh, bass guitar, Luther Grosvenor, lead guitar, Mike Kellie, drums. Beneath these names came that of Pierre Henry – 'Electronics'.

Other credits are: 'Realisation Sonore, Pierre Henry, Recording Engineer, Andrew Johns. Produced by Spooky Tooth/Pierre Henry.'

It is now a £100 value record, according to the 2024 *Rare Record Price Guide* – that amount refers to a copy in immaculate condition, of course. However, the highest amount paid for it on Discogs is £59.

The record effectively killed off Spooky Tooth's reputation and integrity – apart, I would say, from Grosvenor, whose work on it is outstanding throughout. But the laughable lyrics and pomposity of the concept kill the rest of it stone dead.

Mike Kellie said of the record: 'We did our tracks, then Pierre Henry came over one afternoon. He didn't speak a word of English. He listened, seemed happy and went away. Then the tapes got sent to him and he finished them. And what came back is what you hear on *Ceremony*. It's an astonishing mix, but it's just crap.'

Wright was left trying to blame his record label for projecting and promoting it as a Spooky Tooth record, claiming, 'We did a project that wasn't our album. We just told the label, this is his album, not our album. We'll play on it just like musicians.'

But it was released very much as a Spooky Tooth record, predictably flopped, and Wright left the band – which didn't affect his career too badly as his 'Dream Weaver' would make him a huge name and he would again be associated with Spooky Tooth in the future.

Prog-rock website Sea of Tranquility reviewed a remaster of the LP, calling it 'perhaps one of the most controversial and puzzling albums ever released'. I agree with the site's observation that 'take away all of Pierre Henry's nonsense, you have what is essentially a kick-ass album from Spooky Tooth'. Exactly.

I had a look at what the various reviewers in 'the fullest ever study of the 60s and 70s UK music scene', the book *Galactic Ramble*, had to say about it: 'Very weird' – NME in '69; 'interesting experiment' – *Disc and Music Echo*, early 1970; 'a freaky, almost frightening electronic mass, almost a musical nightmare' – *Record Buyer*, March 1970; 'one of the worst records of the era... wilful career suicide' – reviewer Giles Hamilton.

Henry died, aged 89, on 5 July 2017.

IN WHICH I COLLECT MY THOUGHTS

Gareth James has written online about matters connected with the size of one's record collection and how this impacts on the owner, and whether it is good to let the collection just keep expanding or best to exercise a modicum of quality control and culling:

'I think that anything which can be classed as a collection will prompt emotional highs and lows at different points and the guiding principle needs to be around what will help you to enjoy it most. Selling off a pile of records to facilitate the purchase of a more expensive but long-desired title could be just the spark to reignite the jaded listener.'

Indeed it could, Gareth – but having done that in the past, with a following regret when what I have replaced the departed discs with proves not to be as desirable as the records they have replaced, I still find it extremely difficult to make any significant cutbacks in numbers.

The 'I might just want to hear that one day' syndrome is compelling, as well as the fact that the same records can provoke different feelings and emotions in one, depending on how that day has been going when you sit down, or wander about, to listen to something.

I have collected a large quantity of Kate Bush records over the years, purely, I believe, as the result of seeing her live at the Palladium in London early in her career on what was, I think, her first tour, in April 1979, which would also be her last for some considerable time! But that show was genuinely thrilling, spectacular and extraordinary. It almost approached levels and inspired feelings that only Vinegar Joe in concert had ever previously reached.

Ten Kate Bush albums received vinyl reissues in October 2023, with the lady herself declaring, 'It is very exciting to see people appreciating the physical presence of an album released on vinyl. It's how it's always been for me, especially when I was a teenager. The whole buzz of the record store was part of the experience. Buying an album was an event.'

Yes, Kate, for me, too, but for sure buying your LPs when they first came out was all the better for not having to pay £33, £41 and £45, which was being charged for these remastered, 180g copies.

On X/Twitter, one Vince Williams, aka @Golfyfun, seemed to agree with me: 'Seriously? The blurb says that "Kate loves indie record shops". Yet she is charging nearly £40 for a single album? No new material, just bog standard releases on silly colours. Sorry Kate, luv, that's ripping off your fans so you can bog right off! #KateBush #Ripoff'

Spandau Ballet member Martin Kemp could not buy records for eight years when the band split up in 1990 because, he claimed in a 2022 Radio Times interview, 'It made me feel physically sick.' No, I'm resisting the temptation.

Here's a closing thought for you. Walking back home this morning, after buying a newspaper, I suddenly asked myself – why is the word for a vinyl disc pronounced 'record'? Yet, when it is used in the context of the creating of a 'record', it is pronounced 'ree-cord'?

IN WHICH I'M NO LONGER KEPT IN THE DARK

One of the few LPs singled out with a value of £15,000 in the 2024 edition of the *Rare Record Price Guide* is DARK's *Round the Edges* – probably because only a dozen copies of this already vanishingly scarce record were produced by private pressing in a colour gatefold sleeve with booklet. And there were only another 52 pressed with different covers.

No, of course it isn't worth that much money to virtually anyone, other than someone who might have been a mate of a group member and either bought a copy back in 1972 when they were touting it around, presumably at gigs, or found one at a boot sale or record fair and were fortunate enough to buy it because it looked vaguely interesting.

I own a copy which might just be worth £15, as it is on CD – although it does also feature a lyric booklet and a copy of guitarist, vocalist and composer of the half dozen tracks, Steve Giles' insert, 'The Dark Round the Edges Story'.

The album might best be described as more than competent, heavyish, proggish with psych flashes – if not flushes. Well, yes, at least ONE flush – a real toilet flush, which appears during track four, 'R.C.8.'

I have no idea whether those initials have any connection to, or with, the flush, which, apparently, was recorded 'by trailing out microphones to the toilet which, being in an old Victorian terraced house was outside' – one was positioned on the cistern, the other over the bowl in order to ensure a stereo effect.

Actually, when I looked at the CD of *Dark Round the Edges* by DARK, I noticed that after the title of 'R.C.8' is added: 'I see hate'. Fair enough.

The other thing I particularly like about the album is (are?)

the lyrics of track two, 'Maypole', which include: 'The air is thin, you're wearing specs, you look like Michael Caine, but your hair is longer and I'm sure your legs aren't quite the same.'

I did actually correspond with Steve Giles when I was seeking out a copy of a more recent DARK offering from 2014, 'Welcome to the Edge', also worthy of your attention. I did so again to ask whether he might be able to let me have a photo of his group to use in this book... which he generously did.

Amongst the scoops I ferreted out from Steve was that he had ordered a copy of my *Vinyl Countdown*, that: 'I plug my CDs at every available opportunity' and, probably the real 'scoop', that: 'My band has always been DARK – although some labels like to use Dark, or even dark – but the uppercase version is the official one – I think I should know.

'However, just to confuse everyone, the famous album is 'Dark Round the Edges' – by DARK.'

Got it, Steve!

Steve also told me: 'I was initially inspired to play guitar by seeing Hank Marvin in the film *The Young Ones*. I later discovered Cream, and that was the trigger to start playing lead guitar and forming a band.

'Trips into the studio in 1970 and 1971 were to get some of my songs recorded properly, but DRTE was recorded purely because I could see we would probably split up and as the line-up at the time was playing very well together, I just wanted something physical to keep for after the split.'

For a full rundown of DARK material now available via Steve, check them out on Discogs.

IN WHICH COLIN COGITATES

Colin Wilkinson, regular seller of records of various types in *Record Collector* magazine, from whom I have bought several prog/

psych vinyl reissues, explained to me how he got into this role and some of the highlights experienced therein.

Colin told me: 'I originally dealt in ex-Juke Box 7-inches, whilst working as a DJ in the 70s.'

During this time he was returning home in his van after a late-night DJ stint when 'I was pulled over by a police car with flashing blue lights and headlights. nervously, I stopped and stepped out of the van. As the officer approached, I recognised him as a customer in the pub where I was working – he was holding a record, which he handed to me, and said: "We've just put out this single, could you help me promote it?"

He was in a local band with his girlfriend. Of course, I took the record and said '"Yes."'

After a mere '25-year break' by which time, in 2004/5, intending to take 'a Gap Year or two', he and wife Jenny had rented 'a remote farmhouse' in the Highland Council area of Scotland, Colin began selling vinyl again – by accident.

Jenny spotted and responded to an advert in the local paper from someone looking to buy record collections. They had got rid of their record deck in 2000 when relocating to Scotland. Jenny had 'mainly 60s Beatles LPs' to sell, and Colin dug out some LPs and singles – 'including the very rare picture cover original of Genesis' "Happy The Man".'

The dealer arrived from Edinburgh and bought all he was offered. Colin 'told him there were more, so he said to ring him when I'd pulled them out. I rang him in a couple of weeks, but he never returned to buy them'.

Having gathered the records, Colin decided to take an advert in *Record Collector* to dispose of them, together with more which he'd bought locally to increase the quantity in the advert space.

'Quite early in RC, I started advertising for collections, and bought two large punk LP and 7″ collections, so listed Punk/New Wave items separately.'

Colin was often now selling out of LPs and unable to replace them. 'I felt it would be hard for me to compete with large stores and internet sellers on mainstream titles by big name artistes so I contacted a distributor of new vinyl for punk LP reissues. I found they also stocked unusual and rare Prog/Psych/Rock reissues – a very limited niche, not often worth it for big stores.

Amongst my first "Rare Reissues" stocked, in 2006/7, was Comus' *First Utterance+* 12″ EP, which sold well. Then, Leaf Hound's *Growers of Mushroom* appeared on the supplier's sale list, so I enthusiastically took their entire stock of this one – about 25 copies. I now needed to expand the range with more titles, and regular new ones to keep customers' interest.

Jenny searched the internet and found a small distributor who seemed to specialise in unusual titles and labels. I was now able to add new titles each month to the growing stock. We stayed with this new supplier as my main stockist until they sadly closed early in 2022. I had, however, learned early on NOT to attempt to pre-sell small label releases. Release dates were, at best, flexible – so, now I simply sell what I have on the shelf, instead of possibly disappointing customers with delayed releases. We have realised over time that more than a simple Artist/Title/Price List is needed – adding info about the artist/music helps customers, and sales increased as a result. Part of this was the creation by Jenny of our Reissue Catalogue, which she still updates for me.'

I told Colin that it is his Prog/Psych listings which make his regular ad one of, if not THE, first things I consult in each edition of RC, and he explained: 'Whilst I do like the general Prog/Psych genre, I think my decision to specialise here was more of a business decision.'

Much though he might wish he could listen to every record he sells, Colin points out that 'time is a big factor – some get played out of interest, or if they are favourites. But I do play any records with marks on them, so as to be able to describe them correctly to customers, many of whom are now long-term regulars, and it is like speaking to old friends when they call – I do have some who insist on their orders going by overnight delivery so that they can receive them without, usually, their wife or mother finding out!'

As with any business there can be less enjoyable incidents: 'I have had two separate customers return LPs which they had clearly damaged whilst opening. A brand new vinyl record was cut through the sleeve – the cut lined up perfectly with the cut of the mailer where a Stanley knife had obviously been used to open the parcel, and another LP, costing £7, was returned to me SEVEN months later – not because of a fault, but because the customer said he "no longer needed it or wanted it" and could I refund his money?

'An occasional customer had bought the Sex Pistols' "Anarchy in the UK" on EMI. Two years later, he rang me, accusing me of overcharging him, as it was only £25 in the *Rare Record Price Guide* and he wanted a refund. At the time I could sell every copy of this 7" I could find, so I offered to buy it back, including his p&p at the price he paid me. He declined. As I explained to the customer, the Guide is just that – only a Guide to price.'

Colin has what he calls 'a modest collection' of his own: 'It is hard to collect and deal too – you can't keep them all, but want to! I have 200, mainly LPs, by artists including Bowie, Hawkwind, Van Der Graaf Generator and Sabbath.'

The first LP Colin bought was by a now disgraced and seldom mentioned performer, mentioned recently in this book, both of whose names started with the same letter of the alphabet, but 'once I heard Bowie's *Ziggy Stardust* LP, that was me converted'.

Colin recalls perhaps the oddest incident to happen to him connected with record-buying:

'About 2008/9, I had a call from a man with around 200 punk LPs and 7"s to sell. He lived in Peterhead, and I arranged to view them. As I was getting close to his address, the mobile rang and the seller told me I would have to come by a different route as his road was closed by the police, owing to a murder!

"This does not bode well," I thought.

After the detour, I saw a man in a suit waiting for me at the end of a narrow alley, which he took me along, then opened the door to his upstairs flat.

As my eyes adjusted, I noticed the steep staircase, covered in books, crockery, magazines, cutlery – no records, though – which we had to stride over.

"Have you just moved in, or are you moving out?" I asked politely, "No! Why?" said the gentleman, sounding puzzled.

He took me into the lounge, and there was a pile of between 30 and 50 LPs. He explained that the rest were still in the loft, as he'd fallen off the ladder and hurt his leg whilst retrieving these. "Don't worry, though" he added, "there are more in my bedroom" - and off he went to fetch them. As I inspected the records, I found many were in the wrong covers - although the vinyl was generally ok - so I set about reassembling them correctly.

Then it got stranger. I came across a record with no cover - "Oh!, the cover to that is in the bathroom, I'll get it" - which he did. Then another two missing covers were retrieved - one from the kitchen, the other from his bedroom. And so it went on. I found a cover with no disc - "Ah, I know where that is" he said, reaching his hand down the back of the settee cushions to reunite it with the cover.

Surprisingly enough, most of these reunited covers and sleeves were fine... however, although he did later ring to tell me he'd now got the other records down from the loft, I decided not to return to buy them!'

IN WHICH WE'RE CALLING COLLINGS

Turntable.records@hotmail.com - email Angela Collings, if you have records to sell; find her online if you're looking to buy. I'm pleased to include here some of the thoughts of this record-selling 'veteran' now based in Bucks:

'Turntable Records has been delighting the market shoppers of Aylesbury, Banbury and Chesham with bargain vinyl and CDs since spring 2018 and is now available for you to enjoy online.

The weird customers are the ones you remember. I had a customer who despite us having 80,000 records in stock and a high rotation of stock would go upstairs to the vinyl and regularly look through. We always left him to it. He never once bought anything.

After about six months of this, I finally cracked and asked him what records he was looking for, as I could try and source them for him. "Oh I don't want to buy any," he replied. "I just go up and smell them." He was a vinyl record-sniffer.

I had a customer who was collecting the Top 40. Every UK record that had been in the Top 40 since the charts began. He died less than a week after completing his collection – which shows you need to have something to achieve to keep you going.

A lady who brought me in a fantastic northern soul collection insisted I give her only £3. I tried to give her more. She refused. As soon as she had the three coins, she said, "Thank you so much, please show my husband the buying-in book when he comes in and make sure he sees I sold them for £3, that will teach him not to cheat."

Of course, he did come in, and started to buy them back at market price. Business is business.

Selling dance vinyl in the 90s at the height of the club scene was interesting. More styluses than records got stolen. I had to stop many a DJ smoking dubious-looking cigarettes as they literally spun the tunes.

One Saturday morning, a customer came in looking wasted after a heavy night clubbing, with pockets full of cash. He literally dropped about a grand in notes on the floor and went to leave the shop. I thought it best to tell him, as I was pretty sure I knew how he had acquired the money.

I used to get a lot of reps dumping product at my store. It was far enough away from London for them to be able to. I had a handy lay-by they would pull up in, sometimes tour managers before going on tour would bring product in. The heyday of the rep in the 90s was also a golden age for the record dealer.'

IN WHICH LOSSES ARE MOURNED

On 8 January 2016 – his 69th birthday – David Bowie released *Blackstar*. Two days later, his death from liver cancer was announced.

'*Blackstar*, completed in great secrecy during what Bowie knew were his final months, was literally his last word to his audience,' mourned Keith Blackmore of Brighton record shop, The Record Album: 'I am not alone among his legion of ardent, lifelong fans in considering it his greatest work. *Blackstar* is the creation of a man facing imminent death, with fear, courage and, this being Bowie, an elegant curiosity.

It is an often opaque and mysterious record, as much of his best stuff tends to be, but there, at the very end, is a final and uncharacteristically frank admission, in which Bowie explains his philosophy in lyrical terms.

Bowie could write brilliant but readily understandable lyrics with the best of them, if he chose to (just listen to 'Space Oddity' or 'Kooks', or 'Life on Mars?' or pretty much anything else on *Hunky Dory*). But once he had discovered the alluring power of being mysterious he never really gave anything away again – until that final song.'

More recently, I'd spotted Keith's Brighton shop in an episode of *The Apprentice* in which the competing teams were set the task of acquiring a copy of Abba's single, 'Waterloo'.

Apart from the fact that few of the (comparative) youngsters in the different teams initially even knew what a single might be, they both eventually found a copy of the record – one team managing to pay just a couple of quid, the other a little less – although both shops admitted they'd have taken less if pressurised a little more. If nothing else, the item was another high-profile plug for vinyl and hopefully reminded many viewers that records are still desirable and buyable for not too much money.

After Bowie, another of my own 60s heroes departed the stage almost exactly seven years later. Jeff Beck died, aged 78, on 10 January 2023 – following Bowie, Lemmy and Rick Parfitt, who have all expired whilst we have been in New Zealand catching up with family over recent years.

Our son, Steeven, took us to an amazing place called 'Helter Skelter' outside NZ capital Wellington, crammed with every blooming thing you could ever imagine being in a massive second-hand emporium, including scores, if not hundreds of preloved leather jackets, toy train sets, books galore, ill-matched 'pairs' of shoes, lawnmowers, kettles, plus records and CDs by the thousands – but all in absolutely terrible condition. Also, when I showed him three or four discs and CDs which looked marginally playable, I got the impression the proprietor was plucking a figure randomly out of the air, in the hope that, being so obviously a Brit on holiday, I might fall for it.

I'd found some Traffic, Hendrix and Lovin' Spoonful CDs I was vaguely interested in, but finally decided to leave them where they looked to be happily at home.

It was a wonderful place to have been and seen, but possibly not the most hygienic we came across and, oddly enough, we were all arguing over which of us could get in the shower first when we returned to our hotel.

IN WHICH I'M INITIALLY CONNED

Preparing to return from New Zealand in January 2023, I took my traditional visit to the quirkiest record shop I've ever come across, 'Wonderland', in which the elderly and deceptively decrepit proprietor goes out of his way to convince you he doesn't want to sell you any record in which you express an interest – none of which is priced.

I dug through the always overflowing, and completely randomly filled, piles of boxes and yards of shelves. I thought by now – this being maybe my third or fourth visit – I was wise to his ways, but he engaged me in conversation, cunningly flattering me about my knowledge of the records I was pulling out of the packed shelves and indicating that I knew more than him.

Which subsequent events proved not to be the truth.

Although he had loads of stuff, I was struggling to find something I really fancied, until I pulled out an XTC LP in a light green paper cover. I thought it might be a £25 record at home, so maybe 50 dollars here.

I prepared myself to haggle with him. Just then son, granddaughter, Georgia, and wife, Sheila, appeared at the door, looking ready to head for home. I didn't want Sheila to know how much I was spending, so quickly and quietly said, 'Okay, I'll have this. How much?'

He hesitated only until Sheila began to enter the shop, at which point he looked at me – 'Go on then, 70 bucks.' I quickly handed over the notes, picked up the record and propelled Sheila through the door, only then realising I'd just paid about 50% more than I'd meant to. D'oh. Oh, well – can't spend Kiwi bucks at home and just to add salt to the wound, the record had a noisy surface when I got it home.

I vowed I'd return to get my revenge. Don't really fancy my chances, though.

A couple of days earlier, we'd been in a holiday resort on the shores of Lake Taupo in New Zealand, visiting that town's record shop, My Music, with my Kiwi-dwelling son, who had just bought two LPs. I came away with a Tony Joe White CD, but had seriously considered a 4 CD, 2 LP Ramones box set at 100 NZ$ and in terrific condition. A dollar was worth 52p this day.

Eventually, I bottled it and decided against... BUT, two days later, having genuinely had an overnight dream – well, nightmare – that I had gone back to the record shop only to find The Ramones box set gone, I thought I'd better go and check whether that was true.

It wasn't. So I bought it. Relief.

Over one year later, I hadn't even played it, although I had played the Tony Joe CD on a couple of occasions. However, by owning such a set I have the satisfaction of knowing that I can, and will, play it when the time is right.

Still in the land of Kiwis, and I THINK he was expressing delight – it was somewhat difficult to tell – but this is how 'Creeps', a record shop in the Wellington suburb of Newtown, announced to customers that it had changed venues, while I was there in early 2023: 'Woah woah WOAH! Today Creeps reopens. We're gonna try and fill some of the fix from the closing of the legendary Rough Peel store. Swing by anytime from 10am. Hanging around till at least 6pm. And tomorrow 11–5.'

A few days later he was declaring: 'Far out, whatta first week at the new store. Quite unfricken believable. It's like... you go from a small, tight space with great regulars, but just getting by, to a new, way bigger space, lots of potential, lots of new regulars, and more cashhhhhh moneyyyyy. On the mean buzz, that dude behind the counter is super-stoked to be trading in the Wu. He's stood by the suburb that's supported the store. Him and his kid are humbly thankful to everyone who comes in. Cos this dream started out as a record fair organiser, then into a record store. 4 record stores later!!! Loves you's lots!'

Translated, I think the boss was enlarging on how he felt on moving to the larger site from his previous 'bijou' off-street location, where I had first visited him a couple of years earlier, when he'd thrown me out within minutes of arriving as he had to go and collect his kid from school.

IN WHICH I'M CANNED IN CAMDEN

Time for a trip to the record shops of Camden. Hadn't been since pre-lockdown – no, tell a lie – I had, but had got there so early that none, not a single one, of the shops had been open – so this time I made sure not to arrive until comfortably after 11am. I'd gone via Euston Station – where commuters were being entertained at one of the free-to-use pianos being scattered around stations at that time, by a gent in an oversized overcoat with a guitar at his feet, who flamboyantly threw out the back of the coat as he took his seat and began to thump out a boogie-woogie number.

I set off walking up towards Camden, passing a pizza takeaway called 'Lost Souls' with skeletons in the window display – albeit this was February, not Halloween.

First shop I visited was 'Out On The Floor' – the guy in charge, whom I didn't recognise from last time, was chatting to a pal who seemed to be a musician and who was talking about a forthcoming album, which would be released on 'the biggest label you've never heard of – it'll look like we've released it ourselves but we haven't'. There were some interesting records at pretty reasonable prices, but nothing which quite justified a purchase.

Aiming for 'Camden Lock Vinyl', I headed towards the Market, only to find that shop firmly closed, which was disappointing. A couple of places inside the Market were selling records – one of them with an old boy behind its counter (about my age!) who sat silently as I looked at the LPs displayed around the place, which were all priced for tourists rather than locals, I thought.

On to another, where I pondered a CD in the *Upside Down* series which covers mega obscure one-off psych-styled tracks. This was No 9 in the series and seemed to consist of Aussie and Kiwi tracks, but I really couldn't decide whether I already owned it. I had to stretch to reach over to the display to pick it up and I felt a muscle in my calf ping as I did so.

The lady looking after the place was enjoying a very loud conversation with an acquaintance on the phone and paid no attention to me whatsoever, even though I was standing very close to her. I stayed within range for a couple of minutes, but still didn't attract a glance.

I figured if she couldn't be bothered to acknowledge me why should I hand over money to her, briefly pondered just walking out, CD in hand, but being basically honest, just stuck it back

amongst other CDs on display closer to hand, and walked out,
limping slightly from the CD-inspired pulled muscle.

I couldn't find the record and CD place inside the Market
that I remembered being there last time I'd visited, so set off to
'Sounds That Swing' on Parkway. This is a shop mostly dedicated
to rock 'n' roll and its close relatives, but I have often managed to
find an oddity or two to appeal here. I walked in to find the shop
empty, and slightly rearranged since my last visit. The gent behind
the counter was engaged in what rapidly became quite a heated
discussion on his phone to someone who, it soon became evident,
was the owner of the shop.

The two were squabbling about a package which the 'man
upstairs' had brought down, and whose contents the guy on the
premises was unsure about, and wanted to know what he should
do with it. The boss seemed to think he should automatically
know what to do with it, but didn't actually outline precisely what
that might be. Neither of them was prepared to accept being in
the wrong, and neither suggested opening the package up to see
what it contained. The discussion/argument/conversation/row
continued, with each of them becoming variously exasperated,
amused, irate, vexed, while I could not avoid listening and
occasionally sniggering. They both seemed to become tired of the
conversation and it was concluded with no apparent concrete plan
of action.

I'd spotted two unusual items, very reasonably priced, which I
fancied purchasing and had not seen before. They were a couple
of CDs – one by John Mayall, the other by Sam & Dave – which
both came in unusual, brightly illustrated, round, tin can-type
containers, and they were just three quid a pop. I purchased
both, later discovering they had been released in Italy and were
apparently unavailable in this country. I wished there had been
more.

That was the itch duly scratched, so I headed off for lunch at
a pub on Kings Cross Station with a long-standing friend. As I
walked back down the road towards Euston Station I noticed on
the other side of the road a madly pedalling, early 20s-looking
cyclist, heading very fast up towards Camden – on the pavement.

The next thing I heard was a crash as he slammed straight in to an unsuspecting and innocent pedestrian. She had been knocked to the ground, with the cyclist and his machine almost on top of her. She was screaming in pain, and shouting continuously: 'WHY are you cycling on the pavement?' Other pedestrians on her side of the road had immediately come to her aid, so I was superfluous to requirements, particularly as I had no medical knowledge to impart.

I had noticed that rock-blues duo, When Rivers Meet, were offering a free CD (the 9-track EP Collection) for only the cost of 'p&p' – so I signed up – but didn't take too kindly to then being invited to add an 'optional' extra amount to the £3.99 being charged.

Thought that was a little sneaky. Had the p&p come up as £4.99 or £5.99, I'd have bought it anyway, so I don't think emotional blackmail was appropriate – ask for however much you want, then people won't be left feeling slightly embarrassed by just paying what was originally requested.

Anyway, moan out of the way, the CD is excellent, and very good value for a penny light of four quid.

IN WHICH SIMON IS NOTT AN ADDICT

Simon Nott is one of the few people your author knows with the same double set of addictive interests – vinyl records and horse racing – and, believe it or not, there is some overlap between the two. Shortly before the text for this book was due to be handed over to the publisher, I visited a record shop and was handed a couple of records, probably made of shellac rather than vinyl, and containing commentaries of big races probably won by the owner of the horses involved. A story such as this was naturally of interest to Simon, who is a freelance who often works for on-course bookmakers on their betting pitches.

But here Simon tells me about his vinyl varieties:

'My name is Simon and I'm a vinyl addict. I wasn't always addicted, I used to save what I could when I was a young teenager, and when I had enough, would hitchhike the 14 miles to Exeter to buy records.

Don't tell my mum, she'd have kittens, but that bus fare was probably a 7" – hitchhiking was common, and let's face it, it was a no-brainer. Those records were cherished and played until they wore out. My genre of choice was rockabilly. I'd discovered it aged 14, when Matchbox had a hit with "Rockabilly Rebel".

Before that I'd cut my teeth on Gary Glitter. I was very loyal to Gary and felt you couldn't really like anyone else if you like one artist as much as I loved Gary's music. I bought the singles and retrospectively the *Glitter* and *Remember Me This Way* albums, which I played to death. You are a bit of a bastard aren't you, Gary? I can't really look fondly at my musical childhood without it being tainted by your subsequent shaming. I was secretly glad when Gary hung up the platforms, because I was free to learn about new music – punk. Deliciously forbidden songs with swearing and exciting music given to me on mixtapes by an older punk who would have been all of 15.

After weeks of waiting by the radio in the hope that the BBC would accidentally play "God Save The Queen" on the Top 20 show, my mixtape man gave me a new compilation with that banned track on it. I rushed home with the tape, excited to hear it – only to be asked by my dad, "And what makes you think you'll be able to play that in this house?"

I was, from that moment on, a teenager at 12. It's lucky the old boy never heard "Bodies".

1977 was a year of musical mangling. Punk was everywhere, and after 16 August and his death, so was Elvis and rock 'n' roll. I like both. I also admit to hearing Sid Vicious' versions of Eddie Cochran's "Something Else" and "C'mon Everybody" before the originals.

In that time, local shops that sold records were supermarkets, Woolworths and the local piano shop. None any good for music that wasn't in the charts.

During my last year of school, an independent record shop opened. They sold some great stuff, though were doomed to fail – having fag and pinball machines meant that it was the venue of choice for skint schoolkids skiving not buying.

Back to my post-Matchbox awakening. I'd discovered rockabilly. I'd buy compilations, and play them over and over. I remember the first time I heard the *Elvis '56 Sessions* album and Mac Curtis' "Grandaddy's Rockin'" on the Gusto label's *King–Federal Rockabillys* compilation.

My inaugural sense of "collecting" records was when I read with horror in the *NME*, or was it *Sounds* – I'd go hungry on a Thursday and buy them both instead of fags or dinner – that the Polecats had also released their debut single "John, I'm Only Dancing" on 10" pink vinyl. I'd only just bought the 7", but I had to have it. My thumb was out on the way to Exeter at the first opportunity.

I loved my records so much, a lot of them still have an extra groove in the runout where I'd fall asleep with headphones on in bed, the needle rolling around until morning.

Then psychobilly emerged, The Meteors, coloured vinyl, picture sleeves and discs.

There's a gap from then and now. I kept buying the compilations while I was in the Army and annoyed the hell out of my roommates with my obscure 50s favourites.

In the 90s, I was often travelling with bands in Germany. I was also skint a lot of the time so my Meteors, and a lot of other psychobilly albums, were sold to fund beer, while the bulk of my collection still languishes with a mate over there who looked after them... and never gave them back.

Then I started buying CDs, of which I have hundreds. Fast forward to now. I'm bitten by the vinyl bug again, Discogs and Facebook record-buying groups are my crackhouse. I have amassed boxes and boxes of obscure records. I only have to see, "limited to 200 copies", "pressed in puke vinyl" and the like, and I'm compelled to buy it, COMPELLED! Before you can say, "But Si, you'll never play it", I've bought it. They arrive almost daily, delivered by postmen who look at me with a mixture of rage and pity. I justify my purchases because, of course, they'll all be worth more in the future.

Even dafter, wait for it, I have two children under the age of ten, I can't play my precious vinyl in their presence. I mean, come on, imagine a record surviving decades and continents only to be scratched beyond playing by over-zealous offspring knocking the needle.

Yes, I have a problem. My record collection might as well be one of stamps. They just sit there, hoarded in an ever-decreasing space. But there is hope, a utopia; in a few years' time the kids will be at school, my wife at work and I can spin, spin, spin those records, they'll be my absolute delight cranked right up.

This very day I bought two records, one was in coke-bottle green and in a gatefold sleeve, limited edition. Yes, it's serious. I've just self-excluded from my favourite 45s selling group on Facebook, apologies to my dealers especially Sean in Arkansas. It's only for a while, I can handle it, can't I...?'

PS by GS: Simon did confess to me that he'd recently bought '33 singles from the guy I call "my dealer" in the US, including four by Carl Perkins and three by Sanford Clark – they cost from two to twenty dollars each – the justification in my mind is that they (the prices) are in dollars, and I'd easily double my money if I sold them here... I won't, though, will I?'

IN WHICH I MOURN PEOPLE I NEVER MET, FOR PETE'S SAKE!

I'd heard of the sad loss of a man I never met – that of Peter Dunton, the all-too-little-known rock drummer, who wrote and played on, to me, one of the most important records I own – T2's *It'll All Work Out in Boomland*, released on Decca in 1970. Shortly before the LP was to be released, with the band then called Morning, someone discovered there was already an American band with that very name – and they quickly chose the name T2 as a replacement. One of the few records I received to review in the *Weekly Post*, where I worked at the time, that I've kept to this day, it is also one of the even fewer to stun me into virtual disbelief upon hearing it. It was the record I would have loved to create had I been remotely capable of doing such a thing – I wasn't. It was psychedelia with a (very) heavy coating of rock. Original vinyl copies of the record are valued at £300 by the most recent *Rare Record Price Guide*, but I suspect you'd do well to find one in excellent condition at that price.

The group consisted of just three musicians, Bernard Jinks on bass, teenage guitar prodigy, Keith Cross, and the composer of the four tracks on the record, drummer, Mr Dunton.

Peter had also been involved in a number of other groups before T2 – The Flies, Neon Pearl, Please – for all of which he wrote great songs. In his closest brush with fame, he also had a short time with The Gun of 'Race with the Devil' fame. I've managed to collect seven CDs of his music, several LPs and a solo single. I don't think I've ever heard one of his songs I didn't like. He sang the majority of them, too, in a distinctive, straightforward manner.

The news of Peter's death, as a result of a brain tumour, in January 2022, was announced by his partner Jackie. Friend and musician, Andrew Keeling, who played flute on a T2 track, 'Closing Your Eyes', paid tribute:

'A few weeks ago I had a video call with Peter following his operation and found him tired but in unusually high spirits. Ever the optimist, Peter never gave up on his music, once saying to me, "I consider myself as good as the next man." Obviously very modest, too, as I would definitely regard him as an unusually talented musician and better than most "next men".'

Reports suggest that Peter recorded an unreleased solo LP for RCA, from which a single, Taking Time/Still Confused was released in 1973, which I was delighted to acquire recently, apparently recorded at Dave Edmunds' 'Rockfield' studio, on the record label of the same name, and also produced by Dave.

More recently, it seems, he had also played with Sun Dial, the vehicle of guitarist and singer Gary Ramon, who started recording in the 80s as The Modern Art and whose music is described as being rooted in late 60s psychedelia.

I'd call Peter probably the most important late 60s/early 70s musician that most people interested in psychedelic rock have never heard of.

IN WHICH I GO ON A
WATFORD WANDER

On Facebook, broadcaster Darren Harte complains justifiably that: 'A national newspaper (I use that term VERY loosely) called Bonnie Raitt "an unknown Blues singer" in an article after her 2022 single, "Just Like That", won the Grammy Award for Song of the Year.'

He added: 'If they cannot get facts on something that isn't "important" correct, why do people believe, and buy, this tripe on a daily basis?'

Darren had also discovered a single by the St Winifred's School Choir, on offer for a tenner in a local charity shop... form an orderly queue.

Still reeling from the St Wini's bombshell, I went wandering in Watford, and noticed a new branch of HMV had opened. I was impressed with its layout, giving great prominence to vinyl and CDs, as well as stocking record players. I was inspired to purchase a Kinks' CD of their *Muswell Hillbillies* album. Next day, having discovered I already owned the Kinks CD, I returned to Watford, to swap it for a Jack White.

I was en route to the Vinyl Café, where I noticed they had tidied up the storing and presentation of their records. I searched through most categories, only vaguely attracted by a Climax Chicago single, which I half suspected I already own.

Then I came across a Robert Palmer LP I had never seen before. Closer examination revealed that it was some kind of promotional record – and at a mere fiver it was soon transferred into my ownership. It appeared to be called *Armchair Explorer* and was, according to the centre label, 'made in USA'. The record is on the Productions Allied – or, possibly, Allied Productions – label and this copy is numbered 089. It contains 15 named tracks, some from each of his first three LPs, plus a few others which I haven't yet traced to specific records.

In the LP blurb, Palmer claimed bizarrely that, whilst living in Malta as a small child, he was 'taught to swim at the age of three' by Tarzan – well, at least, actor Johnny Weissmuller, who played that role in movies, and was himself a champion swimmer. It played perfectly and is one of the best bargains I've picked up recently.

Following his stint in my all-time favourite live band, Vinegar Joe, with Elkie Brooks (previously in the rather less commercial Dada, where Robert arrived after they'd recorded their one LP) during which the impression did not come across – to me, anyway – that the twin vocalists were bosom buddies. Both eventually went their own way, achieving chart successes in their own style.

I was recently a little surprised to learn that Robert and fellow Island label artist John Martyn were pally and that Robert was involved with the latter's 1984 *Sapphire* LP, recorded in the Bahamas, earning this complimentary namecheck: 'An extra special thank you to Robert Palmer without whose help this album may never have been made.' This is clearly proof that 'opposites attract' as the smooth Robert and somewhat scruffy John, with their very different vocal styles, would not seem a natural fit for each other.

In 1993, Robert became a naturalised Swiss citizen, having moved there in 1986. An interview with Californian partner Mary Ambrose, in 2010, revealed an unexpected side to Robert's non-musical interests: 'He makes remote-control trucks and planes, he builds them himself,' Mary told the *Mail on Sunday* shortly before Robert's death. 'Sometimes he will wake me up in the middle of the night and say, "Mary, I have lost a spring from the plane I'm building." I'll say, "I'll find it in the morning," and he'll say, "But I need it now" so I get up and find it.'

In an interview after his September 2003 death, Elkie spoke about Palmer: 'Robert already had his career mapped out a year before he told us he was leaving the band (VJ). We were just a rehearsal band for Robert Palmer – but it never worked out that way. I got picked on by the media and I was the focal point of the band.'

When the band folded, the two went their separate ways: 'I hadn't seen him for going on 27 years although I kept in contact with his parents. They always kept me well informed as to what he was doing and gave me the latest CDs but yeah, it (his death) really was a shock. I feel on a one-to-one basis I thoroughly enjoyed his company. He was a very, very sophisticated and intelligent guy.'

IN WHICH I TALK OF
GUILTY PLEASURE

I decided to listen to something by one of my 'guilty pleasures' – which, I've always thought, would make a great name for a band. Upon checking online, I discovered that one or two groups have used it, although none of them would claim to be of the household name variety. It has also been the title of a few songs by several artists.

The GP I caught up with on this date is the late Demis Roussos, who first came to my attention when I and a few pals were on holiday a considerable number of years ago, in L'Estartit in Spain. The bar we used boasted two LPs – one by Demis, the other, now an equal GP, albeit rather better known at the time, The Stylistics' *Greatest Hits*. We would listen to both, mainly whilst quaffing a beer and playing on the snooker table. The Demis stuff I was now listening to was his work in the early 70s band Aphrodite's Child which also included in its ranks Vangelis Papathanassiou who composed most of their music.

Demis' role was: 'bass, vocal backings, lead vocal on The Four Horsemen, Babylon, Hic Et Nunc' – the song titles give you some, if only a little, idea of what the music may be like. Entitled 666 which is, as all we Black Magic enthusiasts know only too well, and any Iron Maiden fan will confirm 'the Number of the Beast'. This double LP is now quite pricey, although the CD version is very affordable. It has its moments – the best of which arrive when Demis is utilising full throttle, on, for example, 'The Four Horsemen', which is worth the cost of entry on its own.

Following the demise of Aphrodite's Child, Demis decided to invest in some perhaps more commercial music and, as a result, I rediscovered him warbling 'Forever and Ever', the title track of his 1974 LP – which spent 68 weeks in the album charts – and other middle of the roadish songs, given an unusual edge by his extremely distinctive, almost falsetto vocals. I was surprised when I checked out Demis' solo chart action to discover that 'Forever And Ever' was never a hit as a single. On its own, that is, but it was one of four tracks on a 1976 EP which did top the UK charts.

At this point I should retrospectively apologise for my cultural (mis)appropriation of Demis' Greek heritage when, on holiday on the then very quiet Greek island of Spetses, I dressed up as the great man, with the aid of some towels and cushions, to perform a version of 'Forever And Ever'. This went down well enough with the locals for them to decide, after some discussion, not to beat me up. Mind you, things could have turned ugly had I not – still clad in Demis disguise – persuaded pal JT, on holiday with us, that ringing the village church bells loudly at 2am was probably unlikely to curry favour with anyone.

Another of my long-lasting guilty pleasures has been the work of Luigi Sacco, better known by his stage name of Lou Christie. Lou also had a mean falsetto, and he employed it to great effect on his four UK hits (seven in the US Top 50) – 'Lightnin' Strikes' and 'Rhapsody in the Rain' in 1966, and, three years later, 'I'm Gonna Make You Mine' and 'She Sold Me Magic'.

Lou's middle name might have been Lou-scivious, to judge by the theme of most of his more successful material, much of which was written in tandem with Twyla Herbert, 20 years older than him, whom he had met when he was just 15.

IN WHICH A FRIEND'S STRICTLY FOR THE BYRDS

The Byrds have always been in my top five groups, from their very earliest 'Mr Tambourine' days, through their psychedelic glory days via 'Eight Miles High' and even into their somewhat more difficult 'Chestnut Mare' countryish phase. So, imagine my surprise and delight when a good friend put himself out on, yes, his own behalf – but also very much on mine. This is how Les Hawker explained to me it all happened:

'Any of you like ourselves, who have known Graham for many years, will appreciate when I say he has an opinion on everything and nine times out of ten a strong opinion, which quite often will disagree with your own. Our exchanges regularly stray into music, so when I received "Wow – at last, I'm impressed" in response to a WhatsApp music message whilst on holiday I thought all my birthdays had come at once. So how did this come about? My wife Aydee and I take the occasional cruise, and in July/August 2022 we were booked on the Queen Elizabeth from San Francisco to Barcelona. Those who have cruised will be aware that every evening you receive a newsletter with Daily Highlights for the next day. On Sunday 31 July, on reading this, I went into full "Four Weddings" mode "F*** F*** F*** me." Aydee looked ashen. "What's happened?" "Roger McGuinn's on-board and he'll be singing and talking about his career in the main theatre at 11.00 tomorrow," I replied, with a massive smile on my face.

Roger McGuinn as leader of The Byrds had been heavily influential in my love affair with 60s music and my introduction to soft/country rock, with personal favourites "Mr Tambourine Man", "8 Miles High" and "Chestnut Mare". Even though I'd never seen him perform, I felt an indirect closeness as I had seen

Dave Crosby, his fellow Byrd, many times between 1971 and 2013.

Roger had joined the ship in LA with wife/manager Camilla. During his time on board he gave three one-hour lectures. The first covered his early career, up to "Mr Tambourine Man", the second the remainder of his career and the last a Q&A session. To say I was impressed to see him play and sing well, at the age of 80, was an understatement. In my opinion, too many old rockers continue to sing long past their sell-by dates, embarrassing themselves and making old fans cringe. It was after the first lecture that I messaged Graham and got the "Wow" response. From then until after the final Q&A we were in regular contact, with me giving updates and in reply receiving opinions!!

The second lecture was just as good, and at the end I went into besotted fan mode, skipping down to the front to ask Camilla if it was possible for her to take a photograph of myself with Roger. She could not have been nicer, stopping Roger when he came out of his changing room, getting him to agree and even persuading him to smile. I immediately pinged the photo to all points north to receive this reply from Graham "Seriously, get that enlarged and framed – true Rock Royalty." So, can you believe it? A second compliment.

As my journalistic skills are not great, I thought, why not ask Graham for a question for the last session? Amazingly, it was selected to be asked: "Would Roger agree that, of the contemporary British Groups, the Searchers came closest to the Byrds?" I managed to video the answer, when he agreed, specifically commenting that the guitar playing on "Needles and Pins" influenced his 12-string guitar composing. Knowing of Graham's appreciation of Roger, we wondered what would be a fitting memory for him. Three weeks later and back in Pinner, I went round to his house and handed over a small wrapped gift. Like a two-year-old, he immediately ripped the paper off to reveal it was a CD compilation of Roger's latest work, inscribed:

"To Graham, best wishes Roger McGuinn'"

Thanks to Les and Roger!

IN WHICH COINCIDENCE
LOOMS LARGE

Examining the latest lengthy White Spring Rare Record list of records for sale sent to me in February 2023, put together, as ever, by the excellent Jon Groocock, I find a copy of the self-titled first Glencoe LP, which I immediately order. The group featured Norman Watt-Roy and keyboards man Graham Maitland as well as much-travelled guitarist John Turnbull, who also graced the likes of Arc, Heavy Jelly, and Skip Bifferty.

Later that day, I am browsing the latest edition of the excellent magazine *Fortean Times*, to which I subscribe, and whose 'strapline' is: 'The World of Strange Phenomena'. I arrive at page 18, on which a story is headed 'Spirits of Glencoe' (the second LP by the group Glencoe is called *The Spirit of Glencoe*) and which explains that, 'On 13 February 1692, nearly 40 members of the MacDonald clan were slaughtered by Scottish Government soldiers for being late in pledging allegiance to the Crown, following the collapse of the Jacobite Rebellion of 1689/90.'

That's a proper coincidence – as is the fact that I soon receive the Glencoe record I ordered – and realise that I already own a copy. D'oh! Still, there's a bright side – as a result of checking back on Glencoe, I discover that, after their initial two records, they later changed their name to Loving Awareness, and released a third album – which seems to go for at least 15 quid these days. I'll have to look out for it.

'After I reported last week on the spirited defence of the "banned" song 'Delilah', by Barry Mason, who died in 2021, a reader spotted an appropriate sign listing chromosomes outside a cafe in Aberdeen. "XX = Female; YY = Male; YYY = Delilah", it said. Delightful!' This, from the *Daily Telegraph*, in February 2023, followed a row over Welsh rugby fans being asked NOT to sing the song at the rugby union international between Wales and England, because some, er, concerned people, felt it to be in dubious taste. The row seemed to spark an interest in Tom's 1968 single – but there were still plenty of copies for sale on Discogs – when I looked, there were 1391 of them, starting at 84p. When I saw that, I stood there laughing...

Heard a vinyl joke – 'I went into a charity shop and bought a record, "Sounds Wasps Make". Got home, played it and thought, this doesn't sound like wasps. Then I realised I was playing the bee side.'

IN WHICH WADELL YOU THINK OF STELLA?

Aged just 12 in 1993, Stella Wedell made a cassette tape of her favourite songs of the day, including tracks by the Pet Shop Boys, UB40 and Shaggy. She took it with her on a family holiday to the Costa Brava and Majorca, but lost the tape while they were away. Twenty-five years later, Stella found herself in Stockholm, visiting an art gallery where one exhibit by British artist Mandy Barker, called Sea of Artefacts, caught her eye. It included items Mandy had found on a variety of beaches and amongst them was a battered cassette – which Stella recognised as her own old friend, which had travelled from the Med to the Atlantic Ocean, and to Fuerteventura where Mandy had discovered it on a beach in the Canary Islands – over 1000 miles away. Even more amazingly, it still played! The artist promised to hand the tape back to Stella when the exhibition closed.

Here's a similar type of story, about a 54-year-old woman who, 41 years earlier, living in Jersey, had visited Lady Jayne Records there, to purchase a copy of Boney M's 1976 LP, *Take the Heat off Me*. Lulu Baylee remembered paying £3.23. When her family moved off the island in 1980, Lulu and her parents 'gave away all our furniture and records'. However, they all moved back to the Channel Island in 2014 – and in 2022, when Lulu visited the local Durrell charity shop, she was surprised to see a copy of the Boney M LP for sale – and even more surprised to see it had her name written on it! She duly snapped it up at rather less than the £3.23 original price. Once she'd done so, another problem loomed – and Lulu was left pondering whether 'to go back to the charity shop to buy a record player!' A no-brainer, I reckon.

This message turned up in my email inbox, from HMV: 'Buy 3 or more Vinyl and save 20%. Expires 22 February 2023. Max discount £100. Exclusions apply.' So, now, not only are we having to confront the widespread use of the word 'vinyl' to replace 'record', alarming to those of us of a certain age and upbringing, but also that it appears the plural of vinyl is now vinyl (vinyls is even worse) when, if used in an English context, the plural of vinyl should undoubtedly be 'records'.

Anyway, I ignored the message which, generous though it was, would have meant spending significant money for a couple of LPs and instead checked back on a couple of CDs I'd had my eye on and then forgotten about on eBay – both from groups by which I own several different (both) records and CDs: Crowded House, 5 CDs, 2 LPs; Foo Fighters, 7 CDs, 0 LPs – they were: *Time on Earth* (2007) by the former, and the latter's *Wasting Light* (2011).

How much do you reckon, including p&p? No, under a tenner – well, under a fiver, to be honest. For the two to land on my doormat in three days or less... £3.52. Had to be bought. Bargain, even if I were to play them just once each.

IN WHICH I EXPLAIN A TYPICAL DAY IN THE LIFE, AND MOURN VALERIE

My local charity shop was open, so I popped in, noticed they had some vinyl – yes, most of it the usual Classical, 50s/60s m-o-r (middle of the road), etc – but I found a copy of an early LP by The Move – albeit on one of the cheap price labels. I did have all the tracks, so told myself, 'You don't need it, walk away.' I got a couple of hundred yards up the road before the inevitable happened as my inner voice instructed me to return immediately. The voice was correct. I couldn't bear to leave such fine music from this much underrated group sitting there amongst the debris from recent deaths and departures, so decided to liberate it.

It was just as well I went back. Because, as I walked back to the records, I spotted a pile of CDs – and a note saying they were '10 for £1'. Of course, I bought ten – after all, I would be at a record fair in a couple of months, experiencing life from the other side of the table, and hoping at least to come away with a small profit – and I figured if I couldn't do that from 10p CDs then I didn't deserve to be writing a book involving the buying and selling of CDs and vinyl.

Returning home with a bulging bag I hadn't had on departure would only elicit suspicion and allegations from Sheila that I was bringing more unwanted music into the house. How to avoid, or at the very least delay, such a tirade of abuse? Er, sling the bag in the back of the car outside our house, and drive over to the jewellers in Northwood, where I hadn't been recently. To buy Sheila a piece of jewellery? What a sweet gesture... Er, no. This jeweller offers more than meets the eye.

There's a clue outside the shop, where a box of admittedly dismal discs is balanced precariously. An odd ploy this, as any collector worth his or her salt would have a quick flip, realise they were all dross, figure that what was inside would also be, and do a Dionne Warwick. But I, of course, know better, so went in. This in itself is not the most simple of operations. Because, having pressed the buzzer at the side of the door, one is inspected before the relevant button is pressed from behind the counter, allowing ingress to those of acceptable appearance.

This impenetrable security procedure will, of course, deter any potential jewel thief from disguising him or herself as a vinyl freak by wearing scruffy clothes and carrying a tatty LP under one arm, thus securing guaranteed entry and the opportunity to

steal either a heavy armful of LPs worth possibly about 300 quid
– but only to ageing old heads who can still vaguely remember
the musicians involved – or, alternatively, a very light handful of
expensive jewellery, valuable but light gemstones, beautiful rings
and watches and the like, worth untold thousands, before legging
it unhindered by their flimsy weight.

I hope no villains happen to read this book and plot such a
dastardly deed. I was in. The boss was, too – whose name I was still
unfamiliar with, despite having been there numerous times in the
past. I'm sure you know how such a tricky social embarrassment
can arise – you either don't quite catch the name of the other
person first time round, so are too embarrassed to ask again, or
you are never told their name and they never ask for yours.

Anyway, he recognised me ok and gestured that he'd be
with me once he had dealt with the query raised by his elderly
female customer, about her watch, bracelet, decorative false leg,
or whatever. He was clearly trying to ease her out of the shop. She
was determined to remain there chatting. Eventually she got the
message and departed.

By now I'd flipped through most of the records on display –
some good titles from the 60s and 70s – all familiar to me and
to my now host. Most of which I already owned, or felt were just
a little too expensive given their condition. We enjoyed a long
distance chat. I had to raise my voice to reply to him as he was
behind what was doubling up as a security device or anti-Covid
protection.

He'd been to the Letchworth Record Fair recently, he said,
but didn't really find anything he wanted. He'd also been to
'David's' the long-established record shop in that town, and ended
up rejecting virtually everything he looked at, before fancying a
record he'd never seen before, by someone he'd never heard of,
which he'd bought, and found when he got it home, he quite liked
it. We've all been there. We all tell ourselves we quite like it when
we first play it. We then stick it in the collection, and don't play it
again. Ever.

One of the records I was looking at, wondering whether I
already had it, was by Chicken Shack. Or maybe Savoy Brown.

I don't think anyone could ever quite tell the difference between them with any certainty. Not even WITH Christine Perfect's presence. But we always knew we loved them both.

The LP was called *Blue Matter* – got it yet?

Yes, you're right – Savoy Brown or Chicken Shack. But which one?

You're right – Savoy Brown.

I've got the album, but only on CD. This record was, if I remember correctly, 40 quid, but a little on the tatty side – albeit a check on Discogs reveals you're going to pay around 50 quid for an original UK copy in only 'vg' condition – two letters which can cover a multitude of sins. The jeweller came over and pointed to the record: 'Savoy Brown. Savoy Brown – who remembers Savoy Brown now?' Well, I knew both of us did. But I also knew what he meant. Only people of a certain age remember Savoy Brown. Some of those think they're Chicken Shack. And that situation is not about to change.

And even those people are beginning to die off, so the value of these records can only, in my opinion (probably not his as he didn't immediately try to lure me in by halving the price) go down in value over the next few years. If you're my age and want to own these records, don't expect to be able to sell them on for a profit, as there will soon be far too few potential purchasers prepared to pay plenty of pounds for them.

I'd now come across a bootleggy-looking LP by the Rolling Stones, boasting some unusual tracks but also some unusual marks on its vinyl surface. Later, I investigated online. Of course, it is a bootleg but rather a superior one, is the general judgement, so I'm well pleased I decided to add it to my already extensive Stones' archive. The jeweller gave it an expert going over. 'I can't feel any raised marks. It'll be fine' was the gist of his conclusion. There was nothing there to play it on in order to check.

I'd put it in the 'possible' mental file as he asked me whether I wanted to visit the basement cave behind/below his shop wherein, I knew, always reside literally thousands more records. In no logical order or pattern. The vast majority unclothed, as in not wearing plastic sleeves. Stacked on shelves, in drawers, on the floor, against a wall, in piles. In a room which wasn't, but felt as though it should be, damp. Lit by one strip light and occasionally, when the other one decided to emit a grudging glow, two. Next door to, I think, the basement/kitchen of a Chinese restaurant.

He escorted me down, unlocked the door, and left me to it. 'It' didn't go that well. I had to admit the records were slightly more neatly arranged than in previous visits. But many were neatly arranged on shelves with the open side of the cover pointing out, rather than the more useful spine with the name of the record and performer(s) displayed.

Forty-five minutes later I had examined probably 100 LPs. Only one, by Chip Taylor, had made the remotest appeal to me as a possible buy. Many others had flattered to deceive. Many of them I already owned. Many of them had iffy covers, blemished record surfaces, excessively high prices marked on them. There was nothing I just 'had to have'. I'd decided enough was enough and was about to leave, when in the doorway loomed the figure of not only the jeweller, but also my old pal, owner of my favourite record shop, Second Scene – young(ish) Julian Smith. The same Julian who had recently told me in an online message that he wasn't going to write me a piece for this book. Shame. But I'm not that small-minded. I still like him, even though he happens to be a Watford fan.

He seemed in good spirits and we began to go through boxes and bundles of vinyl together, both of us seeming to find more for the other than for himself. And to be fair, Julian does seem to know what I'm looking for rather better than I do myself – he thrust one record at me, which I had never seen before and by two people of whom I had no knowledge and a third I'd vaguely heard of, insisting, 'You will definitely like that. It's right up your street.' I had to believe him. It was marked 15 quid. Not outrageous.

The next day I played it. What a gorgeous record! First impressions, there is some Crosby, Stills & Nash about it. Very evocative and catchy songs, nice harmonies and some stunning guitar playing. Rather worrying that I am so easy for Julian to read! No, I'm not telling you what it is, I want to be able to boast about it as though it was my own discovery. Absolute bargain.

Although I now suspect every time Julian finds a record in his own shop he reckons I'll like, he'll be adding an extra fiver or tenner to the price!

Shortly after, he found me another – 'Here you go – another one you'll like.' This one was just a tenner – the only LP by Crazy Elephant, who were part of the Kasenetz Katz stable back in 1969. They hit the charts with 'Gimme Gimme Good Lovin'', but it was a short-lived chart career – I don't think they troubled the scorer again.

Finding these two LPs for me wasn't the biggest shock Julian supplied, though – when I asked him whether there had been any repeat of the rather spooky audio and visual happenings recorded in *Vinyl Countdown*, upstairs in the building housing his shop, he told me that, after being exorcised by a friend of the family, the ghostly apparitions had ceased, never to reappear. (Reader: he was wrong!) By this time I had realised that morning was over and we were approaching that crucial time of day when (a) Sheila has some lunch ready, and (b) *Doctors* is soon to start on BBC1. So driving home asap was now required urgently.

I made my excuses and left Julian still digging through the LPs, had to take an unusual route home because of temporary traffic lights all over the place – made it through the door with four minutes to get the obligatory 'Doctors' coffee for madame – and my own cup of char – on the go. *Doctors* is a medically themed 'soap' which had been going for many years without any awareness from me, probably as I was in my office working. But once I retired, sorry, once I WAS retired, I began to watch it, initially with no real enthusiasm. Until I fell head over heels in love with the character, 'Valerie', and the programme became unmissable viewing.

And then, towards the end of 2022 Valerie – well, the actress playing Valerie – left the show. I was devastated but continued to watch distractedly, hoping against unlikely hope that as some soap opera characters have been known to come back after having 'died', it was still not impossible that Valerie might change her mind or suddenly receive a financial offer she couldn't refuse and return to the programme. Sadly, nothing of this nature happened.

Not only that, but the entire series was revealed to be for the scrapyard by the end of 2024.

IN WHICH I PLEAD FOR HEAVY ROCK PROTECTION

No. That's it. I've had enough! Just as some national landmarks are protected from property vandalism, and in the way that authors and writers are protected from plagiarism, I genuinely believe some kind of protection/quality control should be available to writers of popular songs. Or even those who listen to them. Okay, I understand that the writers of songs are paid if someone records a version of one of their ditties, but I do feel that listeners to dismal copies of great tracks when they are played on the radio or TV should be protected from inevitable feelings of rage when terrific, original works of musical art are despoiled by inferior copyists. And it is no excuse to plead that listeners to new versions of classic tracks may well have no knowledge of the original. But when I hear the song which first introduced me to the sound of heavy rock, some 60-plus years ago, being vandalised by one (or more) inferior bunch of musicians, not even hailing from the country of the originals, I have to cry 'no more!'

Planet Rock should know better than to give air space to Van Halen's insipid, uninspired, lethargic version of Ray Davies' heavy-metal-launching 'You Really Got Me' by his and brother Dave's group, the Kinks – the track which changed my life and musical outlook when I heard it hammering out of our usually tinny TV speakers, one day in 1964. Even through those paltry speakers it was a thundering blast of sonic violence threatening to damage the audio flaps on the side of my head. I was never the same person once that riff lodged itself deep into my brain. If that track was a building it would have had a preservation order stamped on it immediately, which would forbid any other group or singer even attempting to sing and play it – the Hammersmith Gorillas in 1974; the 13th Floor Elevators, who tried their hands and failed valiantly with an almost listenable version in 1978 which may, it seems, have been recorded about a dozen years previously and which can be found on the *Psychedelic World of the 13th Floor Elevators* triple CD box set.

But, particularly, those... those 'posers', phoney 'hard' rockers Van Halen, whose 1978 – and I accept this may be only my verdict – inexcusable apology of a version should never be even spoken of again, let alone continue being played on Planet Rock. I was gobsmacked to read, in a *Classic Rock* feature from December 2020: 'Eddie's guitar sound, the tightened-up riffing and squealing licks make the original sound soft and flaccid in comparison.'

Excuse me! On precisely which planet is that the case?

IN WHICH I ACCOST GRAHAM

Graham Coster was my editor decades ago when I wrote a couple of books for the publisher for which he was working. He is now a well-established author himself, and runs his own publishing company. He also moonlights in the blues band, 'Damn Right I Got The Blues' (almost the title of a Buddy Guy LP), blowing a mean mouth harp. We have stayed friends, and whenever we meet up – usually in the pub on a platform at Kings Cross station, the time passes quickly and enjoyably. I managed to persuade Graham to share his vinyl thoughts with me – here they are:

'For some reason, having nothing better to do recently than watch Simple Minds on Jools crank out 'Don't You (Forget About Me)' for yet another time of asking, I found myself wanting to listen again to that hollow, angular music I distantly remembered from the first album of theirs I bought, *Empires and Dance*. But I can't. Only have it on LP. Don't have a record player.

Actually I do have a record player: my dad's – a Thorens turntable that was state-of-the-art back in the 70s, with a brushed-aluminium arm light as a dragonfly, counterweight trembling from a delicate thread a spider could have woven. My first Damned album used to sound great on it. I do have Dad's 60s-vintage Fisher valve amplifier and 70s Spendor speakers, each the size of a small dishwasher, connected up to my CD player, but the record player has sat in the spare bedroom in want of a new needle for a great many years.

But I do still have all my LPs: at least 100 of them. In the kitchen. No room for them elsewhere. Friends are quite amused when they open a cupboard to search for a saucepan and find Southside Johnny and the Asbury Jukes' *Reach Up and Touch the Sky* atop a stack of records. This is not hoarding. Friends also compliment me on my neat-and-tidy flat – I'm not squeezing along canyons of teetering newspapers to go and kip in the bath. But why is it so important to me to know that I still possess all these records I can't play?

I'm sure part of it is the conviction, or maybe just false memory, that if I could still play the record a lot of those albums would sound better than on CD. First Clash album, undoubtedly. Also, my Eddie and the Hot Rods' *At the Sound of Speed* EP has never been issued on CD. Neither has the complete track listing of my ten-inch Chiswick LP of the Count Bishops' 'brutal' (in Charles Shaar Murray's felicitous verdict) live album recorded at the Roundhouse, *Bishops Live*.

But the main reason is it would be just too painful to get rid of them – even though I probably have at least half these albums on CD. Some years ago, in a moment of reckless folly, I gave away my LP of the first Elvis Costello album, *My Aim is True*, on original Stiff, and literally the instant it was out of my hands my heart was in my boots. Why?

What I'd given away wasn't the music. It was that late-teens time in my life: reading *NME* every week, listening to Nicky Horne's 'Your Mother Wouldn't Like It' on Capital every night, buying that first Damned album with the custard-pies-in-the-face cover at Bonaparte Records in Croydon, actually going to see Costello at the Cat's Whiskers in Streatham. I still want that record, with its lilac back cover (Stiff gave you a choice of three or four), back. I have not given away a single LP since. I may have two copies of Nine Below Zero's *Live at the Marquee* on CD – original and fortieth-anniversary expanded – but no one's having the LP I got as soon as the album came out. I was there the very first time they played the Marquee!

Those records stowed away in the kitchen like mushrooms in a mine are an emotional Madeleine cake. That 12-inch Blondie single of 'X Offender' with Debbie Harry in a little black dress: quite valuable now, I gather, but never mind that. That was when Blondie were still a New Wave band and it was cool to know about them. Every single Undertones album right through to the last one (green and white cover, can't even remember the title): I followed – collected – their career record by record just as I did gig by euphoric gig, from nearly passing out at a furnace-hot Marquee during an early residency through to the London farewell at the Lyceum in pre-*Lion King* days, where just trying to dance saw you swept off your feet by the heaving throng and dumped back down on them across the other side of the theatre.

And the LPs – not the CDs I have on the rack – of Bruce Hornsby and the Range's 'The Way It Is' and the first Lucinda Williams and the first Robbie Robertson albums are mementoes of one of the happiest times of my life: the six months I spent working in Our Price Records in Cambridge after finishing my first book. LPs were still mostly what we sold then, customers bringing the sleeves up to the counter in their floppy polythene covers.

In my memory, it is always just before closing time when the Rastafarian called something like Mr Jefferson is plonking down a whole pile of obscure Jetstar reggae imports and I'm having to go out the back and root around for the brown-paper sleeve holding the disc of *Cry Tuff Dub Encounter Chapter IV*.

It was hard work: on a Saturday you'd open at 9 to a queue to get in and then it'd be mental till 6. Sunday off and then back in again on Monday, still knackered – and it was those albums we'd put on then to cheer ourselves up. 'How about...?' Da-da dum-

dum-dum, dum-dum-dum-daa, da-da dum – and on everyone's faces the sun would come out.

Can't go back, which is why I don't need to play them. But the past is hidden away where only I know. Still there.'

IN WHICH JOHN'S NO LONGER JILTED

I love John Shuttleworth – if you aren't aware of his work, google him. His radio shows are works of genius. But before he was John Shuttleworth, he was Jilted John. In this guise, he enjoyed a big 1978 hit single, (number 4) 'Jilted John', a brilliant track completely capturing the angst of being a nervous, naïve, youngish teenager just discovering the appeal of whichever sex was making the greatest appeal to one's exploding hormones: 'I've been going out with a girl, her name is Julie, but last night she said to me, "I love you but there's this bloke I fancy... his name is Gordon" I was so upset that I cried all the way to the chip shop... I know he's a moron – Gordon is a moron.'

Un-PC, maybe, but which of us didn't experience those emotions as a vulnerable teenager? I know I did – her name was Pauline but she was saving herself for Scott Walker! Jilted John, who claimed to have been born in 1959, was the creation of Graham Fellows. JJ's songs of acne cream, unrequited love, and sexual frustration appeared on the now little remembered LP, *True Love Stories* (EMI, 1978). The album also featured an insert game-board on which to play 'mice and ladders'. My copy cost me one quid in a WHSmith sale but is now likely to set you back £20. I wouldn't part with mine for 40 quid – but probably would for 41, if I'm honest – well, for that, I know I could buy a replacement and make a healthy profit.

One of the best titles of any compilation album I own is the *Boil The Kettle, Mother* CD set released in 2004, which includes the Lemon Drops, the Seeds, Haymarket Square, Magic Swirling Ship, and more high quality psych – which was on my playlist this evening, along with some Neil Young/Crazy Horse – *Everybody Knows This Is Nowhere* – plus Chad Stuart and Jeremy Clyde's *Of Cabbages and Kings*, light-psych from 1967. There was also some Fever Tree – 1970's *For Sale* and *Creation* from a year earlier.

IN WHICH I GET THE NEEDLE

Having bought a new cartridge for my record deck, I found I couldn't work out how to fit it – this will probably surprise you, dear reader, but not anyone who knows me even a little. So, into the car, up to Harrow town centre, leave car in car park, lug deck to shop – Harrow Audio, from which I have bought all of my audio equipment for many years. Laugh self-deprecatingly about my total lack of technological nous and return home without the deck.

A couple of hours later, I am summoned back to the record shop where the techno geeks have magically fitted the new cartridge. To celebrate, while I'm there I purchase a new CD player for my set-up. Once I've added it to my stuff, I sample it and am very happy – so don't tell anyone it only cost £179 as they'll think I'm a cheapskate with tin ears. They may, of course, be correct.

Fast forward a year or two, possibly even three, and another, identical, audio aggravation arrives. Having decided to listen to a record or two, I grabbed the first one, a new old reissue, slapped it on to the turntable, pulled the arm over and down on to the now rotating disc, and listened intently to... absolutely nothing.

A quick technical investigation revealed that, of the four coloured wires usually attached to the stylus, two had snapped off, or come away resulting in inability to transmit sound. Okay, short term solution – put on a CD or two. Later, I began the trickier operation of detaching the record deck from the amp, unplugging the whole kit and caboodle (no idea) and preparing for a mercy dash to rush the stuff to the emergency ward, aka Harrow Audio still so-called, despite now having relocated to the wild wastes of

Watford. Before setting off to that little known environment, in which the natives might not be so friendly if they discovered my football allegiance, I had to remove from my vehicle the odd scarf and pennant which might give the game away.

I'd rung ahead to warn them of my imminent arrival at their A&E department, and they promised to have their finest, most qualified, audio experts on stand-by to deal with this potentially fatal incident. On arrival, having missed the entrance to their premises despite having the in-car satnav on, I pressed the buzzer and was greeted and ushered in to the inner technical sanctum, packed with state of the art audio equipment – along with a few shelves of new vinyl at various prices – some more enticing than others. However, most of the performers were unknown to me, although a Black Keys item made some appeal. A gentleman of similar vintage to my own sat me down with the same mixture of sympathy and concern as a top surgeon might exude towards a potential patient. After a speedy but thorough visual check, he sighed, assumed a serious expression as he outlined my options in much the same manner a specialist would adopt if delivering a life-threatening diagnosis to patients. 'Mm. Well, we might well have to send it off for repair... unless... maybe I can fix it here. Let's have a closer look... mm... right, leave it with me and I'll let you know. It could be pricey, though. By the way, have you considered a new stylus?' Indeed, I had. The current one had been subjected to a heavy workload, having been in place pre-Covid, so I had been mentally preparing myself to get round to replacing it when the opportunity arose – as it now obviously had.

I was politely but firmly shown out as I struggled to keep my emotions in check in the knowledge that I'd now have to await the verdict once a specialist examination had been completed. It was a sombre drive home, as I contemplated having left my trusted equipment alone in a strange environment, at the mercy of unfamiliar specialists.

Having been home only an hour or two, I quickly grabbed the landline phone as it rang. I was acquainted quickly with positive news – yes, the problem could be dealt with in situ. Not only that, a decent new stylus had been located at a competitive price, which would, I was assured, improve my sound system significantly. The whole process would be completed by the next day.

After a troubled night's sleep, interrupted by nightmares about distorted speakers and iffy sound systems, I was ready to return to Harrow Audio - where I was greeted like an old friend and proudly shown my now sparklingly revitalised deck and stylus - and handed a bill, which gave me a fiver change from a ton.

I had a chat with the chaps, discovering that the business had been moved from Harrow to Watford largely because of an anti-social element which, they explained, had appeared in the previous location. The local constabulary were unable or unwilling to address the problem but it certainly deterred some potential customers from visiting the neighbourhood.

I returned home to find a pal from my working days, Nick Godfrey, of the *Racing Post*, and also now owner of a record company, Precious Recordings, had suffered something of a disc disaster, having sent his personal copy of a record out to a customer, and now having to ask for it back.

IN WHICH I'M DRIFTING TO PACIFIC

I had been listening to Pacific Drift's *Feelin' Free*, from 1970, Stan Webb's *Jersey Lightning* from 2000, and the West Coast Consortium's 2003 compilation, *Looking Back*. I'm fond of the latter's 'The Day The Train Never Came', but suspect if I had to take one track by them to my desert island it would be the song recorded in 1968, at which time the group probably believed the 'West Coast' to consist pretty much of Newquay and perhaps Land's End. They were then merely Consortium - and I immediately loved their achingly wonderful (if you happened to be in love at the time, which I definitely was) single, 'All the Love in the World'.

Back now to the present(ish) when I am, of course, still in love with the same lady, and had been sent off to buy her some Benecol.

En route, I popped my head into the local charity shop 'just in case'. They had obviously recently acquired the singles collections of a couple, at least, of presumably expired vinyl enthusiasts, on offer at 50p each or three for a quid. I found a couple of interest – covers, that is, rather than the actual records. In fact, I switched records that I fancied into the covers I wanted – because they each seemed to have emanated from record shops almost certainly no longer with us.

One, with details stamped in black print on a white cover, is 'Strood Record Centre: 124 High Street, Strood, Kent'. Into this one I inserted a copy of T. Rex's 'Jeepster/Life's A Gas' on the Fly label, released on 5 November 1971, whose 'B' side is a colour illustration of the two Rex boys. The other celebrated 'BROWN'S RADIO, TELEVISION, RECORDS' with the address: '39 Friar Street, Reading: Phone 62916'. Into this I shoved Elvis Costello's 'Accidents Will Happen'. I took the two to the counter to pay. 'They're 50p each, but three for a quid, why not find another?'

'I know, but the ice lollies in my bag which I just bought from the supermarket over the road are beginning to melt as the heating is on high in here. Anyway, I'm happy just to have these two.'

'No, you have to have another one – go and have a look.'

'I really don't have time.'

'Well, just grab one at random on the way out, then.'

Which I did and which is how I came to own a copy of *Xmas Chimes*, an undated picture sleeve EP on the Dandy Children's Records label. I reckon it is from the 50s (Discogs says the date is 'unknown'), and it features 'Christmas Day Peals from St Clement's and St Martin's.' Lovely stuff.

My postman, Luigi, put his Christmas box at risk today. Not only did he roar up outside, in one of those small, red vans, but strode flamboyantly down the path, hammered on the door, which Sheila rushed to open, and then handed her what Luigi and I had already agreed – or so I thought – would only be given directly to me – a record-shaped package.

Okay, he made some feeble attempt to disguise his actions by trying to convince her this was 'a package of advertising material', but you can imagine how fooled she was (not) by that. Inside the controversial delivery was a copy of the rereleased LP by Quatrain, a group about which I knew little until checking out the *Record Collector* advert by Colin Wilkinson in which it figured with a 'psych' indication, tantamount to offering nuts to a squirrel.

IN WHICH I'M RIPPED OFF BY MYSELF

I decided to visit Amersham's The Record Shop. The interior of the shop had changed considerably since I'd last been there pre-Covid, which I pointed out to the gentleman behind the counter, who gushingly agreed with me. 'Yes, it has.' No further comment or conversation whatsoever was forthcoming until, getting on for an hour later, by which time I had checked out every section likely to contain something of appeal to me.

I'd identified two records as being of interest. One definitely so and the other probably. The definite was *Please 1968/69*, which is yet another example of the underappreciated work of drummer Peter Dunton, whose finest hour was in T2 and into whose career I have gone in more detail elsewhere in this book. Amazingly – well, to me, anyway – I had somehow completely missed this 2021 release on the Guerssen label – 'a collection of demos taken from original master tapes and restored acetates from 1968/69'. There was a slight glimmer of concern at the back of my mind as I knew I did own a CD of Please material – *Seeing Stars* – from 1969, but couldn't, offhand, work out whether that included any of these dozen tracks, all Peter-penned. As it turned out, it didn't. Result!

I'd initially picked the second LP out, thinking that if I bought two I could probably get a small discount, so *Marmalade BBC Sessions 1967-68*, on the No Kidding label, with 16 tracks on marmaladeish-coloured vinyl, accompanied me over to the counter, where I asked the man of few words whether there might be a discount for buying two together if I paid in cash.

'They're both new records. So... no.' Technically, I'm not

sure he was right, with one being from two years ago and the other, I later discovered, also from 2021, and widely available in many other places at £12.50 plus p&p, usually £4.50. Nor was I overjoyed when I later realised I did already have the Please LP, as well, albeit with a different cover, and not on 'limited edition colour vinyl', numbered 74/110. So, I'd spent an hour getting to the shop, bought one record I already owned for 30 quid and another which I didn't already own, but which I could easily have bought for a fiver less than I paid.

But, yes, you're right – had I not gone to that shop I would probably never have known the Marmalade record existed, and nor would I have known that an alternative version of the Please LP, with a totally different cover and in coloured vinyl, had been released. What should I do now? Swallow my pride, keep the two and say nothing. Or try to flog one of the two Please LPs?

Yeah, probably the latter... but what I had learned was that The Record Shop is differently laid out than it used to be, and is now run – or was on this date – by a man of very few words, with an eye on maximum profit at time of purchase over less profit but better customer relations. And who am I to say he has that the wrong way round? My next trip there came in the spring of 2024, when I found friendlier staff, the shop more rammed with records, and purchased a live LP by late sixties' group, Frost.

Later the same day, I was alerted by the guy who runs the El Vinyl record-flogging website that some unusually desirable material was being offered up by a particular seller – here was the write-up which the vendor, 'Barabbas', gave about this record:

'The word (sic) 'Holy Grail' is bandied around a fair bit when it comes to records. However, if there is one record that deserves that moniker, this is it.

An incredible copy of one of the rarest and most sought-after records in the world.

The sleeve is entirely intact. No splits, although there is slight evidence of rubbing on the bottom edge, in the middle, but it is very small. White sleeve has slightly discoloured with age, but one of the best examples I have seen. The disc hardly looks as if has ever been played. Closer to NM than Ex. You are unlikely to ever see its like again.' The cover of the record was graded 'Very Good'. The disc itself: 'Excellent: shows signs of having been played, but barely any marks or surface noise, and labels show only light signs of use.'

Any idea what record was being talked about here? I discovered it was a copy of (The) Can's 1969 *Monster Movie* LP, on the Music Factory (SRS001) label, rated at £175 in the *Rare Record Price Guide*, albeit on a different label and on offer here at: NINE GRAND! Yes, 9,000 of your English pounds! Plus postage and packing. I pondered whether to bid, for almost all of three seconds – maybe not such a bad price after all, though, as Discogs recorded a copy being sold for £10,955.22. Mind you, it also listed one which went for £13.23. Next time I looked at El Vinyl, the £9,000 record was no longer listed.

There was a postscript to a busy day when it was brought to my attention that in 1984, a reconstruction scheme began on the segment of New York's Central Park named Strawberry Fields in tribute to John Lennon, who died when he was shot outside his nearby home – and to take matters from the sublimely tragic to the ridiculously farcical, exactly 20 years later, Ozzy Osbourne was voted the favourite choice to be Britain's ambassador to greet aliens as they arrived on Earth. I'm not sure whether Ozzy recorded a song about this honour.

IN WHICH I REVEL IN DIRT-CHEAP CDS

I bought ten CDs on the morning of 22 March 2023 – they cost me three quid. Half a dozen for £2 at Pinner's St Luke's, and four more for another sov at the animal charity place. I don't really want to add any of these to my collection, though. No, this is happening because I am teaming up with cancer mate Ron to take two tables at the April Record Fair being held at Harpenden's Eric Morecambe Centre. We have often been customers there, but it suddenly struck me that, with both of us receiving partner-based pressure to dispose of significant amounts of our collections, perhaps flogging some there would be a good start.

So, we're now under orders, with a few weeks to go before the big day and are having to make significant decisions in terms of what we are and aren't willing to sell. Of course, my own approach to this is typically obtuse, as I have started acquiring more stuff just so that I can sell it. Which might well mean that, even after the sale, I will end up with more objects than I had at the time I decided to take the tables. Sad, yes, but I'll discover whether this is a route to trimming the collection and also making a profit. I think Ron is really getting involved just to humour me.

I figure that buying up CDs in at least very good condition from the charity shops offering them at 3, 4, 5, or in some instances TEN for 100 English pennies means that I can offer them to the wider populace for £1 each, three for two quid, and still make 100 per cent profit, on the ones sold, anyway. Selling records is more problematic. There are very few which could be sold at a profit in this manner to be had round these here parts, so I am facing up to the fact that I am actually going to have to offer up many discs which have been integral, if rarely played, parts of my collection, and thus my very soul, for many years.

Will I be offended or relieved if no one wants them? Who knows? Will Sheila and Jan wish to come along on the big day to ensure we are selling for real, and not just going through the motions by overpricing them so that we have an excuse for bringing back as many as we take?

Reader – joined by our friend, Roger, Ron and I teamed up at the Harpenden Record Fair in mid April 2024, which was also Grand National day. We all sold well, and made a profit more than covering our table costs. A man with an enviable beard gave me a three-figure sum for several singles – so obscure that even I had barely heard of them – which he bought 'for a friend'. The bearded gent, Jonathan's, mate handed me forty quid for a single by Toomorrow, featuring Olivia Newton-John. I bought a nice white vinyl reissue LP by obscure sixties' duo Twice As Much for a tenner. My Grand National horse didn't make it to the second fence.

I'm browsing online in the late afternoon and take a look at the RareVinyl website, and see a Gary Numan offering:

'GARY NUMAN *Strange Charm* & *Berserker* (Hard to find 2006 UK 26-track CD/DVD set, digi-pack picture sleeve with booklet. Disc One collates rare B Sides and live tracks, Disc Two is a 11-track live DVD [PAL]. Housed in a case with picture inlay and remains factory sealed from new CMFVD1408).'

A CD and a DVD basically – how much do you reckon?

£73.99. Oh, and £5.95 p&p.

Amazon asked less – £64.99 – with free p&p. And I found a copy for £56.25 with free postage thrown in, on ebay.co.uk.

There are so many examples of enormous price differences these days that all buyers of CDs and LPs should be, as a matter of course, checking before shelling out, to ensure they are not left feeling ripped off.

Although I hadn't been since lockdown ended, I felt now would be a good time to let the train take the strain en route to Chesham – where I've always quite enjoyed the fact that two shops selling records lived next door to each other, yet neither of the owners appeared to be able to stand the other.

Arriving in a very damp Chesham, I stood outside Collectors Paradise, surprised to see a notice declaring 'ALL CDS ONLY 50p EACH!' 'Blimey, that sounds good,' I thought – then turned to look at Heroes shop frontage, which, apart from advertising above its window, ahem, 'CLASSIC VINYLS', revealed an entirely empty interior. It was clearly no longer a shop – unless it was a shop selling empty space. It was certainly no longer a record shop.

It seemed as though what I'd identified as the rather less than mutually warm relationship between the proprietors of the two businesses, when speaking to them both, had ended with the departure of the newer arrival, which had opened some five years previously, while CP had been around for many years.

In I went to CP and, rather than the usual youthful, glamorous female behind the counter, there was a lady of rather more mature years, very well covered up in clothing which might almost be described as of a religious nature, sitting there instead. Not that she was anything other than very welcoming – quickly emphasising the window notice by telling me that 'all the CDs are 50p each'. I'd also noticed various discounts on offer for those buying what I was sure were known in here as 'records' rather than next door's 'vinyls' definition.

There were stacks, stacks and stacks of CDs. Some on shelves in a kind of approximate alphabetical order, others sitting in boxes, piled on each other, making it very difficult to see their spines to know what they were and who they were by. There was a little bit of displaying by subject – 'Jazz', 'Soul', for example, but not much. I overheard the lady talking on her phone in a way which was beginning to make me think that the former proprietor was no longer involved. Maybe he'd retired. A lady came in with some items she was interested in selling.

'Dale will be in later' she was told. Ah, that's right – Dale had indeed been the name of the owner when I last visited, and clearly still was. He arrived while I was still checking out the CDs. I just glimpsed him as he walked to the back, opened the door, and disappeared to, I presumed, a rear room.

I'd realised if I didn't want to spend another hour in Chesham waiting for a train, I'd need to make it back to the station within ten minutes. I'd unearthed ten CDs I fancied – some of them, I thought, would be useful at the forthcoming Record Fair, and be bankers to fetch more than 50p each. I'd sorted out CDs by Yes, Oasis, The Coral, The Waterboys, Donald Fagen, Lenny Kravitz, Roy Orbison (double CD in an attractively unusual 'Premium Tin Case'), Jefferson Airplane and Rick Derringer. Which of these could I NOT sell for more than 50p? More to the point, which of these would I later decide I wouldn't sell because I'd quite like to keep them myself? That'd be Airplane, the Coral, the Waterboys, Kravitz (for Sheila to listen to in the car), maybe Yes (it was very early stuff, not the, to my mind, tedious material they'd tended to opt for in recent years) and Rick.

I would hope to make more than the £4.50 I spent overall, via Oasis, Fagen, and Orbison. Anyway, even if I only asked £2 each for them at the Record Fair, that would still guarantee a profit on the whole bundle.

My previous Chesham visits had demonstrated a certain *froideur* between Dale and the Heroes, but it looked as though Dale had gained the last Chesham chortle. Later, I emailed Heroes to find out why they were no longer trading. Mark Lagdon told me: 'Shop was no longer financially viable post-Covid so closed back last May, only doing some bits and pieces online.' I gave Dale a call to ask about his change of CD-selling tactics, and he told me, 'It seems to have taken me years to realise how best to do this. I began selling the majority of my CDs – which had always been at varying higher prices – for £1 a throw, and also offering sales – such as you just were able to take advantage of – when they are 50p each. I do also keep some back which are still priced at £4, £5 and £7. I buy CDs to sell off cheaply, in bulk, and recently acquired 1600 jazz CDs which I'm now selling.'

I asked him about his former neighbouring shop and the rivalry between them. Was he pleased to have seen him off?

'I wouldn't say I'd seen him off – I think he managed to do that to himself.'

While in Dale's shop I'd picked up a copy of *Collector's Companion*, a glossy, readable free magazine, in which local shops, fairs, auctions, etcetera display their wares. A few pages on from Dale's full page ad: 'Established for over 30 years... we look forward to seeing you invest in future collecting' was a four page feature about DJ/designer Rose Daly and her 7" vinyl collection, which inspired her to create and sell t-shirts based on her reggae collection.

She explained that her 'Talk About Love Tee' was: 'Created from a small selection of original 7" records in the Hale London [Rose's music platform] collection. Track titles, publishing dates and artist names are placed alongside the handwritten names of the records' owners, highlighting the importance of the relationship between artist and listener.'

Rose also explained an element of record collecting I hadn't previously been aware of: 'Some of the labels would be blanked out because the DJ didn't want the opponent to see what they were putting on the deck next.' Her father used to mark his records with '73', telling her: 'I thought if I just labelled them then they wouldn't get confused with other people's collections.'

Rose recommended the Eldica Record Store in Dalston, which describes itself as, 'The funk, soul, hip hop, calypso, jazz, reggae & everything in between' shop, where she saw a man digging through records – and there 'was an incredible moment, I think, him turning around and going, "look, look at this". The man had recognised the handwriting on the record. It belonged to his father – imagine that!'

IN WHICH I WHISTLE ALONE – NATURALLY

I walked in to Morrisons – playing over the in-store system was 'Alone Again (Naturally)' by the great, now Jersey-based, Gilbert O'Sullivan which inevitably set me off whistling, entirely involuntarily, much to the, ahem, delight of fellow shoppers. I got the message eventually, though, and switched to whistling Love's 'Alone Again Or' just to give them a laugh. Naturally.

This episode set me up for a jaunt to Camden, where I wanted to check out the relatively new Record Fair I'd been seeing advertised regularly on a weekly Record Fairs Newsletter list I receive: 'Camden Market, Hawley Wharf 1st Floor Camden High Street NW1 8AA (Above SKNFED) (10am-4pm) – David Kozmic Records'.

This was the online blurb about this sale: 'The Kozmic Records record, CD and memorabilia fair has landed in Camden Town. Head to Camden Market Hawley Wharf to peruse all the finest vinyls, from progressive, psychedelic and punk to blues, soul and reggae.'

Before sampling the Fair – and still somewhat concerned at that use of the word 'vinyls', I nipped into nearby Camden Lock Vinyl. Last time I was here it was closed. Today, no problem. Open, buzzing, playing music, a few people in what is a pretty small space. Fortunately, no one perusing my favourite sections of Sixties Rock and Psych. I didn't find anything of Psychnificance (sorry, but I thought that was quite neat – better than 'bromance', for example

– ok, I won't do it again) that I fancied, but delving deeper spotted a sealed copy of *Big Star Complete Third Vol 1* featuring 'all tracks but one first time on vinyl'.

A 2-LP set, complete with 'download card included' – which meant absolute zilch to me as I have no idea how, or what, to do with such a thing. As many of you will doubtless be aware, Big Star's main man was Alex Chilton, probably better known for his Box 'Cry Like a Baby' Tops' days. I was in no doubt that I should buy this gatefold double album, even more so when I realised it would set me back just 15 quid, rather than the 20 or 25 I'd anticipated in this time of rapidly increasing prices. Keen to pay up before inflation resulted in an extra fiver being added, I took the record over to the lady supervising the shop. We had a quick and friendly chat, I handed her a 20-pound note, received back a fiver, and I asked her whether she knew where the Record Fair venue was... she sort of did, vaguely, pointing in what turned out to be vaguely the wrong direction.

Nonetheless, I felt no animosity towards her – we'd parted on good terms, as I had apologised for using her as a human A-Z, and then almost immediately spotted the large banner hung on a building across the road claiming that a record fair was going on in that very building. Avoiding the too archetypal punk, who always seems to be there, charging tourists for taking his photo, and neatly evading a line of cars keen to mow me down, I made it across the road unscathed and climbed two or three flights of stairs. This put me at the entry to a large, much longer than it was wide, room, with various tables of goodies around the edges and some very palatable reggae music booming out, much of it familiar to me from my disco days, which a couple of the stallholders were singing along to.

As I entered the room, I saw a selection of CDs on a table being overseen by a gent of slightly less mature years than myself, which included a box set of Kinks material, which I was examining as the man, wearing a woolly hat emblazoned with a Leicester City FC logo, looked over. I pointed out there was no price on it and how much might it be? He mumbled something about '70 quid', which shocked me so much I put it straight down on the table and pretended I might come back to it after looking at other stuff on his table, much of which was of a vinyl persuasion. This did not prevent the table chap telling me that a friend of his had heard that Ray and Dave Davies had been on a plane flying over Greenland when a dispute they'd been having boiled over into physical confrontation, resulting in the threat that the plane would be landed in the middle of nowhere if they did not desist asap.

Remembering an occasion when I had actually been flying over Greenland, according to the inflight map on the plane, and how bleak and unwelcoming it had appeared, I was unsurprised that apparently this brought the two to their senses, and the flight proceeded with a full Kinks complement. As I tried to concentrate on pulling out records to check whether I might want to buy one or more, he carried on chatting. In an effort to slow the tide, I decided to play on his football allegiance by asking him how a couple of Leicester players, who had also played for my favoured team, were getting on. This sent him into overdrive as he told me he was also a Hearts supporter, and regaled me with the (many) reasons why Leicester will be unable to repeat their 1000/1 feat of winning the Premier League any time soon. In order to escape the ongoing verbal flow, I garbled that, 'I'll have a quick look round and come back.'

And I *did* have a look round. But, while there was a wide range of material which didn't really include much from any wishlist I've ever made, there was a significant number of records I could have considered, if only the prices had not been SO much over what I regarded them as being worth – some of the real 'rarities' which seem to appear at every record fair, so can't really be THAT rare, were way overpriced to my way of thinking.

I'd done the top of the room, one of the sides, and across the bottom, then turned back up towards Hearts and Leicester man, dallied at the 'All LPs a tenner' man, most of whose fare was big-name live records, not usually on traditional labels. The price was tempting but I couldn't find anything which would justify yet another album by whichever particular act it was.

I suddenly realised I was now approaching H and L man again, so did a wheelie, and back-tracked towards another exit I'd spotted which enabled me to sneak quietly away, albeit without acquiring any fresh grooves.

IN WHICH I PREPARE TO FLOG

Another example of record company pricing aggravating and quite possibly also alienating would-be buyers of their products emerged in late March 2023 on X/Twitter, from Gareth, aka @justplayed: 'I still can't quite get over the fact that the 2 LPs alongside 4 CDs in the deluxe book set of Bacharach and Costello, retailing at £180, come in plain paper sleeves. Seriously, which bits are we meant to believe cost the extra?'

Gareth's complaint soon found support, from @cliquetrack, aka Cmdr. Stirling Silliphant: 'It's become a complete corporate ripoff. My enthusiasm for new vinyl has gone. Record companies are mugging us off with mediocre quality product at high markups.' The Cmdr. added: 'new vinyl market will collapse at this rate. They are milking the fan and collector.'

Emphasising such pricing, a clearly gobsmacked @duncanyoung68, aka Duncan 'Stone Cold' Young, showed his frustration with a howl of rage: 'My wife was out and about and she (we) are the last humans alive not to have this. So she bought it. How facking much!!???'

What was the record for which his better half had invested £38.99? It was that rare, sought-after disc, *Abba Gold*. And to make Duncan feel a TINY bit better – a quick look online showed the record available for even better than a penny under 39 quid. I may be wrong here, but when I checked, the almost 39 quid version features 19 tracks on two gold coloured LPs. And when I checked, the contents of a CD called *Abba Gold*, seemed to feature the very same 19 tracks – available on Amazon – at a price of £4.64.

I could hardly agree more fervently about these disgraceful prices, despite the over-familiar defences the record companies seek to put up. Surely, selling more at lower prices and keeping their product attractive to a greater number of people should be preferable to ripping people off who will just decide to spend their hard-earned elsewhere.

I'd begun looking through some of my singles to see which ones I might be prepared to sell at the Record Fair which was now about three weeks away. Some were easily shoved on the 'get rid of' pile. 'Spare The Children' by Studd Pump was a tricky one, with its 'Not For Resale' sticker, along with the release date of 19 March 1971, on the Penny Farthing label – rated at £8 in the *Rare Record Price Guide*, but on Discogs shown as being sold for up to £45, a lowest price of £9.95, and a median price of £30.14... so how much to offer it for? I decided on a 'come and get me' £16 as I won't be upset if it doesn't sell.

But, ex-Gun man Adrian Gurvitz's picture sleeve 'Classic', with a few scratches and a slightly scruffy picture sleeve – one English quid. 'Time to Kill' by the Band? To be fair, I won't go into mourning if I never hear it again – £4. The Sex Pistols' 'No One Is Innocent', subtitled 'A Punk Prayer by Ronald Biggs' with that Great Train Robber on the picture sleeve – a tenner, as I don't remember ever playing it, and it has Sid Vicious 'doing' – in many ways – 'My Way' on the B side. Bargain. One I decided not to offer at the sale was the Thin Lizzy 4-track EP from 1971, featuring Phil Lynott's 'Dublin', 'Old Moon Madness' and 'Things Ain't Working Out Down At The Farm' as well as 'Remembering Part II (New Day)' by Lynott, Bell, Powney. *Rare Record Price Guide* suggests it is worth £300 in top nick and with the picture sleeve. Mine is not in top nick and doesn't have a picture sleeve – which gives it a highest rating of £100 in RRPG. Mine has obvious scratches, but plays through. The EP has sold for a lowest 30 quid, a maximum £573.12, according to Discogs. Can't decide whether I'd be happy selling it for 50 quid plus, or being able to boast that I own it!

I also took a look at the few commercial cassettes still hanging around the place, so decided to price them up as I have reason to believe there are some hardcore cassette enthusiasts still prepared to buy them. How to price the double Beatles Anthology cassette? I decided to try it at a mere six quid. After all, I have it on CD, so no diminution of music if I can sell.

IN WHICH I CHANNEL CHICORY TIP

Who recalls the 1972 Chicory Tip hit single, 'Son of My Father'? If you do, I doubt you will remember many of the lyrics, apart from one of the choruses which bangs on about changing and rearranging stuff, and seems obsessed by the realisation of the male singer that he is actually the offspring of his own Dad.

It's worth checking out the rest of the lyrics and also noting that one of the three writers of the track was Giorgio Moroder – better known as Euro-disco king of his day for his productions and compositions, particularly Donna Summer's 'I Feel Love' and 'Love to Love You Baby'.

Anyway, as his father, on to my own son Steeven's vinyl story:

'I've been "properly" collecting vinyl for about 10 years. I say properly, as I've always had records since developing an interest in music 30 years ago, but it has only been in the last decade that I've really cared about picking up albums on vinyl. What ties me most to collecting music primarily on vinyl is that more meaningful sense of connection with the artist. Playing a record forces you to take the time to actively listen to the whole release, and also the tangible product in front of you can't help but turn your mind to think about the time and effort gone into the product you are holding and hearing.

What kicked me into vinyl gear was an initial desire to own my "top 50" albums in this format. It felt both attainable and a good way to try and experience my favourites in their fullest format. I purchased a quality turntable and speaker system, and away I went.

Collecting music in this format opens up so many more avenues: the experience of going to a record shop, that unique smell, the people (not always a good smell!), and the fantastic stories associated with each and every place you happen to visit.

When I think of the record shops I have been to across the years, they all bring a feeling and so much more of a time and a place in life. Jammin' with Edward in Harrow also had a unique smell (!!) and elicits thoughts of my formative years of getting into music and forming friendships for life. Resident Records, in Brighton, always had an excellent selection and I always associated it with the opportunity to pick up something new, and the joy of catching up with friends.

Moving across the world to New Zealand, and Auckland institution Real Groovy offers an incredible selection, and I also feel fond memories when thinking about the bands I've been visiting the city to see. I'm lucky enough to live in a town, Petone, which hosts its own record shop in Lo Cost Records, which soldiers on gamely providing a quality selection often unavailable in its bigger competitors.

Like most people reading this book I'm sure, having an acquired taste means picking up a complete Top 50 remains tantalisingly elusive (hello *Visual Audio Sensory Theater* by VAST), however, it has meant an evolution of my collecting, basically now picking up anything I love to give more than a cursory listen to on Spotify.

Essentially, I will never complete the 50 and I'm absolutely delighted by that, it just means the search will continue. In the meantime, I'll carry on picking up more treats and without a doubt become more invested in artists, and along the way I will continue to find new experiences unavailable anywhere else. Collecting records is a lifestyle, and thankfully one that can't be changed easily.'

39

IN WHICH I FIND A DINKY ANSWER

I have found pricing up the records and CDs I'm going to take to a Record Fair quite tricky. Yes, the easiest way is to have a look at how much they are going for on Discogs and make an allowance for the fact that there will be no postage and packing costs involved at the Fair. But then there is the probability that most people showing an interest in various title(s) will almost certainly be assuming that the price quoted includes an element that the vendor has added on, so that they can appear generous by knocking it off at the point of sale, and will thus only be prepared to pay a lesser total. So, if I put, say, £10 on a record, will that mean I expect to be offered perhaps £6 and then have to come back with, 'I'll take £8', at which point I'll be offered and will accept '£7', and will have been suckered into ostensibly suffering a 30% discount, although in actuality I'll only be 12.5% down on what I'd realistically thought I might achieve?

I expect a few of you have had this experience – in deciding which records I can bear to part with, I was happy that The Sensational Alex Harvey Band's *Next* was one I could afford to let go without any qualms whatsoever. And to prove it, I sat down and listened to it. Then I wondered whether I should keep it – mind you, I still think I like only three of the seven tracks – I think I'd bet 4/7 that I will take it to the Record Fair, and 6/4 that I won't.

Mark Fry's *Dreaming with Alice* album is usually described as psychedelic, or acid-folk. It is certainly of an otherworldly nature. I own two copies – I don't know why, but I like the different covers of each, so why not! It first appeared in 1972 – Fry was 19, recently graduated from high school and in Italy studying painting when he walked barefoot into RCA's Italian subsidiary offices, played them some songs he'd written on his guitar and was promptly signed to record this album, which was described by *Word* magazine as 'Nick Drake meets Dr Strangely Strange with a touch of Lewis Carroll' which is a fair enough explanation. I bought my first copy in Nantes, France, where we were on a horse racing trip, but I have no intention of selling either.

A word I'd seen bandied about of late, in connection with new LP releases, had left me a little baffled. I really didn't know, and couldn't work out, what it meant. But then I spotted a reference to the word 'Dinked' which directed me to a website, where I discovered that: 'Dinked is a collective of like-minded, independent record shops from all over the UK, working together to promote music we love through limited vinyl releases.'

Nothing to do with the 'Dinky' toy cars of my infancy, then. Sounds like an excellent idea, but if I don't know about it, there are probably quite a few other record collectors who have no idea, either – so perhaps they need to up their publicity. Their website is at dinkededition.co.uk.

IN WHICH I LETCH AFTER RECORDS – BUT FEEL GRAND

It was sloshing down with rain as I walked to the supermarket – hm, ideal conditions to visit a record shop, wouldn't you say? As I was asking myself, the answer came back in the affirmative. So I thought that, as it was celebrating its 60th birthday this year, David's Music, Bookshop and Café, in Letchworth (which, I believe, is an independent-employee trust, although I'm unaware just what that means) might be a good bet for a 30-mile drive – and with any luck I might find something to have inserted into a paper bag marked with the new company seal I'd seen the shop boasting about a day or two earlier online on Facebook: 'Our paper bags are getting a make-over... check out the new stamp. Ooh wee. We're getting jacked from all the stamping.' Nope, no idea what 'getting jacked' means, either, must be some kind of young-person-speak.

David's had also, its website informed me, enjoyed the visit a couple of days earlier by a man and his (guide) dog, adding that: 'We thought we'd treat you to some pictures of Jasper, (the dog) who came in yesterday. Funnily enough the pal he brought with him bought a Pup record (true story). He was a total dream boat. We're here 'til 5.30 today. Bring us your dogs & buy some records.' I'm assuming it was the dog who was the 'total dream boat'.

I researched the 'Pup' reference and believe that PUP (abbreviation for Pathetic Use of Potential) is a Canadian indie/ punk rock band formed in Toronto, Ontario in 2013, originally under the name Topanga. Although I was, naturally, anticipating coming back with vinyl I probably wasn't going to splash out £1,000 as one customer did here a while back when staff member Ashlie Sky accepted that amount in return for a copy of Led Zeppelin's debut LP, complete with turquoise lettering on the front cover.

Okay, no, I didn't get anywhere near shelling out a grand, but I did hand over £29.99 in return for a sealed Rory Gallagher live LP, *Cleveland Calling Pt 2* – a most reasonable £13 in the sale – and a birthday present for Mrs S, an AC/DC jigsaw puzzle, featuring her two favourites – Bon and Angus.

I had a brief chat with the hirsute, friendly lad behind the counter, who wasn't quite sure on which date the shop's 60th birthday might fall. But he knew how to operate the credit card gizmo, and told me who I'd been listening to playing out all the time I was in the shop, although I got the impression he wasn't the greatest fan and it was probably the boss's choice. I can't remember the name of the artist concerned, but the record was officially due out at the end of the week, and the songs were very wordy and story-like. I quite enjoyed his music.

Just like inside David's, there was a bit of splashing out done when I departed, as it was still blooming chucking it down – which meant my brown paper David's bag was running the risk of disintegrating if I didn't keep it shoved under my jacket as I headed swiftly back to the Morrisons car park where I'd left the vehicle.

I was stopped in my tracks as I walked back in, spotting for the first time a notice warning that drivers risked having their cars towed away if they parked in the wrong area and/or overstayed their three hour welcome. I spotted the notice, but no, not my car... panic! Surely I hadn't been in David's for three hours? Well, no, but I had forgotten exactly where I'd put the thing and had a nasty idea that it might have been in the danger area.

Fortunately, the bay I was in was bang next to, but not quite *in* the towing section, so I swiftly jumped in and drove off, fearing for the next few days that I might receive some form of communication demanding payment of 100 quid for being in the wrong part of the car park for too long.

The next day brought another chorus of complaints about record pricing, as the excellent Gareth James from Just Played – justplayed@substack.com – wrote scathingly, in his always readable online blog, about the new Depeche Mode LP: 'The announcement of *Memento Mori* was also notable due to an extortionately priced pre-order bundle of the CD, cassette, red vinyl and signed print that sold out in seconds despite costing £81 before delivery. Such grim gouging of the fans continued with the standard formats – the CD is retailing at £16 and the 2 LP pressing, with only three sides of music and an uninspiring etching, comes in at £43! It has a tri-panel gatefold, they cry! And a tiny bit of foil de-bossing! A 24x12″, heavily creased 'poster'? Yep. But, perhaps, cut the loyal following a bit of a break in these ruinous times?'

I was still searching for items to include on my table at the forthcoming Record Fair when I spotted a CD box set, which I'd acquired several years ago via the *Daily Mail*, which was running some kind of promotion – can't really remember precisely what it was, but I suspect collecting tokens was involved, maybe with a small payment, too. On offer was a collection of a dozen CD albums by Spandau Ballet, Culture Club, Paul Young, Adam and The Ants, Human League, Simple Minds, Bonnie Tyler, Haircut 100, Terence Trent D'Arby, Dexy's Midnight Runners, Heaven 17 and Marillion. Probably the best of them was the TTD – baffling that he never managed to reach that peak again. I'd used the CDs in the car when ferrying people around who wouldn't have fancied listening to my true favourite albums.

But I genuinely couldn't remember the last time I'd taken this out and listened to any of them, and I was considering how much I could put it up for sale at. What would you pay? Great collection, and of its time, of course, but I could live without it, and thought if I asked a tenner I could always reduce if I got an offer of, say, £7+. As I picked the box up to look at it more closely, the internal section opened up to reveal not only the actual CDs – there were no individual covers, just a photographic image alongside each one – but also a white envelope marked 'Bills'. I'd no idea what that was doing there, so I picked it up and opened it, to find a handwritten letter from my brother, Barry, dated 11 December 2016, documenting some payments which needed to be made on behalf of my late Mum... together with some cash. Nine hundred and sixty pounds, to be precise, in the form of 48 £20 notes – obviously sent to cover the cost of the bills. I remembered paying the bills online, but now realised that I had presumably put the money in the CD box for temporary safe keeping – over six years ago, and totally forgotten about it. Until now. What an unexpected bonus someone, picking up the box at the Record Fair and deciding to snap it up for six or seven quid, would have found themselves acquiring when they later looked in more detail at their purchase. And, after finding almost a thousand quid inside the box they would have, of course, made every effort to find out who and where I was, in order to hand me back the cash. It wasn't all completely good news, mind you – I'd put the notes there so long ago that they were no longer legal tender.

I went to the Post Office to enquire whether they would take them off me, and was informed, yes, but only 320 quid's worth – I'd then have to make another couple of trips to different Post Offices or financial outlets, to complete the swap to valid dosh. As I did have an existing account with the Nationwide I walked up to their nearby branch to see whether I could put it into my account with them. When I arrived they were shut, as they weren't opening until half an hour later, at 10am, so I had to go and check out the local charity shops to see what CDs and/or LPs I could find – none at all, as it transpired. Back over at the Nationwide, I was first in the 10am queue. I walk in, and 'May I help you?' says a friendly member of staff. I explain. 'No problem – just put them in the machine over there, it will check how many notes there are and will accept them, despite them being now out-of-date.' She was right. Result!

Only thing is, I now feel I have to open up and check thoroughly every single CD I own (about a couple of thousand) to make sure I haven't done exactly the same thing somewhere else.

IN WHICH ERIC'S FAITH PAYS OFF

Eric Clapton celebrated his 79th birthday today, 30 March 2024... I bet he's surprised to make such old bones! Seen him now and then over the years – first time at Hyde Park with Blind Faith, don't think I ever saw Cream live, though. Later, saw him solo a couple of times at the Albert Hall. I have a good few of his LPs, but don't play them as often as, say, Rory Gallagher's or Joe Bonamassa's. Sadly, also on the same date, one year earlier, founder member of Gentle Giant, Ray Shulman, died aged 73. He was also in earlier group, Simon Dupree and the Big Sound. I remember loving, and buying when it came out, the latter's drivingly listenable single, 'I See the Light' which was only a radio hit in 1966.

When I arrived in nearby Bushey this morning, having just avoided a torrential downpour, there was Second Scene boss, Julian, cleaning the dust off of the records in the large table-top container of hundreds of 'also-ran' records left outside, amongst the meteorological elements to attract passing vinyl browsers who might decide to spend a few bob on an impulse purchase. 'I have to keep checking these records, as stuff that I would previously have happily put on here thinking they were almost worthless – particularly 12"s – have become quite desirable to certain collectors and buyers,' he told me, adding that he also needed to deter giant bluebottles from finding a home amongst them as he had discovered recently when one suddenly startled him by appearing out of the, er, blue. He also showed me the, well, 'stuff' neatly(ish) stored at the side of the shop, advising me to 'be careful of the cat shit' as I manoeuvred my way round.

Safely inside the shop I began browsing and came up with three possibilities – firstly a Ten Years After LP I was not sure whether I did or didn't have, followed by a Love LP, *Out Here*, which I was not sure whether I did or didn't have, then a Roy Harper LP with

Jimmy Page accompanying him on guitar, which I was 99.9% sure I didn't have. Guess which one(s) I bought?

I went for the Harper, of which I played side one on Julian's in-shop stereo/hi-fi/sound system, whatever you like to call it. It sounded very good after two tracks, at which point I said to Julian, 'I really like this' which seemed to send a signal to the stereo and Harper immediately began droning out some spoken poetry! I forgave him for that and still bought the record. Helen, Julian's better half, was also in the shop, and while he was outside I took the opportunity to ask her whether she might be interested in contributing a piece for the book on the trials and tribulations of being a record shop owner's wife?

She didn't commit herself one way or the other! A browser appeared in the shop, asking 'Got any Taj Mahal?' Julian didn't think so. The chap made no comment, had a short look around and left. Then another, rather more talkative gentleman arrived – he does a bit of record selling, in Oxford. He is also something of a follower of the same sort of non-league local football sides as myself. We had a chat about the Edgwares, Hendons, Oxhey Jets and Wealdstones of this ilk.

Then we all began discussing certain Record Fairs of our acquaintance and the relatively recent phenomenon at them, of what we all felt should be known as 'tenner bootlegs', the copious number of ostensibly legit, brand new LPs by all manner of well-known acts, which have appeared in not only Fairs, but also markets. They are almost invariably – when I have seen them, anyway – priced at ten of your English/British pounds and often boast music by very well-known acts. I personally have examples by the likes of Bryan Ferry – this one from a show I actually witnessed – Badfinger, and Procol Harum.

Julian was adamant that they tend to be of extremely poor quality and not worth buying, and told us of a quite young person of his acquaintance who had spent £30 on a double LP of this ilk, only to find their stylus jumping everywhere other than through the grooves it should be following. 'They are made of who knows what rubbish bits and pieces' was his view. Let this be a warning to you that they may appear to be a bargain, and if you are very lucky – as I seem to have been – they may actually BE a bargain, but the odds that they will prove to be no such thing are not very long.

One of the great pleasures of my life since a very young age has been reading the books of Richmal Crompton, about 'Just' William Brown, the permanently 11-year-old boy. She wrote and had them published from 1922 until 1970 when the 38th and final one appeared – with William still the same age. I had decided to reread one of the books, and randomly selected her 1965 offering, *William and the Pop Singers*, in which, it soon became obvious, Richmal – born in 1890 – was becoming aware of the Beatles and their growing success. The title story of this book concerns William meeting Chris, the lead singer of pop group, the Argonauts, whose other members are Ted, Johnny and Pete. Chris has 'gone off' from his band-mates because, as Johnny tells William, 'He's had a classy education and taken classy exams and sometimes it comes over him that he's wastin' his life singin' pop songs.' However, William inadvertently gives Chris an idea for a new song, 'Moon Girl', which he composes in full as fellow group member Ted yells, 'Yeah! Yeah! Yeah!' and the others join in with 'Yeah! Yeah! Yeah!' before Pete offers a solo 'Yeah! Yeah! Yeah!' as does William's pal, Douglas, then William himself.

With 'She Loves You' having been released on 23 August 1963 I'm pretty sure Richmal will have heard it many times, as did we all, and possibly subconsciously written it into this William story. I don't think the Argonauts' song ever made it to record – but it's not too late, the full lyrics are in the book – here's the first verse: 'Moon girl, my moon girl, I'm comin' to you soon, girl, Shootin' up the moonbeams, 'Cos I'm in love with you.'

IN WHICH I WONDER IF I'VE MADE
A RICK

One of my earliest guitar heroes, Rick Zehringer, who would become known as Rick Derringer, revealed on his Facebook page how he felt about records back in the day – and probably still does: 'Remember your excitement the first time you shopped for an album or CD, brought it to your player (hardly able to wait to get there) opened and heard it, completely fresh & new?' This was part of his announcement of a new LP.

This one, he wrote at this time, would be called *Love to Earth* but, when I checked again, it appeared to be ultimately named *Beyond the Universe*. I feared this sounded annoyingly ecological, but it turned out to be a set of many of his better known old tracks, probably rerecorded (I haven't heard it and won't be buying it to find out). Bizarrely, the only copies listed on Discogs are from Germany.

It is seldom a positive step when people begin to talk about themselves in the third person. And, to be fair, my opinion of Rick has rather plummeted since the time I was involved in running the UK Fan Club for him and the rest of the McCoys, whose enormous breakthrough hit was 'Hang On Sloopy' in 1965. I enjoyed them going psych on 'Infinite McCoys', and loved their team-up with Johnny Winter, which made for probably the strongest twin-guitar line-up of any band before or since. But not that long ago, after I'd persuaded *Record Collector* magazine that it would be a good thing to run a feature about Rick, they agreed on condition I could get some good quotes from him.

When I made contact with him he just wouldn't get round to the 'good quotes' part, and eventually I gave up on the idea. Should you read this and change your mind, Rick, I'll see if the RC is still interested – I am, as long as you are honest – I mean, what was that story of you and a gun really all about? Associated Press reported in February 2014 that, 'Rock guitarist Rick Derringer has pleaded guilty and agreed to pay a $1,000 fine after stepping off a Delta Air Lines flight from Mexico with a loaded handgun in Atlanta's airport.'

Rick also produced the World Wrestling Federation's album, *The Wrestling Album* (1985) and its follow-up *Piledriver: The Wrestling Album II* (1987). The albums included the entrance song for Hulk Hogan 'Real American', and the Demolition tag team, 'Demolition'.

Good to see Rick not cheapening his talents for commercial reasons.

IN WHICH I CONTEMPLATE THE END GAME

At the start of April 2023 I was wondering how many LPs/12"s/ singles/CDs/ I should be taking to the Record Fair in just under two weeks. I'd already collected about 100 CDs and 100 LPs together, with maybe 50 singles. I probably wasn't going to bother with cassettes.

Then there's that Jethro Tull framed 'gold disc' my hairdresser gave me, and a few record-related books – the difficulty is going to be getting them into, then out of the car, then being able to ferry them into the venue and onto the tables. Not sure how many separate trips to/from the car this might involve – oh well, part of the fun of being a newbie, I suppose, and something I've never had to contemplate when just visiting Fairs to be a buyer.

Checking through the albums had reminded me of both the delights and the difficulties of owning a large number of LPs and CDs. Not least – WHEN did I get this record, WHY did I get this record, HOW COME I still have this record, and DO I NEED to keep it?

I mean, just WHO are Grauzone and WHAT am I doing with a copy of this record, from which I could not quote you one line of lyric, or sing you one chorus from any track?????

Discogs informs me that my Grauzone LP is from 1981, that their songs have German titles – one of them includes the word 'Marmelade' in its title, and that they play electronic, new wave/post-punk music. No, none the wiser. So, I listen to part of one of the tracks of their record... and it is, to my ears, repetitively awful. But the cheapest copy of this record I own will set you back the best part of 40 quid.

Other LPs, though, I look at them with familiarity and compassion – I even smile at the thought of them, am very glad to have them and would like to make time to listen to them again – but not just now as I have a number of other matters which take priority.

This process makes me realise that owning is as important as listening to the records for me. They are a comfort blanket – knowing they are always there if I need them is clearly as important – more important, probably – than feeling I just have to listen to each one every day. No, I just want to know they are there WHEN I fancy hearing them – even if that never happens again.

And no, it isn't the same that, if I wanted, I could do likewise just by clicking on to YouTube.

These musings result in it suddenly striking me that my generation of record and music lovers is now well into its descent towards becoming 'the past'. Every few days seems to bring news that another iconic, or at least memorable, stalwart of the 60s and early 70s music scene has departed.

It is probably fair to assume that as far as the media is concerned the real 'end of the 60s generation' will be announced when, with all due respect to Messrs Starr and Richards, either McCartney or Jagger heads off into the next world. Should this cause me any angst? Absolutely not. I'm well aware that those of us who grew up with the Beatles and the Stones are well into, at the very best estimation, our last but one decade.

As we grew up we knew that those who came before – the Sinatras, Fitzgeralds, Bennetts, Garlands of those times, were making their way to the exit and forming a not-so orderly queue.

Frank's 'My Way', which presaged the end years was a gigantic hit for him as it acknowledged not only to himself but to his whole generation, as accurately as George Harrison to his, that 'All Things Must Pass'.

There's little doubt that 'our' music will continue to engage with that from younger generations for many years, but it will undoubtedly dwindle to a sideshow compared with the massive influence it has been now for 60-plus years. Most of our kids – maybe even some of the grandchildren – will regard it fondly, but as an anachronism. It will be to them as the songs 'Uncle Mac' used to play for us on the radio when we were little children.

What song will come to be regarded as our 'My Way'? Might it be 'My Generation', maybe 'Satisfaction', possibly 'All You Need Is Love'? Probably not 'Hold On' by Sharon Tandy, though!

IN WHICH I LEARN WHAT IT'S LIKE RUNNING A RECORD LABEL – FRUITY FUN!

Keith Jones gave the world the great little psych-friendly label, Fruits de Mer, launched in 2008, when, as he told me, 'An old friend, Andy Bracken, was already running a vinyl-only indie label in the USA – and we came up with the idea for Fruits de Mer, one drunken afternoon in London.' He went on:

'My love of music and records began in 1967 when I heard two versions of "Bend Me, Shape Me", on BBC TV one after the other, the first by Amen Corner, the second by The American Breed – I instantly knew the US version was far superior and felt compelled to go and buy a copy but what really hooked me was the B side, a track called "Mindrocker", my first introduction to popsike, although at the age of 10 or 11 it felt like pretty heavy stuff for a kid growing up in a mining village in the Midlands.

My first big obsession with music came a few years on, with krautrock - a result of Saturday afternoons in a Virgin record shop in Birmingham's Corporation Street, full of thick, heady smoke; I listened to albums on the Brain label on headphones and my buying habits began with a band called Grobschnitt, moving on to Can, Neu!, Tangerine Dream, Faust.

My collection of krautrock and prog rock albums built rapidly - Caravan and Spirit featured highly; I developed a sideline in buying and selling albums to supplement my paper round.

The 80s were about marriage, mortgage, kids and work. Music largely passed me by. My interest was reawakened by the sounds of The Orb, KLF and electronica - Pete Namlook and his label Fax became my next obsession. I was filling in gaps in both my knowledge and records from the mid-60s onwards - discovering great albums such as *Ogdens' Nut Gone Flake* and *SF Sorrow*.

By 2008 my record and CD collection was taking over the house. I had too many pints in the Stamford Arms near Waterloo, London with Andy Bracken. Conversation got around to launching a label to rerelease classic and long lost psych/prog tracks from the late 60s and early 70s on 7 inch singles. Fruits de Mer Records.

The record labels that owned tracks we were interested in rereleasing had no interest in us - a non-existent label. Andy had worked with a US band called Schizo Fun Addict, and thought they might record new versions of two tracks we had in mind - the intro instrumental to *Ogden's*, plus George Martin's 'Theme One'. Our first single was born - 300 copies, pressed in the US, in wraparound sleeves printed by me in the office. All we had to do was sell them. Help came from Nick Leese of Heyday Mail Order, and *Record Collector* magazine who reviewed that single with a line we repeatedly used: "this is what 7 inches should be all about".

Our first big break came with the Pretty Things. For some reason, Phil May, Dick Taylor and their manager Mark St. John took a liking to the label and got involved in our remake of the classic album *SF Sorrow*, which Phil and Dick named 'Sorrow's Children', contributing an exclusive recording.

My focus/obsession became Fruits de Mer Records. The label's remit now includes new music owing some kind of debt to the

60s/70s, and a heavy dose of krautrock/kosmiche sounds. The focus on 7 inches now extends to 12 inches, double albums and box sets and – just as we launched FdM when vinyl was pronounced dead – now seems as good a time as any to release more music on much-derided CDs. Fruits de Mer isn't a business – asked who our main competitors were, I said, 'Who'd want to compete with a record label that loses money?'

An important moment was when we realised that trying to make money didn't really fit with running a DIY record label. That gave us freedom to run things the way we really wanted to, releasing records that we as music fans would want to buy. Fifteen years is a long time for a DIY record label to survive, but there's life in the old label yet – I still wake up thinking, "bloody hell I'm running a record label" and most mornings that still feels like a good thing.'

IN WHICH CUSTOMER TAKES REVENGE

In early April 2023, with the Harpenden Record Fair imminent, I discovered a decent selection of CDs in Pinner's charity shops – very timely. I also picked up a very fairly priced LP – Eric Clapton's *Timepieces Volume II*, together with its original insert, released on RSO in 1983. How much? Purchased for one quid, while the CDs featured a £2 *The Freewheelin' Bob Dylan* in top notch condition.

I received a Kevin Ayers' single I'd ordered from South Records in, appropriately enough, Southend, and put a photo of myself with said single on X/Twitter and Facebook, for reasons which totally elude me now – however the record shop ended up reposting it. Fame at last.

In April, 2023, I also received an early morning email from Coda Records offering me a three-CD, live Fleetwood Mac set of 41 tracks, performed between 1975 and 1979, for £8.99, with a 20% Easter offer reduction, bringing the price down to just over seven quid. I quite fancied this collection, and it was included in a buy one, get one free offer, which would halve the cost of the CDs – I could also acquire another triple CD, 40-track Fleetwood Mac collection, from 1975–88, while the p&p wouldn't increase.

There were others available which I could switch around to make a varied pair to purchase.

I suddenly thought – yes, but do I actually NEED them? Well, no, I will have many, the majority probably, of these tracks on other LPs and CDs, and although I have enjoyed nearly all of the various line-ups of the band, they have never been higher than the lower end of the Top 20 in my list of all-time favourite bands. Eighty-one tracks across two collections – how often will I listen to them – when even will I have the time to spare to do so!? So, really, no, I definitely don't need these in my collection, but still, yes, I would like to have them for those occasions when I suddenly fancy hearing them.

Which reminded me of the film Sheila and I had recently watched – Ron Howard's *Eight Days A Week*, brilliantly depicting the development of the Beatles' career, and the ultimate effect on each of them, but equally with a soundtrack of song after song, just reminding us how brilliant they were, how well we both knew all the songs and could sing along with them.

But how long was it since I'd actually pulled these records out to play them? This, no doubt, because I had so many 40- and 41-track collections to get through of extremely enjoyable music – but ultimately nowhere near as essential as that of the Beatles and the Stones, the Pretty Things, the Byrds and many others who were influential as I grew from early teenage years to maturity.

So, with my debut as a seller coming up, I was wondering how I'd react when some of the records and CDs I take along are actually sold. Maybe none will sell and I'll realise that if I have so many records, neither I nor anyone else who is a confirmed collector is interested in, why have them in the first place? Having said that, it is constantly surprising how often just reading the information on the cover of a little used record can spark an interest in, or re-evaluation of, the music within! For example, I give you Brian Auger and Keef Hartley, both of whom I have 'rediscovered', having previously convinced myself I had scant reason to play their music.

It was interesting enough choosing records I was prepared to sell – CDs don't seem to hold anywhere near as much emotional heft for me – but, having made mistakes before, with original records by the likes of Arcadium, Bakerloo and Kaleidoscope, there are plenty which I won't now dispose of even if offered two or three times what I believe to be their proper monetary value, and they will still be sitting in the collection when I finally depart – even if I never hear them again between now and then.

On this same date, I spotted an unusual ploy from Record Culture in Stourbridge: 'We've got our "Pay What You Think It's Worth" section in; loads of second-hand records at no fixed price. You won't find a Beatles rarity in there because we're not that bad at our job, BUT you will find nice cheapies.'

IN WHICH WE DISCUSS
A CRATE PROBLEM

Sophie Ellis-Bextor sang about 'Murder on the Dancefloor', but 'Aggro at the Crate Digging' could be a coming record title if the experience of X/Twitter's @52Vinyl earlier in the day was anything to go by. He reported: 'I was at the record fair. Went up to a crate. Fella stood to the side but two foot away and looking in other direction. I start to flick through, the fella turns, looks at my crate and then puts his hand in and starts flicking through. In the crate I am digging through. MY CRATE!

No "excuse me" or "sorry, I was here a few seconds ago, can I just grab that record?" Not a word. So what do I do?

I do what we should all do when we meet twats like this. "Mate, what you doing?" No acknowledgement at all. "Mate, get out my bin and learn some f***ing manners." He turns to me now with a face like rotting marshmallow.

Now he opens his sweaty mouth: "Get your head out of your arse." Me! Get my head out MY arse! Really? So I give him the death stare and off he waddles with his record taken from MY crate!

Anyone else see this kind of behaviour? Up there with guys who put their record choices on a crate, thereby rendering it null and void. I can't tell you how many times I have moved them and then get passively aggressively sighed at when they take them away.'

@billyedwards was moved to empathise: 'So, so many twats. Always. All the time. If you ever ask anyone to budge you get a snarky comment. Hangers on, uninterested and blocking boxes waiting for their friend to move on, the worst.'

This seems to be an ongoing irk for many. On X/Twitter, @bartlebooth45 ranted in late February, 2024: 'Some **** at the record shop yesterday, lent over and started flicking through the bin I was flicking through – at the same time! I've never seen such a breach of record shop etiquette!'

We'd better all start to get used to such unacceptable behaviour, I fear.

I must admit I have yet to experience anything of this magnitude at a record fair, although at busy ones I have found it necessary to utilise elbows to persuade someone trying to monopolise several crates at a time to move over to let me in. Potential buyers can stand chatting with a friend or stallholder, while they effectively, albeit unknowingly, block anyone else's progress towards the merchandise. And there is definitely an argument that the 'Sweat Police' might be gainfully employed at some sales. @FrontierVinyl joined in the X/Twitter chat about this behavioural misbehaviour, declaring: 'There is also quite obnoxious behaviour online. I refunded a buyer on Discogs today because his attitude just stunk. Took a hit on the post as I'd bought it already, but I wasn't having his shite. I stand in solidarity!'

I would tend to agree. My own experiences on Discogs have resulted in frequent trivial complaints from customers clearly looking for a discount or refund, and invariably if they were escalated for a decision from the site it appeared to me that the customer was always given the benefit of the doubt, which is tantamount to a cheat's charter.

Derek Amos compiles a comprehensive weekly listing of forthcoming record fairs. Neither of us can really define the term, and I queried whether a regular listing of an 'event' in London held usually three times a week in the same location, should qualify as a genuine record fair? I believe it is more a collection of dealers rather than genuine 'amateur' or occasional record sellers. Derek (www.recordfairs.co.uk) responded that 'I don't really have a definition' and added intriguingly, 'Would you classify 6 dealers with two tables each as a fair, but not two dealers with 6 tables each?'

Any thoughts, readers?

IN WHICH ROSSI IS QUITE FRANK

Went to see Francis Rossi of Status Quo doing a music and chat show at the Eric Morecambe Centre in Harpenden – terrific, apart from the distracting fact that, when he is speaking in a slightly excited state, to my eyes at least, Francis now bears a worrying resemblance to Sid James. The first half of the 'performance' dealt with Quo's earlier LPs – my favourites, to be frank (or Francis, if you prefer). There was a lot of honesty and surprising detail – for example, that their well-known track, 'Gerdundula', is, he revealed, a coming together of three words – Gerd Und Ula – from a time when he was going through a phase of somehow squeezing in German and/or Dutch phrases into his songs – remember the 'Deutsche car' in 'Paper Plane'?

What WAS that all about? Francis did not elucidate.

But he DID confess that some of his best riffs have come from rocked up versions of songs he learned as a kid, such as one I also recalled (he's about 18 months older than me) – 'Poppa Piccolino' – a song which reached number 2 in the UK singles chart in December 1953 – he strummed the song and then did so again with the now legendary Quo-style 'shuffle' superimposed, and there was a classic Quo riff.

The first half of the show, dealing with their early music, was very informative, and, despite being familiar with the cover of their early and excellent *Ma Kelly's Greasy Spoon* LP, it was news to me that the 'waitress' in what appears to be a 'greasy-spoon' café pic, should have been a real waitress they knew from the gaff, but she didn't fancy doing it. But the 'model' they brought in to replace her wasn't a smoker, so had to be given a fake fag for the cover photo shoot.

Francis' full name is Francis Dominic Nicholas Michael Rossi, (but I'm pretty sure he was known as Mike Rossi in the early Quo days), OBE. Unsurprisingly, the audience was made up of long-time Quo followers – some still sporting the kind of ponytail Rossi once flaunted – but he deliberately drew attention to the bald spot on the back of his now sparsely thatched bonce, as he turned to sit down to talk to the audience.

Francis' relationship with long-term band mate, the late Rick Parfitt, was clearly complicated and he didn't seem to want to address it in any depth, nor was much said about the other group members, although this was, of course, a solo gig. He did play a good few Quo songs, supported by a younger guitarist, whom, I suspect, many audience members would have taken for his son – he did have a ponytail, and played guitar extremely well – but it appeared he was a non-related guitar 'mechanic' who looked after the Rossi instruments.

There was a session during which Francis was asked audience questions, which must have been submitted much earlier, as I saw no invitation to pose one – but had I had such an opportunity I'd have wanted to know why he and his colleagues refused to play, when Sheila (who first saw Quo play on 14 February 1968 – aged 13 – at the NME awards event at Empire Pool in Wembley) and I were amongst an admittedly very sparse turnout to see them at the Farx Club in Southall in, probably, 1969 or 1970. They sent out Alan Lancaster to offer a very brief non-apologetic apology.

My other question, and I would seriously like to know the answer, would be why – when the Kinks followed up 'You Really Got Me' with the almost identical, only slightly less successful 'All Day And All Of The Night', and the Dave Clark Five did likewise after 'Glad All Over', with 'Bits 'N' Pieces' – Status Quo's follow up to smash hit 'Pictures of Matchstick Men', the almost identical 'Black Veils of Melancholy', barely scraped into the Top 50?

Fantastic psych lyrics, though – who else ever managed to combine peppercorn trees, poison gazes and black veils together in the same melancholic song? Come on – psychedelic genius, or what!?

Shortly after this single, they put out another, 'Technicolor Dreams', on the Pye label, marked 7N 17650. If you come across one of these in your collection, it might be worth thinking about selling it on, as the *Rare Record Price Guide* prices it now at £800. For the record, I currently own a modest 8 Quo LPs, and 13 of their CDs.

IN WHICH I'M FAIRLY EXCITED

So, on Saturday 15 April 2023, as the day dawned damp, I was up at 6am to prepare for my debut as a record fair seller, at the Eric Morecambe Centre. Good friend, Roger Plummer, had agreed to help out, even though he lives on the other side of the capital, and he arrived as promised in good time, at about 7am. I'd braved the drizzle to stack boxes and cases of records, CDs, cassettes and books in the car, so we were off and running at 7.15, arriving just before 8am to find organiser Glenn Povey busily organising the car parking in the bijou area available for sellers' vehicles. I was able to insert my Audi into the indicated area – 'don't worry about parking over the lines, get as close as you can to the car next to you' was the welcome instruction. My selling table partner Ron's car, was already occupying a nearby space. We all stood around for a few minutes before, to a small cheer, the doors to the arena opened and we were able to enter the auditorium.

It was noticeable that we three were lugging our records, etc., into the building in carrier bags, boxes and record cases, with great physical effort, while the obviously far more experienced sellers were efficiently utilising high-tech trolleys and cleverly designed, strong plastic cases to move their vinyl into the building. We soon found our allocated pair of tables, which were around the walls, and marked with a handwritten note: 'Graham Sharpe x 2'. We began to unpack various bags, boxes and cases to display our wares on the table tops. We had been allocated one chair, but fortunately, Ron had brought along two collapsible ones, as well, so all three of us were able to seat ourselves once the items were displayed.

All we needed now were customers – the first few of which were fellow sellers, so we repaid the compliment by having a look around their offerings. The masses were permitted entry shortly before ten. First blood went to Ron when he sold a couple of things, although his joy was a little tempered by the fact that they belonged to a friend who had given him some items to sell on his behalf. I was extremely jealous that Ron's table had drawn first blood, and already began to have nervous 'what if no one buys anything from me?' thoughts.

But ten minutes later I had made my first sale, courtesy of a young chap who picked up a Meic Stevens' CD I'd misguidedly bought some years back from, I think, Dale's shop in Chesham, to make up an extra purchase when he was offering a three-for-twelve-quid or some such sum.

I remembered reading of Meic that he was a Welsh singer-songwriter, whose songs had a 'mystical, faintly psychedelic flavour', but probably missed the bit which added that they were 'mostly sung in his native Welsh language', so one play was all I'd given this one, Gwymon, not even knowing what the word meant. Had I checked then and not now, when I've just googled it and been told it means 'seaweed', I probably would never have owned it. And I no longer own it now, as the youthful chap handed over a fiver to become its new owner, without revealing to me whether he had any Welsh roots.

But now I was deflowered in terms of record fair sales virginity, and off and running. I wrote that sale down on the side of a box on the table, and as things picked up soon wrote '2 LPs – £20' but I can't now for the life of me remember what they were! An

LP by the Flying Lizards went next for a mere six quid, before a gentleman excitedly told me he thought he'd read all the books about the Rolling Stones but had never seen this particular one (whose title I've also already forgotten) I'd brought along with me, just in case anyone fancied buying it, as I was confident I'd never get round to reading it again.

I think he got a bargain as the cheapest one I'd seen on the book-auction site, ABE, before coming along was over 30 quid, but I let him have it for 20, along with another he fancied, *Old Gods Almost Dead*, which I reduced from eight to five quid, for a total purchase of £25, down from the £36 I'd originally hoped I might get. But he looked an honest man, genuinely happy to have found a book he didn't know about, and I doubted that I was likely to come across anyone else looking to take the pair – thus a quid in the pocket was worth 30 bob in the anticipation.

I heard a chap looking at my LPs, refer to the fact that one had on it a price sticker from its original selling place, the Sellanby shop in South Harrow, where he used to shop regularly – as did I – since when it has become an ex-record shop, ceased to exist, gone to meet its maker and closed down.

I engaged him in conversation and we soon realised we'd both lived in Harrow back in the day and were both extremely good friends with a chap called Layne Patterson, with whom I was a director of non-league football club, Wealdstone FC. A 45rpm-sized world, isn't it!?

Another surprise bonus during the event was a visit to our desk from Led Zeppelin super-fan, and prolific author of books about the group, Dave Lewis, who bought five singles from me and showed off a foreign copy of a Zepp album he'd just bought, which even he hadn't managed to track down before. I think he said it was the 14th copy of it he now owned, but he might well have said 49th.

I also sold someone 'XM70' or possibly 'XMTO' – can't read my handwriting, and have no idea what either of these two hieroglyphics might mean – although apparently I got a tenner for whatever it was. I do know that I sold two brand new CDs – one by the Vaccines and the other by Alex Harvey for a total of £12.

Perhaps the only rumblings of discontent I would spot during the whole day – and it was still good-humoured – were the comments of various stallholders as we all realised that the background music, being played at a slightly higher volume than the general murmurings of sellers and buyers going about their business, was on a loop, and much though we might know and be slightly fond of the fairly anodyne tunes, we were all thoroughly sick of them by the end of the day!

During my meandering around other traders' stalls I was privileged to be able to look at a pristine, mint promo or demo copy of a single by one of my best loved groups, Kaleidoscope. The Fontana record was 'Do It Again for Jeffrey' from 1969 – not to be confused with Jethro Tull's earlier 1968 'A Song for Jeffrey'. Whoever he was, Jeffrey was clearly a popular boy – popular enough for this single to be priced at £450, at which level I cannot imagine there would be much room for a sell-on profit for anyone – auctioneers excepted, I suppose – so I wasn't about to be in the market for it. However, I looked on Discogs where I came across a 'very good'-graded copy for £150, also noting that the highest amount the record had previously attracted via Discogs was £295.

And I also sold my Jethro Tull gold disc, presented to the band for an appropriate number of sales of *Songs From The Wood* in a Scandinavian country, on which I'd attached a tag saying, 'Make me an offer' – well, it worked, and one came, which I accepted. I'd been slightly suspicious of it since I realised that the side of the album displayed in the frame had more tracks than had ever been on the original LP. Still, buyer beware, and all that – and the middle label is genuine enough.

As I was comfortably ahead of the game in terms of financial outlay versus income I treated myself to a £2 CD version of excellent obscurity, the 1971 *Ginhouse* album, of which I do own an original copy on the B&C label in pretty decent nick. I couldn't resist splurging another 20 quid for a sealed, numbered, double live LP of a Blind Faith concert in Gothenburg, during their short existence as a band in 1969. I'd never seen it before, and, to be honest, was not entirely sure quite how pukka it might be, but it was a very attractive thing and was affordably priced, so

I was happy to purchase it. A search on Discogs later produced the information: 'Recorded in Gothenberg, [I prefer the 'u' version of the spelling] Sweden on 18th June 1969; contains 40-page hardback book, full colour A2 poster & 4 postcard set.' It also refers to it as being an 'unofficial release', whatever that may mean, and lists the lowest price for which it has been sold on the site as £22.99 and the highest £85.05, so mine seems to have been a fair price.

The fair was winding down now as the little hand nudged past the four, so we took the hint and started to pack up our own unsold items to return them to the car. Okay, we hadn't cut down the amount of stuff by a great amount, but we had done so profitably, and it seemed to me most sellers were also going home with the majority of their stock unsold. No surprise there – of course, you need a wide spread of choices to cover the huge variety of requirements and wants of potential buyers, and I can't believe any responsible, thoughtful seller will expect to offload more than a relatively small fraction of what they bring, and if they did they'd probably figure they were under-pricing their stock big-time! After all, when did you ever see a supermarket totally empty at the end of a day's trading? Oh, yes, of course, during the lockdown shortages crisis – bad comparison!

It had been a terrific day all round and very good to get to know some of the sellers. One very affable gent told me he'd travelled down from Newmarket for the Fair (so must have had to get up even earlier than me and Ron) and would be heading to Ely tomorrow to do likewise.

Over the next 24–48 hours I absorbed my feelings about this day, and gradually came to realise that perhaps the most important lesson I had learned from it was that it isn't, in fact, a disaster to allow something which has been there for a very long time, to depart from your collection to enrich someone else's. Probably seeing the look of delight on the face of the man who bought the Rolling Stones book, which he had never seen before, to add to what he had thought was his complete collection was an absolute eye opener. I was so pleased for him. Although I'd have been quite happy to take the book back home there was genuinely no more than a 1% chance of me ever opening it up to read again. The only reason for keeping it would be to brag that I owned it – and who would be impressed by that? Yes, only the man who bought it from me.

Another aspect which convinces me I am now ready to liberate more stuff, was my willingness to give generous 'discounts' to potential buyers, rather than stubbornly insisting I would only part with items for the carved-in-stone prices I'd attached to the covers.

Roger, who accompanied Ron and me to the fair, had brought over with him two boxes of what he described as 'very early Elvis singles' and he was now sounding very bullish about taking a table with us next time out, and trying to sell these and other records he owns.

Not everyone was positive about my foray into seller territory, and my friend John Henwood issued me with something of a warning: 'Have a care Graham, when we "downsized" (what a mistake!) I was persuaded that I had too many books, and umpteen boxes of what I thought less essential volumes went to a charity book sale. So often I find myself looking for one of those non-essentials, which may not have been truly essential, but was very useful/valuable to me if nobody else. Think twice before letting go. You may find yourself scouring the old record shops trying to buy the very one you let go. You could always buy a shed!'

This message gave me food for vinyl thought – since the weekend I had begun to think that it hadn't been too difficult to part with these less essential items in my vinyl armoury, and even to wonder whether this might lead to my becoming willing to sell more valuable items in future. I still think that is unlikely and that what I have actually come to terms with is that the sheer practical problem of where to put ever more records has made me understand that unless I make space I will not be able to add greater numbers.

John's suggestion of buying a shed has a practical ring to it, but sheds, by definition, live in gardens and they and their contents are therefore vulnerable to the elements, as well as to potential thieves. Realistically, though, thieves would have to really know their stuff, otherwise they could spend time and money plotting the perfect vinyl heist, only to discover they've made off with a stash of trash which has been literally put out to grass.

IN WHICH I FIND CLIFF TOPS

Sometimes a single (sorry) word can transport you off in a direction you had no idea you would be taking just minutes ago. I'd spotted a random tweet, asking for suggestions of 'whimsical' music. For some reason, deep in my cavernous mind, something stirred, and the name Clifford T Ward suddenly emerged, which I tweeted back to the whimsical thread.

There it just attracted baffled incomprehension. No one on the thread had the slightest idea to whom this might be a reference. I was thinking particularly of CTW's quite big hit record 'Gaye' as a result of which I had eventually bought three of his LPs, filing them away mentally as 'occasional listens' and probably never brought them back to mind for many years. 'Gaye' was a million-seller, which graced the 1973 Top 10.

Ward, born in 1944, whose long flowing locks helped make him instantly recognisable, followed up with another successful-ish single named after a room in most people of a certain age's homes – 'Scullery'. He also had another, definitely whimsical, single which picked up plenty of airplay but did not dent the charts, 'Wherewithal', which lodged itself deep in my brain and remains there. Ward's first LP, the self-identifying *Singer-Songwriter*, appeared in 1972 on DJ John Peel's Dandelion label, coinciding with the time it was collapsing into liquidation. Clifford was experienced in the business, having served time in several underachieving groups. His second LP, *Home Thoughts*, did better. It included 'Gaye' but the very titles of other tracks show this was not your normal singer-songwriter fare – 'The Dubious Circus Company', 'Where Would That Lead Me?',

'Where's It Going To End' (no ? mark), 'Where Would That Leave Me?' (WITH ? mark), 'Time, The Magician', 'Cold Wind Blowing' and 'Crisis' would all have given a psychiatrist copious material to suggest this was not an averagely contented man. @ThamesChoral, describing herself as 'Record accumulator and general flâneuse', had begun the X/Twitter chat, and responded to my suggestion, that although she was not familiar with his work: 'There is a bench in the grounds of Compton Verney (I think) dedicated to Clifford T Ward and (I've) often wondered if it is the same person.'

Like the story-hungry newshound I've wanted to remain ever since my local paper days, I seized on that reference and investigated at once (googled!), discovering that 'Compton Verney House is an eighteenth-century country mansion in Warwickshire.' Clifford was born in Worcestershire in 1944, and died in 2001. When I contacted Compton Verney's Landscape Manager, Fiona Tansey, she told me: 'I have looked into our records, and have not found a bench for Clifford T Ward.' I solved this small mystery, when I discovered this reference: 'There is a Clifford T Ward memorial bench in the grounds of Witley Court country house in Worcester. The site was chosen by Cliff's family as this was a favourite place of his.'

Ward did not enjoy appearing in public and this helped to hasten his disappearance from the front line of 70s singer-songwriters in commercial terms. But then, in the late 80s, he was diagnosed with multiple sclerosis, which resulted in him having to write and record his final LP, 1994's *Julia And Other New Stories*, at home and, shockingly, as a result of the illness, telling journalist Spencer Leigh, of the recording sessions, that: 'I'm like a bat, I function best at night, but I had to make some of it on all fours.' Clifford died on 18 December 2001. If you would like to know more about Clifford, the Facebook page, 'The Clifford T Ward Project' is worth taking a look at. Good to know he is still being remembered and celebrated.

A little postscript – Clifford T Ward should not be confused with the similarly named, and probably equally talented if less successful, Cliff Wade – who comes highly recommended for his own whimsical work from the late 60s, which is brilliantly collected together in *Looking For Shirley: The Pop-Sike World of Cliff Wade*, issued by Edsel in, I think, 2001.

IN WHICH – SURELY JOHN'S JOKING!

It is one of the most beautiful songs I've ever heard, and I still remember seeing the film for which it was part of the soundtrack, *You're a Big Boy Now*, something of a 'coming of age' movie, I recall, and released a year earlier than *The Graduate*. It was written by Lovin' Spoonful front- and main-man John Sebastian with help from bass player Steve Boone.

Featured in the film is a character named Barbara Darling, and the song, 'Darling Be Home Soon', is the one which really had an impact on me. Loved it, bought the single, bought the LP it came from.

I once saw or read a sketch in which someone listens to the beautiful piano playing of a tune, which he congratulates the performer on, and asks him why he's never heard it on the radio or TV before, and what the tune is called, only to be told, 'I've no idea why they don't play it – but it's called "I Love You So Fucking Much I Feel Like Shit".'

Well, 'Darling Be Home Soon' also seems to me to have a verbal flaw, albeit not as crude as that. But it is caused by John's decision, for some bizarre reason, to rhyme two seldom-used and for a good reason, infantile words – 'dawdled' and 'toddled' – in one of the verses.

It really, seriously, does NOT work – doesn't even make any actual sense, if you think about it. For the life of me I have no idea why, at the run-through stage, that wasn't pointed out in the strongest possible terms to Mr S, along with the suggestion, nay, instruction, that he go away for an hour or two and return with a lyric which wouldn't embarrass anyone who has to sing it.

Despite my problem with the lyrics, a number of respected acts have had a go at performing the song – in 1967 Bobby Darin reached Number 93 on the US charts. In 1969, Joe Cocker had a crack at it. 1972 saw The Association include the song on their *Waterbeds in Trinidad!* LP, while in the same year, Slade included a live version on the *Slade Alive!* record. Then, in 1993, Canadian Celts, the Barra MacNeils, included a version on their album *Closer to Paradise*. So, maybe it is only me who has ever bothered to listen to the lyrics or, having done so, thought there was anything wrong with them.

Writing about this great record with its bizarre lyric sent my subconscious winging off in different directions – eventually coming back to me to say, ooookay – you moan about toddling and dawdling, but you are positively welcoming to a lyric involving a disgusting bodily function involving a discharge from the nasal cavities.

Well, if you put it like that, you're not far wrong – because this is one of my all-time favourite lyrics, which I couldn't quite come to terms with when I first heard it. In the 60s there was no internet to refer to, and you just had to sit and listen over and again to records to pick out the actual words, particularly if they were being sung in an unfamiliar accent, or if, as in this instance, they just sounded so outlandish you genuinely thought your ears must be deceiving you.

But no – after multiple listens it was clearly the case that the group Love's genius and driving force Arthur Lee was actually singing about caked nasal debris turning into crystal (whatever that may be) and an innocent bird about to be assassinated for the unproven crime of trespassing.

Arthur wrote this as part of the track 'Live And Let Live' on the wondrous *Forever Changes* LP, from 1967 – when I was a mere 16 years old and 'snot' was still a word likely to attract sniggers if used at school and a tut at home.

IN WHICH I ENJOY 'NOT RECORD STORE DAY'

I spent an hour and a half of 14 April 2023 catching three trains to get out to the wild wastes of West Norwood. After leaving the tube station, drizzle turned to torrential rain as I walked down the side road and past the man water-blasting graffiti off the side of a nearby building, to enter a shop which had never yet failed to provide me with records I didn't even know existed until I saw them here.

'Here' is the Record and Book Bar, which opened in 2013, and this was my fourth or fifth trip. There was no reason why proprietor Michael Johnson should recognise me, even though we'd been conversing online, so I took a few minutes to re-find my bearings – this place, which also doubles up as a music venue, always seems to have a bigger selection of psych and prog than I generally find elsewhere. This time I had to pick my way around some plastic boxes from recent acquisitions of large collections, to reach my target.

Early perusing wasn't over-encouraging, and I was beginning to ponder buying one LP by a group I really like, Trader Horne, because it featured two tracks not on the original 1970 release. I also hesitated over a compilation LP on a label specialising in the kind of music I enjoy. But things took a rapid step forward when I moved to the shelves round the corner... and almost immediately unearthed a 10″ picture sleeve EP by the Pretty Things, featuring what only a day or two previously I had described to someone as 'probably the greatest four consecutive tracks by any group that I enjoy'.

Although I own a great many Pretty Things' records, this was one I'd never seen before, and it was even more of interest as one of these four tracks was a different version from that used when 'Defecting Grey' was originally released as a single, while the others are 'Mr Evasion', 'Talkin' About The Good Times' and 'Walking Through My Dreams' - if you don't know these tracks you should initially be thoroughly ashamed of yourself, but then make the effort to have a listen to them as quickly as possible.

Ok. What's this? A still sealed Moby Grape reunion LP, 'copyright 1990', called *Legendary Grape*. I must say that 'back together' records are very frequently something of a disappointment. But I do have several Moby Grape albums and this one was only 12 quid (in itself not a sign of impending quality) and I knew I'd beat myself up for not buying it were I to leave it on the shelf. Michael was playing an awfully familiar record, but I couldn't quite place it - ah, some very distinctive guitar playing revealed who it was - great guitarist, the late John Cipollina, in his prime, really, on this Quicksilver Messenger Service track, 'Mona' from the *Happy Trails* LP, but of course I already own that. Now Michael produced a record to show me, that he thought I might fancy - an original Fever Tree LP, *Another Time, Another Place*. I knew I had a double CD of Fever Tree stuff but couldn't for the life of me remember which two albums it includes, (spoiler alert - it turned out that this one was on it) so decided to buy this at the fair price of 30 quid. When I later checked around on my return, the cheapest I could find was £39.99, without p&p - and I don't even recall seeing another one on offer anywhere else I've been, so no problems here.

The final purchase was an LP of 1970 vintage, titled, and by, a group unknown to me, Lightning. Michael jogged my memory by pointing out there was a link to the group Litter, and I do have a couple of THEIR albums which, although I couldn't immediately bring to mind any individual members' names, was a positive sign. It turned out the link between the two bands was lead guitarist, Tom 'Zip' Caplan who played on the 1967 and 1968 Litter LPs before jumping ship or being pushed overboard.

The label name initially counselled caution, as, I am pretty sure, Pickwick was a budget label in the UK, but maybe not in the US, and here it appeared as 'P.I.P.' on the label. Zip gets writing credits on three of the eight tracks, but not 'They've Got The Time' which carries the explanation, 'Written in tribute to Jimi

Hendrix, Janis Joplin, Brian Jones' – on which I have to admit, Zip really nails his solo – which certainly might make the LP of interest to completists of all three of the 'gone too soon' club.

Michael had come up with a smart answer to the imminent Record Store Day, posting that his shop was staging 'Not Record Store Day' and telling his followers, 'It's the countdown to Not Record Store Day... each day until 22 April I'm posting a picture of some gems from our stock. All will be on sale in the shop – none on sale online.'

IN WHICH CASSETTE COMEBACK IS CONCERNING – AS IS REPAIR SHOP

Newspapers in mid-April 2023 became excited by the news that there has been, 'First a vinyl revival, now a cassette comeback.' The headlines appeared as a result of the news that, during 2022, some 195,000 cassettes were bought and sold new – up by 5.2% in a year, the tenth annual consecutive increase – by 2012 annual sales had slumped to under 4000. Apparently, the Arctic Monkeys' *The Car* was the biggest selling cassette while Florence and the Machine's *Dance Fever* was not only third bestselling, but also, oddly enough, reportedly sold more cassette copies than it did on vinyl when it was released in May 2022.

I remember being gutted back in the day, when all the vehicles I was offered as my latest company car were cassette-player-free, albeit mine did – and still does at time of writing – contain a CD player, which is the major reason that despite ULEZ, I intend holding on to the vehicle for as long as possible, otherwise that's the end of my in-car musical entertainment.

And before you ask, no, I have no idea how one's own musical choices can be heard in cars without the assistance of either a cassette or CD player, and absolutely no, zero, zilch, interest in hearing the answer, which I would not understand, anyway.

I wasn't paying much attention when *The Repair Shop* came on the telly this evening – until I heard that one of the items featured was a Mum's broken record player, brought in by her daughter.

I don't usually enjoy this programme. To me it comes over as a festival of frequently fake emotion. People bring in stuff which they've hidden away in the loft, or out in the shed, after their Mum/Dad/Uncle/Grandad/Nan/Mate/Brother/Sister/Cat/Dog passed away.

They didn't know what to do with it, couldn't be bothered to take it to the tip, so just watched it deteriorating for years, having probably made little effort themselves either to have it fixed (might cost money) or chuck it out (might involve effort).

They come up with a brainwave, 'Oh, perhaps I can get on the telly if I ask *The Repair Shop* to fix it, providing I give them some overblown emotional reason why I haven't bothered to have anything done about it before – couldn't face the trauma – too emotionally painful, etc. etc.'

Anyway, this record player was duly fixed, and filmed playing a Nat King Cole record – cue 'aahs', 'oohs' and sobs from the tearfully overcome relative, who declared, assuming I heard her right from my desk outside the room in the hall, 'I wish I'd done it while she was still alive.'

At this point I should reveal that *The Repair Shop* snubbed me when I offered them a great – and genuine – story for one of their recent series, but they decided not to take up the option – much to the disappointment of multiple champion horse racing trainer, Martin Pipe. I wrote a book about one of Martin's racing heroes or, more accurately, heroines – the extraordinarily wealthy, but equally eccentric, successful racehorse owner and multi-millionaire, Dorothy Paget.

She won top races like the Derby and the Cheltenham Gold Cup with her horses – and one of her greatest, if not THE greatest, successes was to land the 1934 Grand National with the legendary Golden Miller, that generation's Red Rum. To celebrate that victory, Dorothy had a record made of the race commentary, which was eventually purchased by Martin Pipe, who had become obsessed with collecting memorabilia about her, which he permitted me to utilise when I wrote the book about her. Sometime after the book had been published, Martin contacted me to reveal that the record of the Miller's National win had been – albeit accidentally – damaged – more than damaged – broken in half. He wondered whether I might be able to find someone who could repair it. I did have someone in mind, but we thought, in the meanwhile, perhaps *The Repair Shop* would like such a challenge, which would also make an excellent story for the programme. So we sent them all the details... but heard nothing.

IN WHICH I'M ZOMBIFIED

I went to see The Zombies in April 2023 – a band I have followed for many years and seen frequently. They were at the Eric Morecambe Centre in Harpenden, close to the band's heartland of St Albans. Sadly, better half, Sheila, was unwell, so I called in cancer mate Ron, who lives locally, to avoid the ticket going to waste. Rod Argent on keyboards, and singer Colin Blunstone have been the beating heart of the group since the earliest days.

I enjoyed the show, but was a little baffled when Argent led them into a version of the song, 'Hold Your Head Up', which was indeed a big hit – but for Argent's group, Argent, and IS NOT a track ever recorded by the Zombies, as far as I am aware, albeit Argent, and fellow Zombie, Chris White, were the composers. The song was well received by the rest of the audience, which struck me as being on a par with, perhaps, a football club like Chelsea introducing a player just signed from Arsenal, who had played for them when they beat Chelsea in a Cup competition, and asking the Chelsea fans to applaud Arsenal's success in that competition.

Colin Blunstone became a Zombie in 1961. His vocals remain powerful, controlled and very mannered in style. His jeans – designer, I'm sure – are still extremely tight-fitting, and it must take him ages to peel them off after each performance. I began wondering why and how the group had ever become the Zombies. Rod Argent explained in an interview with Jim Clash on the website, Forbes.com: 'For the first month or so, we were called the Sundowners. I think that may well have been a western film, in the same way as the Searchers' name was from a John Wayne movie. We were also the Mustangs for a couple of weeks, but never went out on a gig with that name.

One day, our bass player, who was the only one initially who left the band before we were professional (Paul Arnold – who became a doctor) said, 'What about The Zombies?' This was in the days before any of the crop of zombie films, like *Return of The Living Dead*. I just about knew what a zombie was. It had something to do with Haiti, and some sort of voodoo, unsavoury sorts of things. Colin didn't even know that. He hated the name! But I loved it.'

Support act to the Zombies was 70+ singer-songwriter Bruce Sudano, whose name and appearance meant nothing to most people in the audience to judge by the subdued/non-existent roar of approval when he came on stage. He began to surprise us, initially by revealing that, aged 20, he had a 1969 US chart hit with 'Ball Of Fire', which he co-wrote with Tommy James (of Shondells fame), following up as keyboard player in group Alive 'N' Kickin' with the Number 7 US smash, 'Tighter, Tighter'.

In 1979, he then co-wrote with Donna Summer the title track, 'Bad Girls' for the bestselling album of her career. Then, dear reader, he only went and married Donna Summer in 1980 – and they had two daughters, Brooklyn and Amanda, before she died in 2012.

This was not your usual support-artist stage-blurb – not only was he an engaging and clearly talented musician and wordsmith, but his story is genuinely extraordinary.

When a friend heard that Sheila had not been able to attend the concert he sympathised: 'Sorry to hear Sheila's not there to hear She's Not There.'

IN WHICH A LETTER REALLY
TAKES THE CAKE

In late April 2023 I received an out of the blue – (no ELO reference intended, by the way) – but most intriguing message on Facebook, from Rob Sherville of Melton Mowbray:

'I've just finished reading your entertaining book *Vinyl Countdown*. It brought back some real memories for me. I was intrigued by your references to Farx club in Southall – I was also a regular (travelling from the other side of Uxbridge). You might be able to settle a question for me – I saw the band My Cake several times there as a support act, and I've been convinced since that they were Christine Perfect's band in the short period between her leaving Chicken Shack and joining Fleetwood Mac. But I've never been able to find anything about them. Any idea? Thanks once again for a fabulous read and inspiration to restart collecting vinyl.'

Can any reader help, or will My Cake remain a little known slice of musical history?

Vinyl-collecting friend, Mike Hush, visited. I'd promised to take him to a couple of local record shops, starting with the Vinyl Café in Watford – via the newish HMV shop in which Mike bought a very reasonably priced (£14.99) new release of one of the Kinks' LPs, *Muswell Hillbillies*. But it took me a while to get up off the floor from the shock I received when I picked up a Kate Bush CD set and said to Mike, 'Let's guess how much this is?' He suggested 40 quid, I thought possibly a little more. I turned the box around to see a £99.99 price tag.

As Mike went to pay (they had no bags, plastic or paper, to put it in) I asked an assistant whether he had ever heard of the

Zombies. He hadn't, which, given his youthful demeanour, was understandable, so I explained that they were a very well established and popular band, whose origins are in nearby St Albans, and who had recently been playing gigs locally - yet I could find no trace of any of their records or CDs in this nearby branch.

I'm no marketeer, but wouldn't it make sense for someone working for HMV, to be given the job of ascertaining who is playing close to their shops, and to make sure that branches within a few miles' radius of such gig locations, are stocking material by them?

Rant over. We walked up to the Vinyl Café. I was a little concerned when I didn't see their usual amusing sign ('33 1/3rd yards ahead') and feared maybe it would be closed, but it wasn't - the sign was sitting inaccurately in the doorway.

Wandering in we decided the important first task was to order tea and carrot cake, which we did, then began browsing the racks before it arrived on our chosen table. Mike found a couple of LPs to buy, I was slightly tempted by a Richard and Linda Thompson album, but, figured that I hadn't listened to stuff I already owned by them, for some while, so if I bought this one, it may well sit around unplayed for many a week. I absolve the two of them of any blame because I do very much enjoy their work when I hear it. I saw a £3 single of the Zombies' hit, 'She's Not There' - but it wasn't by them - except, in a way it was. The name on the label was Neil MacArthur, which rang a bell with me - hold on, wasn't that a name that real Zombie, lead vocalist, Colin Blunstone, adopted at one point? Indeed, it was - and the 1967 MacArthur version was released three years after the hit version (number 12 UK, 2 USA) by the Zombies. Why? I had no idea. But Wikipedia did: 'In 1968, the Zombies broke up over management issues, shortly after completing the classic album, *Odessey and Oracle*. Blunstone briefly worked as a clerk in the insurance business before resuming his musical career. In 1969, he signed with Deram, and released three singles under the pseudonym of Neil MacArthur, including a remake of "She's Not There", which charted, reaching number 34.'

I next took Mike to the nearby jewellers-cum-record shop, where the gems man was at the door as we entered, already asking me whether I wanted to go down to the basement.

As ever when I introduce 'newbies' to this place, Mike was impressed and astonished, but quick to start dipping into the delights displayed all around him. I managed to add three worthwhile recruits to my collection – the star exhibit, an original copy of a 60s psych LP, Morning Glory's terrific *Two Suns Worth* for only as much as it cost me to buy a reissued copy, which I may now be able to sell on to recoup even the modest outlay here.

My other two were not so storied, but nonetheless welcome new inmates. One of these, *Chilliwack* by the group, Chilliwack, from 1971 is quite unusual, inasmuch as the Canadian group's previous LP was issued in 1970, and was called, *Chilliwack*. Weird, huh? The music on the Chilliwack double LP I bought this day was a weirdish mixture, from a hit (small) single, catchy 'Lonesome Mary' to the utterly bizarre – to my ears, at least – such as the 13 minute 38 seconds 'Changing Reels', described on the back cover as a 'long sectional composition' in which 'the lead vocals in the last section are improvisations, and the song was written around them afterwards'.

Then there is the 17 minute 9 second 'Night-Morning' which 'is the result of a studio full of instruments and microphones set up to record any free-form music we might want to play'. And they did want. Particularly drummer-organist Ross Turney, who 'started to play sounds with hands, head and elbows'. We ascended to the shop to settle up, which happened after a little bargaining for a modest but appreciated discount.

I read a letter from David Britain of Solihull answering a question about music producers faking the length of singles to help gain airplay – he wrote that it happened to the Phil Spector-produced Righteous Brothers' 1964 smash hit, 'You've Lost That Lovin' Feelin''. At the time, radio producers wanted songs of around three minutes maximum – 'playing two ads back to back was considered bad form, so radio stations wanted short songs to space out commercials'. 'Lovin' Feelin'' was 3 minutes 50 secs long, so sound engineer Larry Levine 'suggested we mark the record 3.05, and if anyone asked we could say it was a typo'. Backing this story up is a song written by Billy Joel, called 'The Entertainer' and containing the lines, 'It was a beautiful song, but it ran too long. If you're gonna have a hit you gotta make it fit, so they cut it down to 3.05'.

IN WHICH I ENJOY DAVE DAY

On my way to central London to meet Led Zeppelin authority Dave Lewis, in late April 2023, I made the always exciting discovery of a previously unknown (to me, anyway) record shop, as I was walking down Gower Street, headed for Dave's HQ/office, 'The Spice Of Life' pub in Cambridge Circus. I walked past a Waterstones book shop, noticing that it was promoting a record shop on the premises:

'Gower Records is a vinyl-only shop situated in the basement of the famed Gower Street branch of Waterstones. Carrying both new and second-hand stock, the space covers a broad variety of genres from 30s blues through to classic Brazilian tropicalia and contemporary pop. Music books sit adjacent to the shop itself providing customers with the perfect environment to discover and discuss new artists with dedicated staff, or to simply make use of the turntable and listen to classic LPs on a pair of headphones.'

It was slightly hidden away down a flight or two of stairs, but comfortingly close to the shop's ablutionary facilities, in which the sink taps were not working on my arrival. The toilet lid's underside was covered in stuck-on pieces of paper – by who knows who? One saying 'I support the UCU strike' another, 'HEADCOUNT' plus, 'Together We Are Powerf', on which what I presume should have been the missing letters 'ul' were obliterated. No idea whether this was graffiti, vandalism, or high art. Not, though, your usual bog-standard toilet.

The records were attractively arrayed and displayed, but although I did spot a Beatles' LP there, 1964's *A Hard Day's Night*, and a *Tighten Up* reggae compilation, there didn't seem an awful lot to appeal to my tastes and it may be my fault, but I couldn't seem to work out which were the new records and which the second-hand ones.

To me, the location in the shop smacked of having to be squeezed into a conveniently available space, and as you'd expect from a central London big-name shop the prices were of a premium nature.

Heading off again towards my meet-up, I nipped into the nearby Fopps and half-heartedly wondered whether I should buy a 4 CD+DVD Rory Gallagher box set for £55 – a reduction, it was claimed, of about 40 quid. I looked more closely and there are a lot of 'alternate take' tracks and a 32-page hardback book. But even at a 'reduced price', this seems an awful lot for ultimately not really that much.

Under the gaze of the stern member of staff standing just inside the door, I put it back, then set off for the pub, a couple of hundred yards across the road – negotiated by waiting for some of the slowest traffic lights I've come across to decide to let pedestrians attempt the fraught journey across the road under the gaze of impatient motorists, to the safety of the pavement, and thence through the welcoming doors of Dave's 'office'.

We quickly spotted each other and were soon sat at a table with a pint (Dave) and glass of dry white (me). Our conversation ranged across all manner of subjects – but predominantly health, pubs, music, our writing, long-suffering wives, record collections (his is a little larger than mine), age (mine is a little larger than his) and where in the house we keep our LPs, CDs, singles, cassettes, 8-tracks – answer, every room!

Dave has a curious (to some) love – obsession? – of demo records, and I'd brought him along half a dozen of such pieces of vinyl. He loves reading the dates and other tiny, but vital, messages revealed on the labels. This is how he later told his Facebook followers about our get-together:

'It was great to have a meet with author and record collecting comrade Graham Sharpe at the office also known as The Spice of Life. While in the vicinity I popped over to the nearby Fopp

Records and was pleased to find a copy of the album *Good Morning Starshine* by Oliver. The title track was a massive hit in 1969 after its use in the *Hair* musical. Some foreign tourists sat near us and enquired about the album – I relayed to them how *Good Morning Starshine* had been a hit back in 1969 – one of them googled it and found it on YouTube and they were instantly enlightened to its 60s charm. I'm also holding a batch of early 70s demo singles which Graham kindly gave me – from his time as a journalist on a local newspaper. Graham received review copies in his role as the paper's pop columnist.

All in all meeting Graham was a much needed tonic. Thanks for listening, mate.'

IN WHICH I HAVE A FEELING ABOUT EALING

Genuinely, but somewhat bizarrely, I woke up next morning, thinking: 'I must visit that record shop in South Ealing I haven't been to since before lockdown.' I checked the address and decided to follow the feeling. That shop was, and, hooray, still is, 'Sounds Original' on South Ealing Road, just down from the tube station. Here's some info about the shop:

'In 1978 Paul Green, long-time record collector, turned his hobby into a business. Originally trading at record fairs and through mail order before opening Sounds Original in November 1983, in what was previously a sweet shop for the Odeon cinema, turned nightclub and more recently a church. In May 2000, the opportunity came to relocate to larger premises half a mile away, our current location. Having built up an international client base it is ideal for record collecting tourists, who often pop in on their way to and from Heathrow.'

It isn't far away, as the crow flies, from my neck of the woods, but always feels like it should be easier to get to than it actually is. I had to drive to Eastcote, to wait on the platform to catch a Piccadilly Line train, only to find myself suddenly involved in a to-the-death stare-out with the ringleader of four probably truant-playing kids of, what, 14 or 15, intent on looking and behaving 'ard – to the extent that the station announcer had warned them over the station's loudspeakers, but to little effect.

I was just leaning against a pillar when I noticed him beaming back bad thoughts as we gazed at each other, me thinking 'Right, you little twerp, this is one psychological battle you won't be winning.' And he didn't. Nor, possibly fortunately, did he then decide to take physical reprisal with the help of his two female and one male accomplices. As a Met Line train came in, they swaggered swearily on to it, flicking Vs at anyone looking at them, and blowing vape smoke left, right and centre as they went. A female station staff member was standing next to me and we both indulged in a bit of 'what's the world coming to?', 'can't see them turning out well' stuff. Then a train rolled in to transport me to South Ealing, via Acton, from where I emerged for the stroll down to Sounds Original, opening at 11am, and already with a couple of flipping, rack-riffing customers in place, while jazzy music of a type I associate with that mid-80s TV series The Beiderbecke Affair, starring James Bolam, was playing unobtrusively, and appropriately as, in that series, the storyline involved the hero buying jazz records from a 'dazzlingly beautiful blonde' who calls at his door raising funds for the local Cubs' football team. When the wrong records are delivered, a hunt begins that draws the pair into unforeseen intrigue.

I took my bearings, identifying sections to investigate, starting on the 70s, where I was soon nodding approval as interesting items appeared, all seemingly in Mint or Mint-condition, yet very fairly priced – not least, I thought, the copy of Badfinger's 1979 Elektra label Airwaves LP, which revealed itself with a price tag of a mere tenner. I remember, vividly, buying one, decades ago, from a long-gone record seller in Rayners Lane clearing out its entire stock at 10p or 20p a go.

I flicked over a Barclay James Harvest LP definitely not yet in my regularly growing collection of their work. This one, *Victims of Circumstance*, boasted a striking cover I'd never seen before, and a strikingly attractive price of £7.50. That immediately became a 'definite'.

Alongside, to my right, a gentleman of a certain age appeared to have fallen fast asleep whilst leaning over to check the section of records to the rear of the compartments. I'd detected no movement from him for a number of minutes. But suddenly he stirred, coming awake with a start, declaring: 'No luck... oh, well, I've looked at all the LPs.' He then walked up to the counter to engage the man I took to be owner, Paul Green, in low vocal conversation; the little of which I could overhear appeared to involve the route he had taken via bus and tube train to arrive here, from a starting point in or around Edgware, where I was born.

He did seem to have earlier found something to buy, and calculations were going on as I carried on riffling, now turning up a *Grace Slick And The Great Society Vol 2* LP in an excellently preserved Columbia label sleeve, explaining on the cover that it contained 'newly discovered recordings (from 1966) of the group which forged the "Sound of San Francisco".'

I was confident that I already owned Vol 1 and had had no idea there was a Vol 2 to collect.

I wasn't over-confident the eight tracks of music contained within - one of them credited to G Slick, D Slick, J Slick and D Milner - were going to be that thrilling, but that is part of the appeal of collecting, you're never quite sure and the anticipation can be sufficiently satisfying to justify the outlay even if you end up realising you've bought rubbish!

The Great Society would, of course, lead Ms Slick to Jefferson Airplane and with the cover notes promising that I would soon be able to listen to 'Grace's wailing on recorder on Daydream Nightmare' I enjoyed an anticipatory thrill!

There is also reference in the back cover notes to Grace's brilliantly barmy comment about The Great Society being 'Conspicuous only in its absence' - man, how 60s can you get!

So, that's two purchases in the bag... and here comes a third as I pull out an LP which, I suppose, I ought to admit to already owning on CD. This one is an absolutely smashing condition, limited edition gatefold cover LP rerelease via *Record Collector* magazine's own record label, of the 60s British obscurity, *Making Up For Lost Time* by The Riot Squad – AND it came complete with a handwritten 'Certificate of Authenticity' showing it to be Number 004 (just possibly number 9) of 750 copies released, and signed by the mag's editor, Ian Shirley. It was priced at a smidgeon under 20 quid, again terrific value.

Now I looked at the CD racks – no joy there, albeit very affordable prices – then the 60s singles, where I unearthed a most desirable Island label picture sleeve (of the group) copy of what is really an EP as it boasts four of this group's best songs, including one which really takes me straight back to the 1968 movie of which it was the theme song. Again in terrific condition. Got it yet? I doubt it, as I haven't really given you enough info – but this is a 1978 release of mainly 1967 tracks, by one of THE great 60s bands, Traffic – featuring psych top notchers, 'Paper Sun' (sung by Steve Winwood), 'Hole In My Shoe' (sung by Dave Mason), 'No Face, No Name, No Number' (Winwood) plus that rites of passage movie theme, 'Here We Go Round The Mulberry Bush', which features all four members of Traffic singing a joint lead, though the bridge and parts of the chorus have Steve Winwood singing unaccompanied. The only downside to this 4-tracker was that the offer on the back, '80p OFF any TRAFFIC album at all Virgin stores', seemed to have run out – it finished 'July '78'. Just missed it by 45 years, give or take.

I wonder which other four track mini-collections might offer a similar overview of the greatness of, for example, the Beatles (Strawberry Fields/Penny Lane/Rain/Paperback Writer, perhaps) and the Stones (Paint It Black/19th Nervous Breakdown/Have You Seen Your Mother/Baby/Standing In The Shadow?/We Love You, for sure).

As I walked up to pay I heard the owner being told by the other customer still in the shop, 'We've all got to die sometime and get old.' Accurate, although maybe in the wrong order, but Paul had a good response – 'Yeah – he was 85 yesterday.'

'Who?'

'Duane Eddy.'

The same Duane Eddy, of course, whose single '(Dance With The) Guitar Man' was the first I ever owned. Sadly, Duane Eddy died four days past his 86th birthday, on April 30, 2024.

Up at the counter, Paul totted up the total payment due, I asked whether there might be a discount for cash, and he duly obliged with a small one, but seeing as I'd felt the prices were not exorbitant, that's fair enough. He even gave me a branded plastic bag to carry them in.

I departed for the tube station. As I walked past a nearby charity shop, I thought I'd better nip in – just in case. Once there I saw no CDs or LPs but spotted an Elvis Costello autobiography. I began to flip through the pages, but suddenly heard some barking coughs coming from the front of the shop, then a female voice loudly explaining, 'That's my Covid cough. I've got long Covid but can't shake the cough off.' I was outside and on the station platform before you could say 'Covid cough'.

IN WHICH I TAKE TIME OUT TO LISTEN

It was a little concerning to receive a message from Discogs in late April 2023: 'Discogs has recently detected an increase in scammers in the Marketplace, and we're taking action to address the issue. New sellers on Discogs will undergo a waiting period to reduce fraud attempts. If you see suspicious activity, please report it immediately to Discogs Support through this form.'

On the positive side I had decided to stay home after a few trips to record shops in recent days, in order to address what I and, I'm sure other collectors, often worry about – when will I find the time to hear what I've been buying? That is, ultimately, the object of the exercise, of course, but it is probably fair to admit that sometimes just realising you now own something you've been after for a good while, can be enough of a buzz to make actually playing the records slightly less important, as you can now do that whenever!

But I now listened to yesterday's purchase, Volume 2 of *Grace Slick with the Great Society* LP. I expected it to be rather less rocky than it turns out to be and I am 100% happy to have acquired it – but if there was 101% to be offered to a record, it would be for the original 1968 Morning Glory LP, *Two Suns Worth* I found whilst delving in the depths of the jewellery vinyl jungle. This record does have a few slightly crackly areas, whereas the reissue one I have doesn't – but I know which one I'd sell off first, and it ain't the more recently released one. This record, unlike so many I've bought which come with the same 'psych' references, genuinely, for a change, does deserve that description.

Unexpectedly, the 1971 *Rosebud* LP by Jerry Yester, Judy Henske, Craig Doerge and John Seiter, I'd recently found, turned out to be something of an eight quid delight (this, I soon discover, was a bargain price) – really, care of Ms Henske, who plays a large role in the writing of all ten inventive tracks and whose vocals are a constant joy.

On the back cover there is a reference unlike any I've seen elsewhere, concerning bass player on the album, David Vaught, explaining: 'For those people offended by David's absence on the front cover, be not, for he is a late joiner.' Lovely, and catches the mood of the music somehow.

Waiting in an Audi dealership for them to replace the wing mirror which fell off of my car for no immediately evident reason on Wednesday, I began flipping through a magazine I had not read for many a year. Edition number 473 of *What Hi-Fi?*. I've never been a hi-fi buff. Never quite understood the apparent eternal search, by some, for the perfect sound.

When I first heard the music which I came to love so much, it was via small transistor radios, and on record players with built-in tinny speakers. When these were turned up to their maximum volume they vibrated and shook as they poured out as much sound as they possibly could.

I'm not going to try to pretend that there is no difference between the many set-ups of amps, speakers, turntables and headphones – plus the other add-ons which are available these days, but I am more concerned by the music to which I'm listening, and not the precise way in which each of the individual ingredients may sound. I bought my current hi-fi set-up at the recommendation of the chap in a local shop, and it cost just under a grand in total.

Some readers are probably choking on their drink or food at the heresy expressed here. But reading through the magazine I saw stuff like: 'The Sonos is still over-pleased with its low-frequency response, but it controls the attack and decay of bass sounds more effectively.'

If you say so. That was written about a wireless speaker costing the best part of 500 quid, although I couldn't quite work out whether it was being critical or complimentary.

Another article about amps asked, 'Will the amp suit your headphone listening needs? And will you need to save some cash back for an external phono stage for vinyl replay?' Not a question I've ever previously asked myself. A positive comment on another amp explained: 'It ducks and weaves its way around tricky compositions, tying all musical strands together in a way that is authoritative and skilful without ever losing its sense of fun.' Okay, okay, I know I am being facetious here, and I get the difficulty of describing much the same things in a different manner – a bit like the many methods employed to explain the tastes of various styles of wine. But when another article explains that, 'it doesn't always work simply to stop at five-star products, bung them together and expect everything to work perfectly', you do wonder whether the more you try to compare different essentials within a system, the more difficult it becomes to decide which you need over those you might want.

As another article pointed out: 'It is no good spending hundreds of pounds on speakers if you then don't allow them to perform properly. Take care with positioning to get them to sing.' Would that be the speakers' positioning, the listener's, or both?

Sheila had been struggling with a coldy, flu-type virus for the best part of a fortnight, but the good wishes she received yesterday for her birthday, on Facebook, and the pleasant weather, prompted her to declare she fancied a walk to our local garden centre. I was drafted in to accompany her, and soon realised how much in common her own favourite pastime, and mine, had in common. She wasn't looking for anything in particular but walked around the whole place, which was packed with plants, trees, seeds, shrubs, bushes and gardening equipment of many types, noting as she went, the ones she was expecting to include on her list of required new items, ranging in price from a couple of quid to serious dosh. Wisely, I kept quiet when she was perusing what I inevitably regarded as un-necessary and/or over-expensive items. I knew not doing so would inevitably prompt a short, sharp discussion I was unlikely to emerge from with any joy (her middle name – well, Joyce).

IN WHICH I EXPERIENCE 'MONKY' BUSINESS

An email arrives from friend Mike H, telling me of his trip, during the weekend to: 'A new(ish) record shop in Tunbridge Wells, which has been open about a year. The guy running it has been trading for about 30 years... good selection of records – I bought seven for £60. Very helpful, knowledgeable and welcoming... will certainly go back. He does local Record Fairs. Trades as Sugarbush Records.'

Maybe I'm gullible, maybe I just WANT to believe everything I'm told, but today, yet again, I am about to listen to what I would very much appreciate turning out to be a previously unknown work of genius from many years ago, which was never issued close to the time it was recorded, for whatever reason. Some – okay, a couple, maybe – of these 'undiscovered classic' records have turned out to be the works of unheralded genius they were claimed to be – but they are few and far between. Most of them deserved to languish in obscurity.

So what would I be feeling about this one which, I am given to understand, was recorded 'circa 1970'. Why, then, have I never heard (of) it before? Because what I am about to listen to has been 'lovingly restored from the only known copy; a battered acetate found by accident 15 years ago, inside an MOR LP sleeve in a junk shop by Damon Jones'.

I have no idea who Damon Jones may be. Nor how and why he might have bought an MOR record from a junk shop 15 years ago, whether or not he'd noticed at that point that it had inside a battered acetate. Nor of how or why he then even knew of Bright Carvings, let alone why he eventually decided to draw it to their attention, and why they then decided to issue it in a limited edition of, of course, 227 copies. Nor how and why it was decided to name the group, in the entire absence of any reason to do so, as 'Monk'? Nor how I came to swallow this yarn and buy a copy, admittedly not for an outrageous amount of money.

The back cover of the record promises: 'Top tier music from c1970, sitting on the cusp of psychedelic into progressive rock, a heady mix of great songs, stinging, jamming guitar and psychedelic effects.'

I'm a sucker for psych of almost any description, so, of course, I'd bought a copy, desperate to hear the 'trippy lyrics peak on the "apocalyptic" title track, "Through an Electric Glass Darkly".' I've now heard it and, to be fair, it is something quite special, albeit maybe not quite living up to its cover notes – but only not quite.

There is a slightly muddy haze hovering over the whole thing, the singing is less than Premier League quality, the songs are slightly predictable once they get started, but undeniably there is a definite feel of 1970 to be had and enjoyed. It took me back to the days of my local venue for such bands, the Rayners Lane Commune, man. The cover depicts the band members as a vocalist and three guitarists, one of them with a twin-necked instrument, but there is also definite organ-playing to be heard. I hope that the 226 other copies will be speedily snapped up and that someone will help to publicise the release in the hope of luring out more details about the group. The least you can do is check on Discogs whether there are still copies to be had and if so grab it quickly. Bright Carvings could be a label worth watching.

A reminder from excellent 'record cover artist', Morgan Howells, aka @SuperSizeArt on X/Twitter, that: 'On this day (2 May) in 2009 a rare Motown seven-inch single sold for £25,742, ($38,378), setting a new world record. "Do I Love You (Indeed I Do)" by Frank Wilson was one of only two in the world. Motown boss Berry Gordy had all other copies destroyed after Wilson moved on up.'

Country musician Ernest Tubb, who introduced the electric guitar to the Grand Ole Opry, opened a record shop in Nashville bearing his name in 1947. It survived until Wednesday night, 4 May 2022 before closing its doors for the last time. There were subsequent reports that it would reopen, but as of mid 2024 it doesn't appear to have done so.

IN WHICH I MEET A MUSICAL HERO

A trip to the Spitalfields, London, Record Fair on 5 May 2023 proved memorable, as I met one of the unsung (less sung possibly a better description) vintage vinyl heroes of the rock and blues scenes for many, many years. Browsing at one of the stalls, distracted by the record being waved around by the stallholder – a copy of the second May Blitz LP, on which was written a price of £380 – I didn't immediately recognise the silver (grey?) haired gent standing right next to me, protesting to the would-be seller that he had never heard of either the record or the group.

I do have an original copy of the debut May Blitz LP, which I treasure, but only a CD of this one – however, I was not remotely tempted to splash out the asking price. And nor was the chap at my side who, now I turned to look at him, was very obviously the terrific Chris Farlowe, a vocalist hero of mine across most of his lengthy and varied solo and different group incarnations

BOUGHT A REISSUED, PRISTINE COPY OF CAT STEVENS' 'NEW MASTERS' LP from My Music in Taupo in New Zealand – disappointed his 'Father And Son' track isn't on it – as I'm father to the son, (Steeven), also in this photo…

JON GROOCOCK AND INFANT SON BEN, IN 1981 – Ben was already a Left Banke fan – back when early starts wheeling and dealing with London locals happy to swap little valued records for modest amounts of cash, meant Jon could sell them on to dealers, ensuring he and Ben didn't go hungry! Check out the Bright Carvings label, via which he now resuscitates otherwise unknown vinyl obscurities to the delight of psych-prog addicts such as your author.

WE ALL KNOW ABOUT COLOURED VINYL, but in New Zealand 'vinyl art' appears to be a growing trend…

CATCHING UP with Herb the only mobile travelling record shop boss, in Tawa.

LO-COST is a record shop based in Petone, a few miles outside of Kiwi capital, Wellington. Rumour has it that this shop, and nearby Wonderland, in Wainuiomata are owned by two brothers. Lo-Cost is logically laid out and everything is priced; Wonderland is eccentrically packed, heaped and piled with vinyl, whose prices have to be negotiated.

'HALCYON DAZE' RECORD SHOP IN NEWTOWN, SYDNEY, OZ – great window, but no chance of reflecting on the inside, as it was shut – when many others locally were open and selling – and I was buying!

SCREAMING LORD SUTCH & LITTLE RICHARD: My long-term friend David 'Screaming Lord' Sutch (pictured here with rock'n'roller pal, Little Richard when they teamed up for a Wembley Stadium concert) was a keen record collector – albeit mainly of his own vinyl works! For me, easily the pick of his lengthy recording career were his 1970 'Heavy Friends' LP, featuring contributions from Jimmy Page, John Bonham, Jeff Beck and Noel Redding; and, perhaps surprisingly to lovers of the style, his tremendous psychedelic version of 'The Cheat', a 1966 single which is well worth searching out. Original, well preserved versions of each can now command three figure sums, but reissues are affordable.

I LOVED the early seventies band, Vinegar Joe, fronted by Robert Palmer (far right) and Elkie Brooks. I've never seen a more exciting group, but sadly their electrifying live act did not translate in to commercial success, so the two went off to enjoy separate solo careers, via somewhat differing, albeit still very listenable, styles of music.

A SLIGHTLY SHABBY RECORD COLLECTOR collects his thoughts before entering the ever so slightly shabbily-fronted, but vinyl treasure-packed internally, Across The Tracks record shop in Brighton where, fortunately, such shops survive in healthy numbers.

HAD TO SIT DOWN, I was so excited to find vinyl in this Pasadena mall in the States – which resulted in a classic Moby Grape purchase, and in a mad moment, a later regretted and apologised for Tiny Tim LP. Sorry, again!

IN OSLO FOR A BRIEF TRIP, there was 'Norway' I wasn't going to visit a record shop… and RAKK & RALLS was the one I chose… great choice of vinyl available…

MY PAL ROGER PLUMMER, with his pride and joy ROCK-OLA stereo jukebox after it literally survived a riot…

CHRIS PITT is a great fan of horseracing – and Pentangle. He sneaked into an after-gig dressing room to persuade his idols and original members Jacqui McShee and John Renbourn to sign the band's 1970 release, 'Cruel Sister'.

A GEM OF A SECRET VINYL STASH, located behind and underneath the jewellery shop in Northwood… tell them I sent you! But don't mention that a May 2024 visit produced a £12 purchase of an obscure 1968 pop-psych LP, a little gem which can now go for £100+.

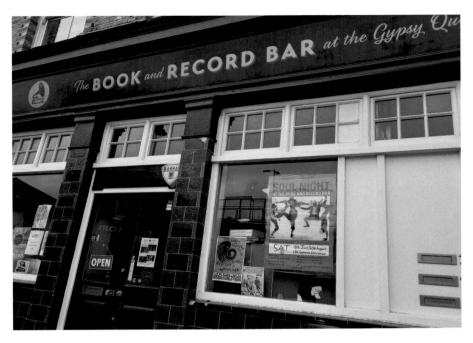

THE BOOK AND RECORD BAR is well worth the trip to Norwood High Street – opened in 2013, it boasts 'bring your own record nights', live bands and a radio show, the West Norwood Broadcasting Company… it also used to boast many great psych LPs which I liberated to add to my collection.

THROWING A LITTLE LIGHT ON DARK – one of the best bands (most of) you've never heard of, in action in 1972, when their great 'lost' LP, 'DARK Round The Edges' (worth five figures should you be fortunate enough to come across an original vinyl copy) appeared in tiny numbers. Leader Steve Giles has since made it, and other albums, available - and I strongly recommend that you step into the light and acquire one or more of them.

CLAIRE HOWELLS explained to me for this book how she kept her Wolverhampton record shop, Vinyl & Vintage, going during the dark days of Covid when, like so many others, they opened and closed on a number of different occasions. Here she is, with friends and colleagues celebrating the shop's ultimate survival.

WHAT A WAY TO END A SUCCESSFUL DAY'S VINYL DELVING – with a thirst-quenching, record-listening visit to Newtown's classy vinyl bar, Sake & Sounds, featuring a record deck in the counter, and records on the shelves. Even tough-to-please Mrs S loved it!

and exploits. I thrust out a hand towards him, declared: 'Thanks so much for all the music over the years,' and was thrilled to be rewarded with a very quotable response: 'Pardon?' So I said it again. This time he smiled, nodded, completed the handshake, offered a 'Thanks very much' and went on his way, leaving the stallholder somewhat disgruntled that his attempt to flog the £380 record was a non-runner. He did 'dine out' on the story, though, as when I came back round to his stall somewhat later, he pointed at me, and said to another customer, 'He'll tell you – it was Chris Farlowe!' I could hardly dispute that. It was only when I bothered to check Chris's age (born in October 1940), that I discovered his real name – John Henry Deighton.

I sampled the wares of every one of the probably two dozen-plus, or so, dealers, buying a brand new but old Badfinger double LP, *Kansas City 1972*, which is a live FM broadcast from that hugely famous venue, The Cowtown Ballroom (?!). It cost a tenner, on the Parachute Recording Company label, and, I suspect, possibly not entirely authorised. I also found a CD of radio broadcasts from the infancy of the underrated Alan Bown mob. I didn't recognise most of the tracks and as I already had three of their LPs, all of which I enjoy, at four quid it seemed a no-brainer. Played it as soon as I returned to my car afterwards, and it is excellent. Later, I read in the sleeve notes some remarks about an arcane question which has always bothered me (yes, I know, 'saddo'!).

One of my three LPs by the group – at one point The Alan Bown, at another The Alan Bown!, as well as The Alan Bown Set, – is *Listen* for which, according to the sleeve notes of my just-purchased CD, the vocals were recorded by Robert Palmer – who had in turn rerecorded those originally on their previous album, *The Alan Bown!* – which had been originally recorded by Jess Roden. (Still with me? – there may be questions, later.) Palmer then left and HIS vocals were rerecorded by Gordon Neville, including those for 'Pyramid', a single as well as a track on the LP.

However, every time I listen to 'Pyramid' I am convinced my version is by Palmer. As he is no longer with us, of course, I think that 100 per cent verification of who it is singing on *Listen* is likely to remain unclear. Maybe both versions were released at different times.

A friend, Roger Plummer, pointed out to me that when Esoteric Recordings released a 're-mastered edition of the classic 1970 album *Listen*', they were quite clear in media material that the album 'featured the unique vocal talent of Robert Palmer... Palmer's final album as vocalist for the band'. But the allmusic.com website reckons: 'Lacking the funds to start from scratch with Palmer's replacement, Gordon Neville, the band had to simply rerecord the vocals over the original instrumental tracks.'

Curiouser and curiouser. I wrote to Esoteric Recordings for enlightenment... still awaiting a reply. Then I contacted an X/Twitter site for Palmer fans, called 'Addictioners', and soon received a response: 'It's a pity, but we should assume that with Palmer out of the band, there was no need for his recordings and they were likely trashed. But listening to Neville's singing, I often wonder if the whole album is an exercise in Robert Palmer impersonation.'

By the way, I read an excellent piece by one Gary Marlowe from May 2021, about Palmer, in which he wrote: 'One day a blues band called The Alan Bown Set found itself without a singer for a show at the Scarborough Spa, borrowed him for the night and kept him. Until then, he was Alan Palmer, but he changed to Robert to avoid confusion with the name of the band.' However, other sources suggest his Christian name was Robert, but his middle name was Allen. Who knew? Not me.

Anyway, back to Spitalfields. A potential purchase got away. It was a Pretty Things compilation LP of some of the more unfamiliar tracks on the *Bouquets from a Cloudy Sky* box-set of LPs and more, which I bought as soon as it came out, but have never removed from its packaging for reasons I cannot explain. Hence I thought that to buy this LP might give me a flavour of some of the music I hadn't yet heard, from the box-set, and maybe encourage me finally to open it up and listen to it. The compilation had a £12 sticker on it and when I checked the disc it looked immaculate, although the record cover was very grubby. I asked the guy behind the jump whether he'd be prepared to accept a tenner for the record. The shrift I received in answer was of a shorter duration than struck me as acceptable, and his expression whilst delivering it was not of a friendly nature. 'Nah.'

Discussion over. If he'd changed his mind and said, 'Oh, go on then,' after that bad-tempered and hostile response, I'd have told him to 'F*** off.'

I also looked at a double CD of the group Copperhead, featuring one of my favourite guitarists, John Cipollina. It had no price tag on it. I asked the chap at the stall, who pointed to two leather-clad, young guys who looked as though they might be children of a couple of Ramones, and suggested I ask them. So I did. They both looked at the CD as though they'd never seen it before in their lives, thought briefly about it and one asked, 'A tenner?' I didn't want a second 'F*** off' to be delivered had I offered, say seven or eight quid, so just said 'I'll think about it' and put it back, deciding to save it for another day. I've never seen another copy since.

During my time at the Fair I would estimate that some 95% of sellers were male, and between 85–90% of buyers likewise. I hadn't visited for a couple of years, since pre-lockdown, and felt there was a higher percentage of sellers offering 'sale' or just generally lower prices, designed to attract more business. I recognised some, but not all, of those offering their wares today, but some of the regulars I remembered seemed to be absent.

IN WHICH I DISCOVER SECRETS

Donovan Leitch was born on 10 May 1946. He seems to divide tastes within the world of music lovers and was widely accused of being merely a Dylan wannabe in the earlier days of his career.

However, to my ears he has produced some world class music over the years – not always, of course, but please tell me you also love 'Hurdy Gurdy Man', his amazing psychedelic 1968 track which made number 5 in the States and 4 here, one of his many

chart successes. It was stunningly produced by the frequently
underrated Mickie Most – who used to live up the road from where
I live now – where there is a current-day house called Hollies, but
I don't think that's where either Mr Leitch or Mr Most lived. Or,
indeed, the Hollies.

Donovan's follow up, the underrated 'Atlantis', also had its
charms – once you get past the irritating spoken intro, but he then
teamed up with Jeff Beck for his next single, 'Goo Goo Barabajagal
(Love Is Hot)', which restored both him and Jeff to the, er, Top 12.
In Jeff's case that was the highest any of his singles reached.

I've begun recently to think of second-hand/used/preloved
record collecting as being slightly less brutal, but no less accurately
described, than vinyl grave-robbing. After all, almost never are you
aware of how the records in the shop, advertised in the magazine or
online, have come to be available for you to own. Has the original
owner died, moved, needed quick cash, fallen out of love with
records, been robbed of them, decided they no longer enjoy them?

It doesn't really matter to you. The owner is no longer there
in person to care or worry about what will happen next to those
items they once felt responsible for, that they have probably paid
money to own, treasure, boast about, and consider as a welcome
part of their lives. Until someone else comes along to adopt them,
the records have become vinyl orphans.

Whatever the reason, they are now at your mercy and the
decision about whether they will accompany you home to begin
a new life in which they are at the very least wanted and looked
after, or will stay where they are, unloved, unmourned, merely
waiting patiently for someone else to decide to take them on, is at
this moment purely up to you.

You're most unlikely ever to find out what particular reason is
responsible for their arrival on the shelf of vinyl through which
you are flipping, any more than a visitor to a cemetery or graveyard
can know more of the person buried or scattered there than is
revealed on a headstone or memorial.

Rather like fishing, when you make that initial strike, prior
to the equally enjoyable actions of reeling in the prey, checking
its weight, taking a photo before sending it back into the water

to be caught again by someone else – or in the vinyl instance, picking out an interesting-looking cover from its design, quickly checking its condition, deciding whether it holds an attraction for you as it may complete a set by a singer or group, looking at the price, deciding whether it is easily affordable, a bit pricey, or outrageously dear – you are in complete charge of the next move.

And when you get home you'll either regret buying it, or not buying it – or be 'over the moon' you did or didn't do exactly that.

IN WHICH I'M DISAPPOINTED
– THREE TIMES!

I schlepped up town to visit three London record shops – the first of which proved a little disappointing, the second extremely disappointing, the third the most disappointing of all – as it was no longer in existence.

First stop was a long-established record shop, just over the road from Notting Hill Gate tube station. On the way up I was reading my copy of Nick Hornby's vinyl-filled book, *High Fidelity*, in which the hero is a record shop owner. This shop's website explains: 'One of the oldest surviving independent record stores in London, 'Music & Video Exchange' – formerly 'Record & Tape Exchange', established in 1967, has certified a status as a frequent destination for record collectors around the world.'

I hadn't been here for a few years, but the feel was exactly the same, almost as though the clock and calendar had been turned back a decade or three, four, maybe even five or six! The main character in Hornby's 1995 book would immediately feel completely at home here – I couldn't be sure that Nick didn't base his depiction of the shop in his book on this very one.

I started by perusing the '60s Rock – Pop – Folk – Psych – Garage' CD section. Prices reasonable, some very good, but nothing which jumped out as a 'must buy'. As I flipped through, up came a note – 'Looking for The Doors? They have their own section in rock + pop A–Z above.' I was not looking for the Doors.

Then I turned my attentions to the various LP and 12" sections. There was a US Garage and Psych section but I couldn't see a UK equivalent, so asked the staff member, who had been assiduously sweeping, cleaning and vacuuming the floor around me. He helpfully managed to locate the relevant section – which was gloriously... empty! Beginning to think there wasn't much else I fancied I took another look at the US Garage/Psych stuff and pulled out something I'd glanced at briefly before – a group called London Dri, and their LP, *Western Skies*, sub-titled 'Los Angeles Psychedelic 1967–69.' Cover notes explaining that this band had released just one single, in August 1967 – 'a reworking of a Jewish folk song' – did not exactly enthuse me, but they went on to explain that between 1965 and 1970 the group recorded 'several songs from "garage-rock" to classic US psychedelia to Who-styled mod-pop'. At £13 and in pristine nick I thought it was worth a gamble, and I'm listening to the album as I write these words. The back cover of the LP, released in Germany on the Break-A-Way label, calls it '11 killer tracks in their distinctive London Dri style'. That may be slightly over-egging the vinyl pudding, but the music is definitely authentically of its time and very listenable.

The band were from LA, so where their name came from remains a mystery as the fairly comprehensive sleeve notes make no mention of an answer. It is a relatively short album, as the notes explain these are really the only professional sounding recordings to survive.

Mine is hand-numbered 94 of an issue of just 100. The only other copy I could locate for sale in the UK online was number 97, for £29.99 and £6 p&p, so I figured I'd paid a very reasonable amount.

A few other customers wandered in to the shop before I left, and a foreign-sounding pair were attempting to sell some Bowie records, but the cleaning man, now behind the counter, explained to them that the person who made offers and decisions of this nature, would not be in today.

I departed, and set off to walk to my second target, a Rough Trade shop in nearby Talbot Road. Arriving some 15 minutes later I recognised this shop having been there before, a few years ago, and particularly having to go downstairs to check out the stock of interest to me.

This time there was no stock of the remotest interest to me, and it took me just a few minutes to decide this wasn't a shop I'd be keen on returning to. To be fair there were a number of other browsers who were browsing more happily, so, mea culpa.

Right, off to the third shop I'd set myself to visit. It wasn't there. It closed down some while ago. It was now a former record shop, which had gone to meet its maker. I nearly lost my way walking back to Notting Hill Gate tube station – in spite of, or more likely because of, my inability to persuade my phone to show me the way back – only to be rescued by a lady with two very young children in a pushchair, whom I ungallantly interrupted in her mothering duties to ask for directions. She was, to judge by her accent, American, but politely and patiently, whilst also capably coping with the kids, pointed me in the right direction, and didn't appear in the least put out to be interrupted in her duties.

Oh, I've just read the London Dri inner sleeve notes again – they got their name from 'an old gin bottle'.

When I arrive home I get a visit from an old pal who pops in on a regular irregular basis. Paul tells me he is currently reading *Vinyl Countdown*, and thinks the stuff about me 'wearing' a bell as a mid to late 60s 'hippie' is almost as hilarious as the name of one of the groups I write about in that book – and this – the Electric Prunes. Philistine!

IN WHICH DEATH IS
NARROWLY AVOIDED

Having survived an attempt on my life by an alarmingly poorly secured wayward steel fence, blown straight into my path by a gust

of wind, which I was just able to deal with, thanks to the fact that
I wasn't looking at my phone, and was able to make use of my still
razor-sharp(e) reactions by immediately thrusting out my hands
and somehow hopping backwards, I made it to the door of my
barber, only to discover that Karl was away on holiday.

What to do instead? Well, obviously, nip over to nearby Ruislip
Manor, home to Sounds of the Suburbs record shop. The first
thing I heard once through the door was a conversation in French,
between un homme et une femme, who were looking through
a whole pile of records, and being occasionally quizzed by shop
owner Tony, who was making good use of the common British
tactic of addressing foreign types by repeating words which they
have already shown they don't understand, but which we invariably
believe they may grasp if we repeat them more loudly, but slower. It
didn't – and never does – work.

However, said foreign pair were not remotely phased and still
managed to find a good selection of records with which to return
home. This was apparently their second trip over, and Tony seems
to be doing well with foreign-based customers, telling me about a
Maltese chap, 'one of the top continental DJs' who buys regularly
from him, as does a Dutch source – but who now only visits once
a year, rather than, as previously, two or three times. Some of the
blame for this reduction appears to rest either with the effects
of Brexit, and/or the amount of duty and added-weight costs of
taking vinyl back to Holland.

Meanwhile, a man who was staging an interesting conversation
with himself, consisting mainly of uttering the names of various
groups and artists, whilst not picking up any of their records,
eventually decided to depart, complaining, 'There's too many
records.'

He was replaced by a much more laid-back gent asking 'I don't
suppose you have any cassettes of Elvis – maybe the Beach Boys, or
Tom Jones, or some other easy-listening stuff?' He was told: 'Yes, I
have loads of cassettes of all types – and I definitely have some Elvis.
Hold on, I'll find it.' Many of these had come from a recent house
clearance, I was later told. 'I want them to play in my lorry – which
still has its original cassette player, and I don't want to change it, so

I need stuff to listen to.' I empathised with this reason, having kept hold of my ageing car, mainly on the grounds that it still boasts a CD player. The happy lorry driver departed with plenty more music to listen to on his travels. Another customer recently asking for cassettes was apparently, 'a young girl who'd just passed her test in an old car, which still had a cassette player'.

I was struggling to find anything to purchase. Tony has a double LP of singles previously released by the White Whale label which I quite fancy. He has had it for literally years. But it is priced at 20 quid, which I think is too much. Every time I'm here I tell myself to ask for a discount, but somehow the time never seems to be right. I might take this book in to the shop when it is published and show Tony this paragraph, as I'm confident the album will still be there, and perhaps I'll get it for a tenner as no one else seems to be remotely interested – and surely a tenner in the till is equal to 20 quid in the record rack?

I was somewhat distressed by reading in *The Oldie* magazine, a 'Digital Life' column by Matthew Webster under the headline 'A digital LP? Music to my ears'. In it, the writer debates whether he wants to continue paying out to 'stream' (I think that's the correct terminology) stuff from Spotify, or to collect CDs instead: 'Buy a CD and it's yours for life. Stop paying Spotify and you'll lose access to the music.'

'Hold up, man,' I immediately thought, 'what about your vinyl?'

Then I read this astonishing declaration: 'I have finally admitted that the vinyl LPs I have been cherishing since school days will have to go. I am selling what I can on eBay and using the money to buy CD versions of the albums I'll miss. I then copy them onto my computer.'

Whoa, there, man – have you seriously thought this through? You're writing for a magazine whose readers are overwhelmingly just over 50 – or more likely well over 50 with an appropriate mindset for that age group. You're telling me that you are now prepared to get rid of objects which you have treasured enough to look after for probably at least 35 or quite likely, many more years?

If you do that, Matthew I can guarantee you WILL regret it, possibly later rather than sooner, but for sure the decision will return to haunt you, particularly as you come across as someone with a proper regard for the music you like. The crucial mistake you're making is to 'buy CD versions of the albums I'll miss'. No. Just no. KEEP the LPs you'd miss most, get CD versions of the others – which you'll probably also be able to find in charity shops for mere pennies if you make it an enjoyable project to track them down. But I worry that you've already made the decision and that you'll now have to carry on and make the error, before it turns into a burning regret and you begin the pricey process of trying to rebuy the records you are about to discard as though they were unimportant impulse buys, which, I suspect, they weren't.

They're an important part of the process by which you became the person you now are.

Webster ended his article with the line: 'I'll be back in control.' I doubt that very much. He's far more likely to wish he hadn't LOST control of his senses and made that fatal error.

Also on this day, I was not best pleased to note that we record collectors were again being attacked for our hobby – if it wasn't bad enough already to be labelled weirdos, saddos and dinosaurs, we now have to deal with a claim that we all have ADHD which, initially, is explained as 'attention deficit hyperactivity disorder'.

The reasoning here is that 'hoarding disorder' is, according to one Dr Michael Mosley, 'a mental health problem affecting around 2% of the population'. The article goes on to admit, 'it's not clear what causes hoarding disorder but new research has linked it to ADHD'.

What a total load of, er, nonsense. Just because we collect stuff – and even if others don't, we know where everything we need and want is – well, usually – we're obviously hopeless hoarders, with a disorder. A diagnosis which fits almost none of the record collectors I know.

As for our collecting being a mental health problem – well, it appears it is others who don't collect who have the problem, not us. The article refers to someone named just as 'Clare' who, it alleges 'almost certainly has ADHD'. Why? Because 'she says she holds on to stuff because she thinks, I'll need this someday'. Yes, so do I – I buy records because I want them to be there when I fancy listening to them. What's wrong with that? According to the article 'If you haven't used an item for at least a year and you don't have specific plans to use it soon, put it aside for the skip or a charity shop.'

Oh, please, enough with this nonsense. I am a happy disorder hoarder. Get over it.

IN WHICH REBUS IS NICKED

In my spare time, I love to read Ian Rankin's great 'Rebus' novels, featuring as the main character, John Rebus, a detective with a love (and large collection) of vinyl which chimes with so many of my vintage. Here's a wonderful example from *The Naming of the Dead*, a 2006 Rebus adventure, in which he takes a shower, during which he 'couldn't decide which track off "Argus" to choose' but finds himself 'humming "Throw Down the Sword"'. I'm sure many of us have found ourselves in such a situation. Or, how about this from the earlier, 1998, *The Hanging Garden* – 'What did it matter if you could reel off the track listing to every 60s Stones album? It didn't matter a damn.'

But, of course, it did to Rebus – and to me!

Rankin's text elaborated why he felt record-collecting mattered to Rebus – 'Obsessions came easy – especially to men – because it was a cheap way of achieving control, albeit control over something practically worthless.' I'm not so sure about the 'cheap way' reference, mind you.

In the first few novels, Rebus showed a liking for jazz, but by the fourth, *Strip Jack*, in 1992, he had begun to admit a partiality for the Rolling Stones; from that point on, his favourite music becomes folk and rock from his own – and his author's – youths. Rankin, knighted in 2022, has used Stones' LP titles as Rebus story titles, too – *Let It Bleed*, *Black & Blue* and *Beggars' Banquet*, for example.

In the books Rankin's own different musical tastes often emerge via Rebus' younger fellow cop, Siobhan Clarke, who seems to favour the likes of the Clash, Big Country, Peter Gabriel, and even Rory Gallagher.

Saints of the Shadow Bible was published in 2013, and contains this lovely exchange. Rebus is quizzing someone:

'He tells me you met at a party.'

'That's right. I went there with Alice and got talking to Forbes in the kitchen.'

'Just like the song, eh?'

'What song?'

'Before your time,' Rebus admitted.

On page 75 of this book, Ian Rankin twice demonstrates his love and knowledge of vinyl, writing of Siobhan Clarke – 'She slid some of his LPs back into their sleeves' – and of Rebus – 'Rebus was putting an LP on, turning down the volume. Miles Davis, she thought – from the period before he got weird.'

In Chapter 4 of *A Song for the Dark Times*, the 23rd Rebus book, published in 2020, Siobhan tells their mutual colleague, Fox: 'John says he wants it put on his gravestone: "He listened to the B sides."' Now, that is a fitting tribute to any music fan.

In 2017, 57-year-old Rankin became lead singer for the group Best Picture, who released a debut single, 'Isabelle' on Oriel Records, also featuring Al Murray as a backing singer and Number One single-scoring Bobby Bluebell on guitar. No copies were available on Discogs when I checked in early 2023 – so, clearly a collectors' item.

In a November 2012 interview with Euan Ferguson for the *Guardian*, Rankin gave the game away: 'I am, of course, a frustrated rock star – I'd much rather be a rock star than a writer. Or own a record shop.'

IN WHICH I'M PRETTY UPSET

Sadly, it was far from a rock 'n' roll death which deprived the world of Pretty Things' singer Phil May in May 2020, at the age of 75 – which, personally, I think is too old to be messing around with bicycles. But for some reason, Phil had deemed it desirable to get on his bike, only to take a tumble and end up in hospital where he expired, due to complications from the emergency hip surgery he had to undergo.

The Pretty Things suffered hugely critical and often positively aggressive media coverage when they first came to public attention in 1964. Singer, Phil May, and guitarist Dick Taylor – an early Rolling Stone – were usually the targets, and as a spotty, self-conscious teenager, I empathised, particularly with Phil, whose shoulder-length tresses, shocking for the time, made him an instant target for criticism, if not outright condemnation.

The group first hit the singles charts, albeit the lower end of the Top 20, with the raucous 'Rosalyn', followed up with the excellent 'Don't Bring Me Down' reaching a similar placing, before they opted for a slow blues track, 'Cry To Me' – and I retain a vivid image of being at my Aunty Winnie's house, sitting on the carpet in a shaft of sunlight, in 1965, listening to this atmospheric single on the radio, which may, or may not, be accurate – I suspect it is, but am not planning to be regressed hypnotically in order to prove it beyond doubt!

'Midnight To Six Man', 'Honey, I Need', 'Progress', 'Come See Me', 'A House In The Country' were all minor hits, maintaining their career level, but hardly preparing most listeners for one of the most remarkable singles of the 60s, 1967's 'Defecting Grey', a psychedelic classic, with an album's worth of wonder compressed into a single, such was the invention and innovation displayed over the few minutes – but there was almost equal delight on the B side, in the shape of the soaring 'Mr Evasion'.

Amazingly, the charts were not troubled by this double-sided monster 45, nor its successor, which maintained the creativity burst with 'Talkin' About the Good Times', backed by 'Walking Through My Dreams'. I did then, and have again many, many times since, played these four tracks successively and been left delighted and entranced by their brilliance, but wondering why so few others were aware of it. Also around this time, and as alter egos, The Electric Banana, the May-Waller-Taylor triumvirate, created a superb series of recordings for the De Wolfe music library to be used in radio, films and television shows. They produced a total of five albums between 1967 and 1978.

In 1969, the Pretty Things appeared in a film starring Norman Wisdom, *What's Good for the Goose*, telling the dubious tale of a 'middle-aged' – elderly would be a more appropriate description – businessman falling for a swinging chick, as they were known in those days. Dick Taylor was not impressed by the ageing comedy actor: 'He couldn't leave a room without pretending to trip over, doing one of his pratfalls. God, he was a pain in the arse!' But, 'he had a toke with us', recalled May.

A triple CD compilation, 'The Complete De Wolfe Sessions' was released by Cherry Red in 2019 with, in my eyes – ears, really – 'It'll Never Be Me' and 'Alexander' the highlights.

However, the group had also been building up to the game-changing release of the Pretty Things' first – and perhaps anyone else's – genuinely psychedelic concept LP, 1968's S F Sorrow, (all tracks written by May-Taylor-Waller-Povey, + Alder on several) which would bring them garlands and acclaim and continue to resonate down the years – as would its almost equally as impressive 1970 follow-up, *Parachute*, which did make the Top 50 LP chart, whereas S F Sorrow didn't. You would probably have to pay the best part of a four-figure sum to acquire top quality copies of these two groundbreaking records now – fortunately, I bought them at the time, probably for a total of not much more than a fiver.

Parachute is often said to have become *Rolling Stone* magazine's Record of the Year, but this may well be an urban myth. It was in

1975 that Steve Turner, a writer for that publication, wrote that it had been 'a *Rolling Stone* album of the year'. But *Parachute* was not listed amongst the magazine's Albums of the Year for 1970 or 1971. According to an authoritative website on the subject, the 1970 winner was Black Sabbath's *Paranoid*, followed in 1971 by The Who with *Who's Next*.

The band's awe-inspiring streak could not be prolonged, though, and their next LP, *Freeway Madness* marked a phase of their career which resulted in sporadic great moments, but no further propulsion into heights of greatness. I couldn't betray the band by jumping off their bandwagon, although Dick Taylor did temporarily, and I continued to enjoy their LPs as they came and went, and to attend occasional live shows, including a memorable one at the 100 Club in London in, I think, 2014 – well, the album recorded at that show came out in that year.

A few years before Phil's death a friend and fellow 'Things' lover, Martin Wilson, was out on his rounds as postman in the Cambridge area, and was 'delivering and chatting to a woman, who said to me "We've got our Pretty Thing in the garden again." I asked what she meant and she said "Phil May of the Pretty Things – he's back again – he's in the tent over there. He often comes and stays here. He's a friend of the owner of the local pub, the Blue Ball Inn."'

Martin asked 'whether I could get Phil's autograph', but she was a bit concerned that he'd be asleep. 'I pressed her about it and she took me down to see whether he was up – he was awake, but a bit bleary-eyed, we shook hands and made small talk. I thought, "I need his autograph" so rummaged around in my bag and found a Recorded Delivery book. I tore a page out and told Phil I was sorry but this was all I had – he took it and wrote his autograph, drawing a picture of a flying guitar next to it. Of course, I still have it – it has pride of place in my collection alongside Bill Wyman's, which I got when he opened his burger restaurant, 'Sticky Fingers', in Cambridge.'

It is a great pity that Phil (Dennis Arthur) May (birth name Wadey, but raised by relatives called May) never wrote an autobiography, or even that no one decided he was worth a biography. In February, 2023 came news of a Pretty Things' boxset, *The Complete Studio Albums 1965–2020*, set for March 31 release on the Madfish label.

'For the first time' begins the info blurb (yes, I think, tell me more at once) 'the complete studio album recordings of The Pretty Things.' Okay... but, to be honest, underwhelming, really – after all, I and, I'm sure, most of the group's longstanding followers already have them. But when I read on, apparently I haven't – 'All albums have been remastered for vinyl' (really? I could have sworn the copies I bought were on vinyl) 'and feature replica original artwork' – so, the same artwork they originally had, then?

Yes, but 'each album comes with an album-specific 4-page insert with rare photographs and original single sleeves'. There's more: 'Housed in deluxe slipcase style box the set also includes an exclusive pull-out print of the band in their prime.'

Okay, so these are all the LPs I already have and, I'm not sure about you, but I don't think most other records I now own, which have been remastered, sound any better than the originals I know and love. Still, let's see what the damage will be... 'For the first time in one set, the complete studio album recordings of The Pretty Things'... wait for it... £275.

I do already have a Pretty Things box-set, released back in February 2015, which consisted of: Box Set, Compilation, Limited Edition; 11 x CD, Album, Reissue, Remastered; 2 x CD, Compilation; 2 x DVD; Vinyl, 10″, 45 RPM, Compilation.

This was released by Snapper Music and when I checked on Discogs in February, 2023 the cheapest copy on offer, from a UK seller which was not mint and unopened, was £298 + postage. My own copy is, as I write, properly 'Mint' – unopened, still in its wrapper, and the closest one for sale matching that is £495, with a caveat:

'BRILLIANT BOX SET WITH EVERYTHING IN MINT CONDITION, CD'S UNPLAYED, BOX IS ALSO MINT BUT DOWNGRADED AS IT HAS BEEN OPENED.'

Decide for yourself which of these two box sets is, or was, the better purchase option. But please know I will not be remotely tempted to buy the new one; also please know that I can't really tell you why my copy remains virgin, undefiled, unopened, almost ten years since I bought it. I never intended that to happen and am struggling to explain the logic behind this situation. I did not purchase it with the sole intent of making a profit – in fact I cannot now remember how much it cost on release, although I am pretty sure it wasn't anywhere near £275. And feel free to buy the latest one, I'm sure it, too, will increase in value over time.

Perhaps the best tribute to Phil came from his long-time musical muse and partner, Dick Taylor, with the release posthumously in 2020, of the album fronted by the pair of them, described uncompromisingly as 'The Pretty Things', supported by five 'additional musicians', *Bare As Bone, Bright As Blood*, which appeared with the message on it: 'In memory of Phil May.'

I'm not about to forget him.

IN WHICH I SUFFER A
SPOOKY TEMPTATION

It is not particularly unusual for me – or, I'm sure, many of you reading this book – to become obsessed by an LP and to listen to it several times on the spin, wondering why I've (you've) forgotten all about it for a number of years. It happened again, this time when I picked up a few old self-recorded CDs to play in the car en route to here, and, even, to there. The music in question is that played by the band Home on their debut LP from 1971 entitled *Pause for a Hoarse Horse* (by the way, ignore the Discogs' description of this band's music as 'country rock' – I really don't think so!). The individual track of that title is indeed about a four-hoofed equine – and one on which lead guitarist Laury Wisefield's playing is just brilliantly precise and controlled but absolutely spot on to complement the vocals and thrust of the songs.

He really works the strings on 'Red E Lewis And Red Caps' and although this track contains a mention of one Jim Page – ('I hope he remembers when he was a younger age') which may or may not be a Led Zepp reference – I cannot decipher all of the lyrics, but the mood of the track is just compellingly hypnotic and completely original and it doesn't outstay its welcome.

When I checked with the record's liner notes I read that, 'the band worked closely together for six months to ensure their musical definition was, well, well-defined before going into the studio' – and I can well believe that. I have two of their other LPs, *The Alchemist* from 1973, and 1972's *Home* and it is a positive pointer to their (what we used to call) togetherness (man!) that on all three they sport the same line-up – although Laury does become Laurie along the way.

And how come I'd remained ignorant of the facts – until I did a little research when I was writing this piece – that Mr Wisefield went on to join Wishbone Ash once Home folded, while their bassist Cliff Williams became a member of mildly successful group AC/DC. When I read that I thought I'd catch out Mrs Sharpe, a keen AC/DC fancier, so took the covers of the Home LPs to show her and asked whether she could recognise any of the group members. It took her about 8 seconds to locate Mr Williams and add to my rock education by telling me that he worked with both Alexis Korner and Graham Bond.

I rounded off my listening today with the Temptations' *Psychedelic Shack* LP: 'Psychedelic shack, that's where it's at... Right around the corner, just across the track, people I'm talking about...' Now this is what 'funky' means, BUT, strange to report, on this very day I suffered one of the weirdest moments I've experienced in a record outlet – and it was directly related to the Temptations – one of whose LPs, *Masterpiece*, from 1973, literally vanished in front of my very eyes.

I'd visited a recently refurbished and redecorated local charity shop, which has a fairly large record section and had come across this Temptations' album, offered at a very affordable three quid, albeit with some splashes of something unidentifiable on the cover. But the disc itself seemed almost pristine. As I took a quick peek at Discogs to see how much a better copy might cost me, one of the shop guys pointed out to me the very basic record player they had added to their facilities, and invited me to play anything I fancied on it – which I did, putting on £1 bargain, *The Stars Sing Lennon & McCartney*, on the cheap label, MFP, and featuring the likes of Peter and Gordon, Cilla, Billy J, The Fourmost and, er, Bernard Cribbins, performing tracks by the mop tops. 'Okay, I'll have that, and I'll take the Temptations' LP, too,' I declared to myself. 'Now, where did I put the latter?'

It was nowhere to be seen. Nowhere at all. I went through every section of the container holding the LPs, the Rock section, the Jazz section, the Easy Listening section – all of them. No Temptations anywhere. Nowhere it could have gone. I was baffled, and a little spooked, to be honest, but it didn't turn up. Another of life's small vinyl mysteries.

IN WHICH I NAME WHAT I SHARE WITH ELTON

It isn't something I often tell people, but I share a name with Elton John – yes, one of my two middle names is Reginald, not sure why Mr Dwight was handed the name, but mine was in honour of my troubled godfather of the same name. When I hear of artists with similar nomenclature, I tend to pay them just a little more attention than usual – which might account for my early championing of the Troggs, courtesy of Reg Presley.

So, the late Reg King of The Action – who died of cancer in 2010 aged 65 – was on my radar quite early on, and I was pleased when Grapefruit Records issued a very comprehensive, but little known, overview of one particular stage of his career.

Reg, sometimes Reggie, fronted what was known as a mod-cum-soul group initially, much to the liking of Paul Weller amongst many others, but which eventually moved towards a more rock-oriented approach. Reg left The Action in 1968 (they went on to morph into Mighty Baby) then in 1971 produced a magnificent, but virtually ignored eponymous LP, which he also arranged, produced and wrote, which received rather more attention when Circle Records reissued it with seven bonus tracks back in 2006.

This album's very striking cover featuring demonic, winged and long-tailed creatures with fangs, and bare-breasted ladies, makes it stand out from first glance, but a close perusal of the contents of a new version revealed that I would be effectively paying 22 quid plus p&p, yet only one of the 3 CDs included would be offering different material from my 2006 expanded version. Might it be pushing things a little to also suggest my middle name also explains my partiality to reg-gae music?

I was watching an episode of lunchtime soap *Doctors*, in which I have never noticed any character with the name 'Reg'. This one was featuring newly bereaved, retired copper, Rob, who had just left the long-time family home and was lodging with a friend, one of the eponymous 'Doctors'. Moving his possessions in he reveals a couple of boxes full of tatty looking records, one of which is a 1980 Specials EP, 'Too Much Too Young', but he bemoans the fact he no longer has anything on which to play it. His new landlady magics up a portable record player and they are soon skanking away – other tracks on the record are 'Guns of Navarone', and a 'Skinhead Symphony' medley of 'Long Shot Kick The Bucket', 'Liquidator' and 'Guns of Navarone' – all tracks which mentally zoom me straight back to a late 60s disco, ska-ing, reggae-ing and rocksteady-ing away on the dancefloor. The originals were my favourites of the time, but these sympathetic cover versions are pretty good and make me consider finding a copy to buy, until a quick check reveals it would probably cost me the best part of 20 quid to do so.

It is difficult to work out precisely when bluebeat became ska – or vice versa – and then when one or the other morphed into rocksteady, before the arrival of reggae. Whatever it is/was called, the beat of the music is similar, and in my disco days it was easy to dance to, as that seemed purely to involve moving one's shoulders up and down whilst shuffling on the spot – until such time as any of us whose hair was growing over their ears, were forced to move rather more quickly to avoid the flailing fists of skinheads or suedeheads, who seemed to have an inbuilt prejudice against longhairs. But however much I disliked the usually boneheaded, aggressive skinheads I couldn't do much about liking the music which they seemed to have adopted as their own. I have collected a few records in these musical modes over the years and decided to have a look through them. I was a little surprised to find that several are worth an interesting amount of money in the mid to high double figure range, and one maybe best part of three figures.

This one is a triple LP collection, released in 1971 called *The Trojan Story* which, according to the label stuck on the front of my copy, declaring 'SALE PRICE', cost me £1.45. When I checked on Discogs, copies in similar excellent condition to mine which, I don't believe has ever been played, were going for between £75 and £125. Mine also contains the original comprehensive track detail sheet.

A good proportion of my LPs of this type are collections by various star names of the day – such as Derrick Morgan, Laurel Aitken, Max Romeo, Dandy, The Rudies, Ken Boothe, The Gaylads, The Maytals, Bruce Ruffin, and many more – almost exclusively male acts.

Lovers of 60s soul music may remember a various artistes 1968 Atlantic label LP called *This Is Soul* which sold at a bargain price – and did so in vast quantities, as it contained many of the biggest disco hits of the time such as Wilson Pickett's 'Mustang Sally' and 'Land Of A Thousand Dances' which topped and tailed it, Arthur Conley's 'Sweet Soul Music', Ben E King's 'What Is Soul?', and several more, including tracks by both Carla Thomas and Aretha Franklin. I seem to remember it cost 12/6d – just 1s 1/2d per track.

Anxious to avoid any allegations of breach of copyright or unjustified imitation, the world of reggae waited until 1969 before coming up with the idea of a 12-track, budget-priced record featuring many of the big names of this music style, such as Laurel Aitken, The Upsetters, Max Romeo and Derrick Morgan.

This LP was on the Pama label which, to differentiate itself from This Is Soul, called their offering This Is Reggae. I'm not entirely sure how much it cost but I'd take a wild guess at, perhaps, in the 12/6d region. This Is Soul had featured an atmospheric front cover, with a photograph of a male soul singer, crouching and clearly pouring his all into the song, lifting the microphone in his right hand, with its twisting lead, towards his wide open, giving-it-large, facial orifice, in front of an evidently enthusiastic mixed-race audience, with the colourful photo overlaid with jigsaw puzzle-style lines and a colourful depiction of the record's title.

In complete contrast, This Is Reggae featured an atmospheric front cover, with a photograph of a male reggae singer, crouching and clearly pouring his all into the song, lifting the microphone in his right hand, with its twisting lead, towards his wide open, giving-it-large, facial orifice, in front of an evidently (not quite so) enthusiastic mixed-race audience. Both tremendous records which offered terrific value – the latter is now likely to cost you about 30 quid if you can find one, while the former is more readily available as it has been reissued.

Possibly my favourite ska LP is what, in 1967, became only the 22nd LP I owned – and I think I wanted it mainly because it featured a track which both appealed to and appalled me. The record is FABulous Greatest Hits by Prince Buster, for me a ska classic which now will also set you back around 30 pounds, depending on what condition you're prepared to accept.

It appealed to me because all of the tracks are insanely catchy – and appalled me because the second side's 'Al Capone' featured the refrain, 'Don't call me Scarface...' Which had been adopted and adapted by some of my acquaintances to highlight the small facial disfigurement of my then 'almost' girlfriend. Almost, on account of the fact that her heart really belonged to another – some annoying bloke called Scott Walker. I still think of Pauline whenever I happen to listen to that track. I have no idea what became of her. Can't even remember her second name, although I can confidently eliminate Walker from the possibilities.

Perhaps the classiest of reggae singers was the great, multi-talented Jimmy Cliff, whose self-titled Trojan label 1969 LP was a frequent visitor to my record deck, particularly to hear 'Viet Nam', Jimmy's self-penned protest against that particular conflict, and perhaps ultimately his best known songs, 'Wonderful World, Beautiful People' and 'Many Rivers To Cross'. Or maybe 'The Harder They Come'. Perhaps 'You Can Get It If You Really Want' or even his version of Cat Stevens' 'Wild World'.

Probably my scarcest LP of this nature is the rock-steady *Dandy Returns* by Dandy, on Trojan, from 1968, which might well make three figures, depending on condition. Mine looks pretty immaculate in the playing surface region but the cover doesn't quite correspond. I have a few collectable reggae singles, notably one found for under £2 in a local 'pop-up' shop, Derrick Morgan's 'Moon Hop' on the Crab label, rated at £40 by the *Rare Record Price Guide*.

I also own a couple which will be contenders for the Filthiest-Single-Using-Clean-Language Cup competition when I get round to introducing it – which are Lloyd Terrel's 'Bang Bang Lulu' from 1968 on the Pama label, and Max Romeo's 'Wet Dream' on Unity, from the same year.

You will, no doubt, have your own favourites, but remember, this is not a male-, nor reggae-only, contest, and I would have to nominate a Dana Gillespie LP I recently purchased for its versatility and invention in this category – in fact, she has made several of this nature! If you doubt this, check out her 1984 Ace Records release *Blue Job*, an album of double entendre blues standards. She chose the album's title and songs – and as a result began to enjoy a new career path as a bawdy blues queen.

IN WHICH HAT'S THE WAY TO DO IT

I took a fairly straightforward tube train trip from my home to Ealing for that location's Record Fair. Despite a recent haircut, earlier in the week, I decided to don a head accessory in case of a surprise downpour, or potential sunstroke should the forecast scorcher materialise. This is something of an affectation which was imposed originally on me by my much-missed mother-in-law, who bought me a rather fetching trilby-style item for Christmas or birthday some years ago and which I now regard as a trademark, complete with permanent Remembrance poppy.

I gradually grew into hat culture, possibly because of my football allegiance to a team known as The Hatters, but probably not! Today I was wearing said item, and heading – sorry – towards a destination of a church in Ealing for the Record Fair. Walking to the venue, I passed a lady of a certain age – a little less mature in years than myself, she definitely smiled at me in a friendly manner after taking in my cranial adornment. I think hats have helped me over the years when in record buying situations, if only in endowing me with the confidence to bargain, in an effort to obtain a discount, and certainly in shops where I have been a regular visitor the staff seem to recognise the headwear rather than me, but familiarity, however achieved, can help smooth the clinching of a deal mutually suitable to both sides.

I must confess, though, that my original inspiration for considering taking to matters hat-related was the legendary Man With No Name, the hero of the amazing *A Fistful Of Dollars* film and its several follow-ups – er, follows-up? – starring the laconic, fearless, man of few words, played by the equally charismatic Clint Eastwood, who, you may not be aware, has had ten LPs released in his name. The first, *Cowboy Favorites* in 1962 does what it says on the cover and has the great man crooning away on such zingers as 'Along The Santa Fe Trail', and 'Tumbling Tumbleweeds'.

Once at the Fair, not overburdened with exhibitors, I see that the most popular stall is the 'everything a tenner' one, with a hefty, varied range of titles, most sealed and clearly brand new. I spy titles by the likes of the Byrds, Quicksilver Messenger Service, Bad Company, the Doors and dozens of others – most offering live radio broadcasts or shows. Far be it from me to suggest that I would be most surprised to learn that the artists featured would benefit from the sale of these records which, I'm sure, play to the highest possible standard. I decided, though, not to buy any of them.

Instead, I listen to a conversation between two chaps half-heartedly flipping through the discs, chatting about the fact that one of them recently made a coffee-shop sighting of a member of Ron's favourites, The Shadows. It is unclear of whom they speak, although I don't think it was Hank Marvin. But the only clue is that one says perceptively:

'He'll be getting on now.'

'Yes, 80, I imagine.'

'At least 85, I'd reckon.'

'Well, he can still get out to drink coffee okay. And he had a woman with him.'

'I doubt it was his Mum,' I think to myself, but resist saying to them.

Meanwhile, another potential buyer, digging alongside me complains to the stall-holder by waving a record cover at him and declaring: 'I hate picture discs, haven't you got any proper copies?' The stallholder, unsurprisingly, seems lost for words.

I move to a different stall, where I spot an attractive, boxed and sealed Blind Faith double live from Gothenburg LP. I recognise it as the very same attractive boxed and sealed Blind Faith double live from Gothenburg LP I bought at the Harpenden Record Fair recently, for £20. This one was £55. Oh, by the way, if you have a copy of this – however much you paid for it, may I just point out that this gig took place on 18 June 1969, while Blind Faith's debut gig in Hyde Park was 11 days earlier. It was now my turn to be lost for words – as at that very moment, I heard someone apparently speaking to me:

'Graham – I THOUGHT you might be here!'

I looked up, and there was Oliver Wilson, my sometimes best friend Martin's son.

'Ollie! Great to see you – you're looking really well.'

And he was.

We chatted away and I discovered Ollie and his fellow AFC Wimbledon-supporting friend were en route to the Sounds Original record shop not far away in South Ealing, which I'd visited not that long ago.

'You'll like it,' I told him. 'I'm sure you'll find something to buy.'

We agreed that our meeting place here was far from the most exciting and tempting of record-selling venues either of us had visited. I'd now done my circuit of the room, and apart from the Blind Faith shock, had also noticed that the £4 brand new, sealed Alan Bown Set CD I'd also acquired just days earlier, was being offered for EIGHT quid here.

I decided I could live without buying anything, shook hands with Ollie, had a photo taken with him, and headed home. Later that afternoon I received a text from Ollie, after visiting Sounds Original, telling me: 'Spent small fortune! Bizarrely, he keeps the good stuff behind the counter, not on show. He kept asking what I'm into, then produced rare stuff on demand. Good shop – I'll have to go back.'

Paul Vernon wrote a piece on the British Record Shop Archive website in May 2017 about the recent death of record shop owner, Chester Dowling: 'Chester was a record seller for many years in a number of different outlets, reportedly starting locally to me at Wealdstone Market from 1970–72, then moving to Rayners Lane until 1976, after which he went northwards to Far Cotton, while he also ran the Luton Record Fair for almost 40 years.'

Vernon related a story of a 70s scam involving hyping the price of UK 78s of Bill Haley's 'Rock Around The Clock' on the Brunswick label, by suggesting they were worth some £40 each. He explained:

'This had its origin in an early evening local TV news show, wherein a bloke was interviewed about "rare records", and advised viewers to check if they had a copy – the following week, Exchange & Mart and Record Mirror were filled with small ads for them, all at 40 smackers! But there was another ad offering it for the bargain price of £10. That was placed by the TV interviewee, holding multiple copies.

A week or so after all this, a bloke and his dog turned up in Chester's record shop with an unsleeved copy, and said, "How much will you give me for this then?"

Chester took it in hand, squinted at it and replied "Fifty pence."

"FIFTY PENCE??" said the astonished owner. "You know damn well it is worth at least forty pounds!"

Replied Chester: "You want to know the true value? I'll show you," and he took one of several copies off the shelf, showed it to the bloke then shattered it across the top of the cash register.

"THAT'S how much it's worth, mate, now f*** off.'"

On a visit to 'Second Scene', I'm failing dismally to find anything to make my buying juices flow with any great energy, until Julian tells me he's created a 'Pop Beat 60s' section, which he advises me to peruse – and where I very quickly spot a copy of *For Certain Because*, an often overlooked or underrated Hollies' LP on which all the tracks are penned by Clarke-Hicks-Nash, the Hollie-Trinity of the group. I immediately plonk it on the in-shop stereo system and am impressed. Marked at 30 quid, I buy it for £25 – possibly three quid too much, but I always feel guilty if I don't buy something, having spent an hour or more wasting his time with inconsequential chat about the this and that of vinyl.

Talking of the Hollies, Graham Nash's latest LP had come out in May 2023, and he described it thus on Facebook: 'I called this album *Now* because that's what this work is. It's me. Now. In this moment in my life. It's no small thing getting to be my age. It's not easy. I wanted this work to show that even when you reach this point in your life you feel no less creative or passionate about what you do, and how you exist in the world.'

Graham was born on 2 February 1942. I know that some might think it to be in poor taste, but when I read of high-end rock performers still at it in their 80s, I can't help but wonder how I'd have replied during my days working for a bookmaker, if a punter had asked me to offer odds about which member of the Beatles or Stones would be the 'last man standing'?

I don't think my bosses would have approved of me actually quoting odds for people to place bets on, but as a purely speculative talking point, I think, as I write this, I'd make Jagger (born 26.7.43) 6/4 favourite to see off the other three, with McCartney 2/1 (18.6.42) second most fancied, and the apparently indestructible

Keef 3/1 (18.12.43) third, with the oldest of them, Ringo, (7.7.40) the 12/1 outsider. Apologies in advance in case one or more of these – or even myself – has passed away when you read this.

A week or so later, there were two records I quite fancied owning, whilst at the St Albans Street Market. Both were 10″ singles or, I suppose, more accurately, EPs. Both offered at least four tracks. Both were by groups I've collected on and off for many years. Both appear to boast material not available elsewhere. Both were priced up at £15 each. I showed them to the gent in charge of the stall, who my cancer pal Ron, told me he thought would do a deal.

I held both records up to show him – 'I'll definitely have the Pink Floyd for £15, and if you'll do the two for £25 I'll take the Soft Machine, too.'

He hesitated, thought, and said, 'I'm sorry. They're expensive to get. I can't do that.'

'Okay, no problem – I'll take the Floyd, then.' I flash my wallet and take out a £20 note and hand it over.

'Er, well, hm, okay, I'll do the two for £25.'

I hand him another tenner and get a fiver back.

We part on good terms. Ron's already acquired some LPs and singles to his liking.

Job done, with Ron's daughter, Penny, joining us, we retire to the local Wetherspoons for tea, and bacon sandwiches, where I tell them that while I was waiting for Ron to arrive I'd seen what looked for all the world like the ghost of former Lynyrd Skynyrd lead vocalist, Ronnie Van Zant, right down to the hat, the flowing locks and a flowing coat.

Later I play my two 10″ purchases. The Floyd has two acetates, 'Lucy Leave' and 'I'm A King Bee', (yes, that one!) and 1967 out-takes of 'Silas Lane', and 'Experiment', both instrumentals. With one B or 'Other' side track, a studio session from October 1966 of 'Interstellar Overdrive'. The Softs' record is of an appearance in Paris in 1967 for TV show *Bienvenue* which was broadcast in August 1968.

A little uncertainly, I'd agreed to buy a copy of Keith West's relatively unknown 1967 single, 'Sam', in a picture sleeve, together with a 4 CD compilation in an LP sized box, *Acid Drops, Spacedust & Flying Saucers* – which I'd been after ever since foolishly missing the chance to buy one from a Cambridge shop some years earlier when it seemed too expensive at, if I remember, around £30 – for a combined price of 55 euros from a European seller. I was apprehensive about how long they would take to arrive, if at all, and whether I'd be faced with additional charges. Answers – not long, and no.

Tunes kept popping up in my head, and when one appeared I carried on whistling whilst asking myself – 'Has there ever been another song which represented such an unexpected change of direction for the group who created it?' Not that the group ever again recorded (at least not that I heard, to be fair) anything remotely like it, despite the fact that it received such a positive reception. It came out as a single in 1972, and was called 'Crazy Horses' – the group, of course, the entirely previously unhip, untrendy, frankly naff, Osmonds. It was sung by Jay Osmond, who said, '"Crazy Horses" was way ahead of its time. It's a song about ecology and the environment: those "crazy horses, smoking up the sky" are gas-guzzling cars, destroying the planet with their fumes. We shot the record sleeve in a junkyard, surrounded by big old cars.'

The group also found their song banned in a couple of countries – South Africa, where government censors interpreted the word 'horses' as referring to heroin, and France, where authorities assumed the lyric 'smoking up the sky' was about drugs.

IN WHICH I SHOP RECKLESSLY FOR POSTER GIRL POSTA

I boarded an overground train from Hatch End, the plan being to get off at Queens Park to join a Bakerloo tube train through to Oxford Circus. The lady stepping off the train at the same time as me, turned and said, 'Why DO they do that. WHY do they do that?' 'That' was to close the doors on the tube train at the very instant we were all disembarking from our overground conveyance, thus ensuring that we would now have to wait for the next one to arrive. I smiled at her, sighed, and said, 'Because they CAN!'

Fortunately, the next tube soon arrived. Once there, I took a short walk to check out the two well-established record shops within 100 yards or so of each other – Reckless and Sister Ray. The latter, named, of course, after the Velvet Underground song of that name, has been in business in Soho's Berwick Street since 1989. Berwick Street was once at the heart of a thriving hub of several other independent record shops, including: Daddy Kool, Shades, Red, Tag, Black Dog, Ambient Soho, Black Market, Kubla, Liberty, Vinyl Junkies – all long gone. Just across the road is Reckless Records – where they have been buying and selling vinyl records and CDs on Berwick Street since 1984. The shop boasts of 'buying collections every week, and our buyers are often travelling all around the UK finding the best titles (sometimes we go further afield!). We put thousands of great vinyl records and CDs out a week so there's something new for everyone every day'. So much of record buying/hunting depends on the mood you're in, and I remember on my previous trip to this neck of the woods just not feeling the vibe, and leaving with nothing purchased.

Today was different. I first arrived at Reckless, early enough for the shop still to have a peaceful mood. I was able to browse untroubled. Being in such a high-profile location, just a short walk from Carnaby Street, means that there is seldom a shortage of vinyl-fancying tourists in either of these two almost neighbouring shops, so it is only logical that with so many customers there is no necessity to keep prices low, unlike in different areas. However, I spotted one of the few Joe Bonamassa albums I don't possess, on CD for a reasonable tenner, and paired it with a Coral EP for a (k)nicker, departing content that this was a wisely invested 11 quid.

Into Sister Ray which, unlike Reckless, is on two levels, with the CDs upstairs, vinyl down. They have a hefty section for new 'psych' and 'prog' CDs. Again, with no pressure from fellow customers, I went through the absolute lot, emerging with a CD which had been on my wish list for some while – it pairs the first two albums by Dana Gillespie together for a tenner, under the title *London Social Degree* – the title of a Billy Nicholls' song which she tackles well, albeit not quite matching the original.

It is evident just by initial perusal of the words and pictures in the accompanying booklet that Dana's striking looks were no hindrance to launching her career, but that she is still around and performing is testament to the fact that she is certainly not a one-trick pony, and there is much strong material on this set.

As always, there are very reasonably priced CDs prominently placed on the counter which leads to the payment section, and as I passed this on the way down to the vinyl basement, I spotted and grabbed a copy of the 2016 Madness CD *Can't Touch Us Now*, which was on sale for a mere £2.99. This came out seven years after the band's marvellous *The Liberty of Norton Folgate* but has a similar feel to that epic and demonstrates the way in which this group has maintained its jaunty approach to the world but become adept at dealing with more serious matters than just continuing their early 'nutty boy' ethos.

I went through the complete complement of psych LPs, but must admit to being deterred by some of the prices adorning the few I was attracted by. Flipping through the more affordably priced singles I spotted a reissue version of Fairfield Parlour's lovely 'Bordeaux Rose' which I already owned on that Kaleidoscope 'spin-off' band's sole LP – but that is now so valuable it is something of a risk to play it. At four quid it was easy to pick the single up to take to the counter, where I handed over £18.98, before heading back to Oxford Circus station.

Back home I pulled out my purchases to have a listening session, which went really well until I got round to the 'Bordeaux Rose' single – which was nowhere to be found. On the train back I'd read a large format freebie trendy paper, before deciding it really wasn't written for someone of my age, with no idea who most of the people featured might be. So I folded it up and put it back in the bag with the CDs, but then changed my mind, removed it and stashed it on the seat next to mine for a future traveller to enjoy.

I could only think that I must have pulled out the single along with the unwanted paper and left both together on the train. But then it occurred to me that when my CDs and record were on the counter where I was paying, just maybe I'd picked up the CDs but not the single, so I looked up the shop's email address and sent them a note:

'Afternoon. Slightly bizarre question... I was in the shop this morning, and purchased two CDs, plus a reissue 7" single of 'Bordeaux Rose' by Fairfield Parlour. On returning home I have the two CDs, but not the single. I have checked indoors and can't find it, so two scenarios present themselves. One, I somehow lost the single out of the bag I'd put it in en route home, or Two, I may have left it on the shop counter and only picked up the CDs when paying. If you did happen to notice the single on the counter, perhaps you could let me know so that I can return to collect it. These things happen, and at least I do possess the actual music of the single on an LP! Cheers.'

I received a speedy response:

'Hi Graham;

Yes we have it here – I've had it popped aside for you.

Kind Regards

Leo @ Sister Ray'

Excellent – and not only did they have it, they offered to post it to me to save having to make another trip up town. I accepted their generous offer. It had been my own fault. So, that's what I call peerless customer service.

Today I discovered that one of my early 'crushes' after seeing her in a film which was influential for me, *Here We Go Round The Mulberry Bush*, the actress and singer Adrienne Posta, was actually born Adrienne Poster. For this information I am indebted to author Kingsley Abbott, in whose book, *500 Lost Gems of the Sixties* I read that she released a 'Spectorish' single called 'Shang A Doo Lang', a Jagger-Richards song, on Decca in 1964, co-produced by Andrew Loog Oldham and Phil Spector.

How could I not have known this; why do I not possess a copy? Part of the reason may be that, when I looked at Discogs, I found the single now sells for £87! Listening to it, I enjoyed the kitchen-sink production and Adrienne's vocals but it seems to be all chorus and not much song. It is also the shortest track, just under two minutes, on a 25-song CD compilation entitled *The Girls' Scene* which I found online for £6.24 and snapped up.

IN WHICH DECEASED GRANNY SINGS WITH GRANDDAUGHTER

In 2023, a most unusual record was rereleased, having originally appeared in 2012. *Tyneham House* reappeared on the Clay Pipe Music label, inspired by the story of an English village in Dorset which was requisitioned from its 225 residents by the Ministry of Defence in 1944, for the purposes of military exercises. People were never allowed to return. The reissue is on 10" coloured marble vinyl, with a booklet. Explains Clay Pipe's website: 'The pastoral, wistful yet ineffably disquieting music of Tyneham House is made by artists who wish to remain anonymous here, save for their eponymous title.'

If you think that is an odd thing to make a record about, *Fortean Times* magazine offers details of an equally offbeat LP, *Domestic Sphere* by Josephine Foster, whose voice is described as an 'unholy warble' and who, on one track, 'is accompanied by the crackly vocals of her own late grandmother'. The magazine also highlights Cate Brooks' *Tapeworks* which is 'a love letter to a 60s tape recorder salvaged from a Lowestoft junk shop in the late 90s' and on which the owner had recorded a TV performance by Billy Fury 'and the accompanying chirrups of a budgie'. Whatever turns you on...

I received an email from long-time friend Michael 'Pud' Pullin, in which he reminds me of something from our dim and distant days as teenagers: 'How can we forget the Small Faces' *Ogdens' Nut Gone Flake* which he played every time anybody went round to his house? I doubt if there were any grooves left on it, as he wasn't noted for looking after his collection.' The 'he' to whom he refers is our mutual friend, and near-neighbour of Michael's back in the day, John Maule, now a long-domiciled Aussie. Michael's email prompts me to tell Sheila, another Small Faces fan about it, and she immediately reveals or reminds me – I honestly don't think I knew – that John gave that *Ogdens* LP away when he left to become a Ten Pound Pom, to none other than my sister, Lesley. Oh. Did he? And that would be the same sister who, when I spoke to her some years ago to ask whether she still owned that LP, and if so, might she be prepared to let me have it, told me yes – but it would cost me. A three-figure sum changed hands.

Had I known/remembered it had been John's – who has many talents, but looking carefully after vinyl was never one of them – I'm sure I'd have offered considerably less cash to my ever so slightly younger sibling. And how could I have known Michael Pullin for some 60 years, without becoming aware of the link he has to one of rock music's legendary songs? Let him tell you himself: 'The third record I ever bought was "Morning Dew", a 1967 single by Episode Six, popular in Europe but never charted. The song was written in 1962 by Bonnie Dobson, but was, to be brutally honest, nicked by Tim Rose – who altered a couple of words and promptly claimed it as all his own work. Bonnie came to Britain in 1969 and, in her later years, she worked at Birkbeck College in London, as an administrator. This was also where I worked as the Print Manager, and she often brought work to me to be printed. She went by her married name, so I had no idea who she was. Then, one day, she came into the print department, where I just happened to be singing the opening verse – badly – and the story came out. Before she retired from the college, she successfully went through the High Courts and won the right to have her name included on the credits for "Morning Dew". So, it is now credited to Dobson/Rose. I noticed recently that a good copy of this single by Episode Six sold for £26.50.' Great story about a great song.

I found my copy of The Who's 1966 single, 'Happy Jack', this afternoon – and was soon listening to Daltrey singing: 'he lived in the sand at the Isle of Man' – well, WHAT a coincidence! I hadn't played this record for a double (probably treble) figure number of years and what had I been watching on the TV just last night? Only a mini-series set on the Isle of Man!... And while I'm on the subject, what's that shout of 'I saw yer!' at the very end of 'Happy Jack', by Townshend, all about...? I don't know if it is/was the case, but I found an online explanation claiming that: 'It is said that he had noticed drummer Keith Moon trying to join in surreptitiously to add his voice to the recording, something the rest of the band would try to prevent.' But surely he'd have shouted 'I 'eard yer' if that had been the case?

By the way, true to their word, the good folk from Sister Ray record shop did indeed send my missing single back to me, and it arrived at a cost of £1.85 postage to them, and probably another 50p for the admirably sturdy cardboard envelope – easily offset by the many pounds' worth of goodwill from me they earned by making this much appreciated gesture. I duly immediately played the single – Kaleidoscope spin-off group Fairfield Parlour's 'Bordeaux Rose', backed by 'Baby Stay For Tonight' (both Pumer/ Daltrey-penned). Both sides are lovely – okay, they can sound a little twee or mannered these days, but that's how they were. I loved these songs then – and still do.

But then up came the second coincidence of the day, as I randomly visited one of the three Flashback record shops in London – the Essex Road, Islington branch – and what did I come back with? More than I thought I would, for sure, and included was a Kaleidoscope single of two 'offcuts' from their *Faintly Blowing* LP – in a picture sleeve mirroring that original album cover. It was quite a straightforward trip to the Angel tube station, and a shortish walk to the shop. It is on two levels, with comprehensive sections on the ground level, leading me to assume that downstairs would be just crate-digging territory for those difficult-to-get-rid-of titles – but it was no such thing.

Having taken my bearings, I started looking through 60s and 70s rock stuff. There were a few people in the quite spacious area, including three or four staff members behind the counter, and a similar number of browsers. But, having for once, decided not to wear a hat for today's jaunt, I was feeling underdressed as I was surrounded by head-covered people – three customers in caps, another, wheeling a bike and wearing a cycle helmet appeared. Behind the counter, two of the staff had hats or caps – apart from the female member who did, though, have a fine head of hair.

A man came in with a few singles to sell. He was dealt with politely and efficiently by the young lady within a minute or two. She offered, and he accepted, three quid. But then she had to ask him a string of questions, to which he responded very politely, presumably, I imagine, to keep a record for the shop accounts and to deter anyone from trying to flog dodgily acquired vinyl.

I had by now located the psych-prog LP sections and was finding them rewarding, identifying half a dozen I was interested in, and choosing three of them as certainties: two compilations – one called *Dustbin Full of Rubbish*, which included a couple of Tomorrow live broadcast tracks and similarly appealing obscurities, by the likes of Spiggy Topes, and Steam Beating Association; the other, *Free Flight*, a double set of even more 'Unreleased Dove Recording Studio Cuts 1964–69' obscurities in an appealing gatefold cover, in most acceptable condition. I rejected the LP I spotted by Aussie group, TFS – aka Tropical Fuck Storm – apparently also the name of their record label.

I then descended into the lower area, to find another staff member behind a counter, his hair tucked into an enormous woollen hat of a type favoured by Rastafarians – and from where I then acquired the previously mentioned Kaleidoscope single, and also snapped up a newly reissued psych group LP by a Canadian band I had never heard of, The Dorians.

He was friendly, checked my records, asking me had I also done so – I hadn't, but then did – and he sent me upstairs to pay.

Before I went, I looked around the record covers on the wall, particularly noticing a shabby looking Pacific Drift LP for a three-figure amount. There was also, coincidentally, a very bright and undamaged Daddy Longlegs' LP, *Oakdown Farm* cover on the wall. I'd been looking at my own copy of this only the previous evening, thinking that it was well preserved, albeit having some kind of stamped message defiling the cover, and that as the *Rare Record*

Price Guide identified it at a value of £250, mine was probably worth around £150, the record surface being in excellent order. The one in the shop here with the superior cover was priced at a mere £79 – maybe the record itself was scratched – to be honest, I couldn't be bothered to ask, as I wasn't going to buy it in any case, and I certainly didn't want to find out that their copy was in better condition than mine, yet being offered for rather less than I would like to believe/hope mine is worth.

IN WHICH, AS A COLLECTOR, I COLLECT A COLLECTION OF COLLECTING COMMENTS

I was doing a little internet browsing and googled a certain record shop. Looked at its website and saw the following comment from a customer, and I quote as written:

'To be honest the guy that owns it is a bit of a rip off merchant I sold him some old Reggae records that they said they was asking for and I know that some I had were rare and old and when I took them to him he offered me cheap money and said that they was not old enough being that my records were from the late 60s going through to the 70s how old dose he want them concidering true Reggae didn't start till roughly 1968/69 makes me think he really dose not know what he is on about or as I said a rip off merchant, by the way I excepted his offer because I needed the money so beware when you go there.'

Of course, I'm not going to identify the shop, as I have no idea how accurate this comment may be – although there is possibly a clue in the claim that despite rubbishing the offer made, the 'customer' then accepts it, rather than taking his records elsewhere. Just demonstrates, though, how vulnerable to such criticism businesses are these days. I've been to this shop on a number of occasions and had no problems with them, although haven't tried selling anything there.

I have often wondered whether my urge to collect records is just down to personal enjoyment of the activity, or a symptom of some deep-seated psychological problem. Today, I came across an online article by Shirley M Mueller MD, who wrote this about 'The Mind of a Collector', on the website Psychology Today, headlining that: 'Scientists don't yet understand if the predisposition to collect is hereditary. If collecting is similar to smoking addiction, which has a behavioral (*sic*) component, they may have pathologies in common. The insula is a brain region implicated in conscious urges such as smoking and collecting.' Added Ms Mueller: 'No one really knows if there is such a thing as a born collector. We certainly don't understand if the predisposition to collect is hereditary, which would be required to be a born collector.

Be that as it may, the question is important and, hopefully, will be the thrust of future research. In the meantime, however, I postulate what will likely be found based on addictive smoking as a model. The latter is a plausible pattern for collecting as both can be addictive, collecting being behavioral (*sic*) and smoking with components of both physiological and behavioral addiction. We know so much more about smoking addiction and cessation that a working prediction related to collecting may be possible.'

She added: 'If my hypothesis is proven to be correct, writers and others will indicate that the tendency to collect is due to a specific brain network rather than a collecting gene per se.'

When one Pascal Massinon began researching at the US National Archives in late 2012, he compared the experience to his love of record collecting: 'Dry fingers, dusty hands, and dirty knees. Common ailments for record collectors scouring through "new arrivals" bins and passed-over shelves for rare used LPs. Historians don't always favor (*sic*) vinyl, but many of us are compulsive record collectors of one kind or another. Hoarders all, we're on the lookout for elusive documents, long-lost insights, and words that haven't been read since they were first put to paper. The obsessiveness required to hunt down both rare LPs and historical documents hit home when I joined archivist Kate Mollan in the stacks at the National Archives.'

Under the headline: 'Anyone got room for my 1.75m records?' *The Times* ran a story on 13 January 2020 about 70-year-old Bob George who founded, in 1985, The Archive of Contemporary Music, in Lower Manhattan, where he 'has amassed three million sound recordings' of which about 1.75m are on vinyl. He was seeking a larger home for the collection.

Keith Richards has donated to the Archive – but the copy of the first Stones LP which George prizes, didn't come from the guitarist – he found it 'under a pile of half-sodden newspapers – Keith Richards' signature appeared to have been erased by dog pee'.

George is endeavouring to collect 'everything sung and strummed since 1945' and told Will Pavia, who wrote the story, 'Today, someone said he had 50,000 78s, and did we want them?' I'm pretty sure they did.

Richard Capeless is a vintage jazz record collector – with a difference, explaining in a 2020 article for Deep Groove Mono (dgmono.com) why, for him, less is more: 'I have long been aware that I am not a typical collector. Where most experienced collectors create the circumstances for impressive photo ops posing in front of a solid wall of tightly packed album spines, my minimalist values have kept my collection extremely small. The less-is-more manifesto is largely driven by a preference for a deeper connection with less music over a more surface-level experience with a larger number of records. But my perfectionism also plays a role in my modesty, probably to a bit of an extreme. Call it reverse-hoarding, call it a gift and a curse, my obsessive tendencies make it difficult for me to see the forest for the trees.'

As far back as 1957, American newspaper the *Saturday Evening Post* wrote about 'renowned New York record dealer Sam Goody, who discussed and described his regular customers: "It's pitiful, sometimes, if they've got it bad. Their eyes get glazed, they go white, their hands tremble. They're oblivious of everything around them. They take out a record, study it, push it back, move away and then move back to the same record again. As I watch them, I often feel that a dope peddler is a gentleman compared with a man who sells records.'"

That's most of US, for sure!

Toronto filmmaker Alan Zweig made a 2000 documentary *Vinyl*, declaring: 'I want to go through every pile of records in the world. That's the problem.' In the documentary, he interviewed a man who, running out of space, felt he had to throw 2,000 records away, because he didn't want anybody else to possess them, telling the filmmaker: 'I even picked a dumpster that I didn't think anybody would find them in.'

In a November 2019 article, Kevin Mitchell, of Canada's *Saskatoon Star Phoenix*, who was named 2018 journalist of the year at the National Newspaper Awards, confessed of his 3000 strong LP collection: 'They're fun, or they can be. They stimulate the brain's thrill centres. They provide glimmers of satisfaction. They can also be endlessly frustrating: a chore, a burden, a daunting fixation, a blessing, a curse.'

Kevin also has something of a phobia about cleaning his records: 'I ponder the hundreds of discs still waiting to be cleaned and processed. And now, an unexpected thing happens on my turntable – some sibilance on the S's, perhaps, or a series of ticks, or surface noise that sounds like bacon sizzling – and I regret it all.' I contacted Kevin after reading his article, and in permitting me to quote from it, he told me: 'Always glad to hear from a fellow vinyl enthusiast! And thank you for the kind words. Yes, by all means, feel free to quote from the article. I love seeing books about this strange hobby of ours getting out into the wide world, so best wishes with the project. I just picked up 30 more records at the local symphony's annual book and music sale, so the compulsion continues.' I suspect Kevin is probably now closing in on the 4000 mark!

He's also a very organised collector: 'It lines a wall of my basement, 3,000 vinyl records, neatly shelved, grouped, alphabetized.' He estimates the collection, which he calls 'the behemoth, the big old beast', weighs three quarters of a ton! He is a little more specific about how he likes his records to be before they are played – as pristine as possible is the answer. He says: 'Far too many wait their turn in the queue – and the rule is they can't be played until they're cleaned.' However, even Kevin is outdone by another Canadian, Dave Doolittle, who 'owns approximately 35,000 vinyl records. He stores them in an empty schoolhouse in the Saskatchewan community of Maymont'.

Great for all of we like-minded vinylholics to come across proof that we are far from alone in our obsession/compulsion/addiction/hobby/call it what you will, but we all know what it means, however it is described.

IN WHICH I'M FUL-Y COMMITTED

I decided on a visit to Fulham today, Thursday, 1 June 2023, to visit On Broadway, a shop whose owner at the time of my last visit, pre-Covid, has, I have been told, since died. A relatively straightforward trip via one overground, two underground lines – and I'm deposited outside Fulham Broadway station, peering at a 'You are here' map, trying to ascertain in which direction the shop may be. A little confused, I walked away and back on three occasions before being satisfied I was heading in the right direction.

I found Dawes Road – On Broadway resides at number 161 – quite easily in the end. And set off happily along it – until, confusingly, it split into two differing directions. As the house numbers seemed to be carrying on seamlessly into the left fork I went that way. Of course, that was the wrong selection, as the numbers soon dropped to very low single figures, causing me to retrace my steps, cursing, before regaining the correct route, which brought me to a shuttered number 161. I wasn't that concerned. It was 5 to 12 and the shop was due to open at midday. I had obviously arrived a little before the doors were to be thrown open, as promised by the times printed prominently on said blue shutters: 'Thursday – Sunday, 12–6pm.' This strident message clearly outranked the much smaller, scruffier one typed on white paper and stuck on a side window, declaring: 'Fri–Sun, 12–6.' Or did it?

I checked my copy of *Record Collector* – it clearly stated Thursday to Sunday. As it was a few minutes past 12 I rang the shop number. It rang and rang, with no recorded information message kicking in, and no one answering, to say, 'Sorry, running late, hang about and I'll be there soon.' It was clearly 'Clash-time' – should I stay, or should I go?

I took the latter option and set off back to the Station, hoping that perhaps this was a mere cosmic joke at my expense, with a positive punchline which would be the sudden appearance of a charity shop, into which I would wander, there to find a treasure trove of original 60s psych LPs, only recently brought in by the grieving husband of a long-time vinyl collector whose recent tragic passing was now offering him the excuse of 'I'm afraid I'm now downsizing' to dump the unloved discs which held no appeal whatsoever for him, who begrudged them being stored in every available orifice of their dwelling. But, this being upmarket, Premier League, Fulham, there was not a single – or even LP – 'chazza' to be sighted.

To defray potential delay on the journeys to and from London, I'd brought along a book I'd been meaning to read – *Mug Bookies* by David Watts and Johnny Winall (can that really be a bookmaker's true name?). As well as his activities as a turf accountant, Johnny describes his days playing drums in a succession of 'almost made it' bands, and how, when working as a Business Development Manager, he visited a client company which produced compilation LP records, and there met Dick Rowe, of Decca record company – famously the man who, in 1962, had turned down The Beatles, because 'guitar groups are on the way out'. Explained Johnny, 'I couldn't resist asking Dick questions about the Fab Four. For many years I told the story of my exhilarating 1988 encounter. Twenty eight years later I realised that I had been duped when it came to my attention that the real Dick Rowe had passed away in 1986!'

Arriving back on home ground, I went to turn left towards my house, but a little voice in my head suggested turning right to visit the local charity shop. Just in case. I did. A swift look through the 5 for £1 CDs produced a couple I was interested in. But they had also adopted that annoying tactic of individually pricing the only ones I could summons up any real enthusiasm for at £1 or £2 each, and I was in no mood for such little games.

I glanced at the '5 for £2.50 or £1 each' box, full of the usual LP dross – Max Bygraves, Liberace, Cliff Richard, classical stuff, Hawaiian bands and the like. What was this, though, a Bonnie Tyler LP I don't recall having seen before? She has a decent voice and the occasional above-average song. I didn't know the album, *Secret Dreams and Forbidden Fire*, but it had involvement from Jim Steinman and Todd Rundgren, together with a couple of E Street Band members backing her. Not a bad album overall, but as I later found, the version of 'Band Of Gold' – oh dear! Dreadful. Unsubtly hammered drums, yelled vocals. No empathy with the lyrics. No subtlety in arrangement or vocal. An overwrought mess.

I also found a very decently preserved David Essex LP, *Out on the Street*. I knew I had four or five of his early LPs – but this wasn't one of those. It was an in-very-good-nick 1976 gatefold. I confess to a sneaking admiration for the man's work over the years. Probably a lingering consequence of seeing him star in the musical *Godspell* when he were nowt but a lad. An excellent buy, even better when I got home to listen to it.

I went over to pay my two quid to the young girl behind the counter, whose reaction suggested she'd never seen such exotic items, let alone knew what they might be. She dropped Bonnie on the floor, alarmingly, but didn't seem to have damaged the sleeve: 'You'd have been sacked if you were working in a record shop,' I joked – to an entirely baffled expression. I handed over two £1 coins and headed happily home.

Having settled down to watch *Doctors* I was irritated when the phone rang – 'Surely everyone who knows us knows better than to ring during *Doctors*?' I said huffily to Sheila, but answered it anyway. It was Viv, my mate Colin's wife. 'We're on our way down to Devon, just gone past Bath – I've had a phone call. Someone's found your phone.'

'Found my phone? I haven't lost it.'

'You have. In a charity shop.'

'Ah' – a quick check. 'Crikey. How did they get your number, then?'

Viv had no idea, and nor did I, but, having received an entirely unsympathetic reaction from Sheila to this news, she agreed to walk down to the shop with me to retrieve the mobile, enjoying every bit of the apologising and self-hating which I had to indulge in to demonstrate my gratitude to the good folk in the 'chazza', one of whom, a gent of similar age, admitted, 'I've lost mine twice recently,' to condescending looks from his colleagues. I gave them a tenner to put in the till – or their Xmas drinks kitty for all I cared – and departed, having been ritually, deservedly humiliated. All the fault of that bloody shut shop – wouldn't have lost the phone but for them.

I double-checked their *Record Collector* ad – which not only said they were open on Thursdays, but also listed website details saying the same thing, so I rang the mag and asked whether they might be able to correct the shop opening details in time for their next edition? I also emailed the shop to ask them why they don't seem to think it would be helpful to tell people they may actually be closed at times they advertise themselves to be open.

It'll be a good while until I can be persuaded to revisit 'On Broadway', I told myself.

However, next morning they'd made an effort to ingratiate themselves back into my good books with an email – 'Really sorry you had such an annoying experience. We will indeed change the detail in RC. I'm sure that others have been caught out. We are open only on Friday 1 to 6; Saturday 1 to 6; Sunday 2 to 6. Please accept £20 worth of records of your choice when you do return. Please email me so if I'm not there I can tell whoever is behind the counter of this arrangement. I know that doesn't really compensate for your wasted time, again sorry.' Okay, if you put it that way, I can't hold a grudge for long – not if bribed, that is, so... on 9 June, I was once again en route to Fulham.

I decided – having twice checked, once in a diary, once in a newspaper, that today was a Friday – to head back. I strolled up to the shop once again, with my phone telling me it was now

12.23pm. The shop was once again firmly shuttered. Surely not?! I looked at the sheet of paper stuck on the inside of a window but visible from outside, informing me:

'Friday 1pm–6pm; Saturday 1pm–6pm; Sunday 2pm–6pm.' Ah. My fault this time, having assumed that when they opened on Thursdays it had been from noon, I had foolishly assumed the same opening hour would apply on Friday. Right, this time very much my fault.

Now I had over half an hour to wait for opening time. What to do? I'd walked past an inviting looking hostelry called 'The Mitre' en route, so I retraced my steps, and entered this posh-looking gastropub. As I ordered, fearing my preferred glass of dry white was likely to leave me with little change from a tenner, I was a little surprised at how quiet the pub was, with just a group of youngish customers in situ. I asked the barman (person) whether this was an establishment recognising that cash is still legal tender? He accepted that it might be, but added that here only a card would suffice, making me fear even more the actual cost of the vino. The afternoon improved as he said, 'That's £5, sir.' How dare (s)he assume I identify as a 'sir'? The wine tasted most acceptable, and a pleasant half-hour passed as I sipped, listening to a playlist, including the Arctic Monkeys and, er, no idea – I only recognised them.

I noticed that a couple of walls of the bar were covered by framed LP covers, and it soared in my estimation – look, there's Roxy Music's *Manifesto*, here's Lennon's *Shaved Fish*, Cream's *Disraeli Gears* – Prince is over there, R.E.M on that wall, the Eagles up here.

This put me in just the right mood to stroll back to 'On Broadway', happily now properly open. Their website explains: '1982 saw the opening of the first 'On Broadway' on Fulham Road, before a move to Dawes Road in 1988, where we currently reside.'

My eye was immediately drawn to display cases of CDs, and as I looked through them there were a good number I quite fancied, most at £3 or £4 – Black Keys, Nick Drake, Tyrannosaurus Rex, Rescue Co No 1, Stackridge, Luther Grosvenor, Jeff Christie...

wouldn't mind any of them. A lady had been talking to the gentleman slotting records into their correct sections, who I took to be Mr S, who had apologised in the email to me. The lady departed, so I walked over and introduced myself – we shook hands, and he apologised again, clearly completely genuinely. Had I visited his shop before? I told him, yes, but not since before lockdown.

Mr S was a fellow Graham and we were soon getting on like the proverbial burning domestic residence, with me rather apologising for complaining, but he reminded me that I must select 20 quid's worth of stock entirely free of charge. 'The least I can do.' Graham's fellow owner, John Thorpe arrived for work, somewhat slower on the old pins than was once the case, but Graham humorously described the pair as 'two happy old guys making occasionally sensible comments about records' which sounded a decent description. They go back literally a long way, well over half a century, with John (long-standing fan of John Coltrane and Miles Davis) and Graham's first venture a record shop/stall, called 'The Sky Is Crying' – named after the Elmore James' 60s blues song of that name – and specialising in singles, which was in business until around 1973.

When John moved on to 'Cheapo Cheapo' in London's Rupert Street, Graham had a stall outside, as highlighted on the British Record Archive website. 'Cheapo' was owned by the late Phil Cording, 'he wore the same orange turtle neck jumper for 30 years', remembered Graham, who recalled walking in to Cheapo to sell a James Brown LP which he received 12/6d for, 'only to end up working there for "30 bob a day". Phil owned the shop but was also training as a nurse.' Graham and John – who was one of the first people ever to see a youthful Mick Jagger performing on stage 'with Alexis Korner's Blues Incorporated at a venue in Ealing Broadway' – are very clearly a team.

I later read online that Graham had been a headmaster, and was also brother-in-law to Cat Stevens – and he is certainly a driving force for 'On Broadway', founded in 1982, albeit also well aware of the vital input from John. I'd picked out an unusual 10" Status Quo six-track EP as my first 'purchase'. I had the cover, and Graham was trying to work out where the record itself was filed, as we noticed a tall, young man, clutching a crash helmet walking up the shop towards us. Sounding nervous, he began, 'I'm organising an event at Abbey Road, for a group of people from 40 to 80 in age, and was wondering if you'd have some stuff I could use to add atmosphere to the place – maybe some vinyls...'

He got no further, as Graham jumped on his use of the word, 'vinyls', pointing out that no self-respecting lover of records believes it to be a legitimate term: 'The plural of vinyl is vinyl,' explained Graham to the now even more nervous young man, who then compounded his situation when he asked Graham, 'What's that little machine, there?' 'It's a record player,' explained Graham. The tall man eventually took his leave, promising to return the next day, but almost certainly hoping against hope he wouldn't be asked to!

Graham had to rush off now, and took his leave, suggesting that I collect the records and/or CDs I fancied and let John sort them out for me – which I did, ending up with £21 worth after John refused to accept my proffered £1 coin! It was time to take my leave, and I departed, carrying the Quo EP and CDs by the Black Keys, T Rex, Nick Drake and Jeff Christie – now very pleased I'd taken the trouble to complain last week, as it had resulted in being able to strike up an acquaintanceship with Graham and John, which I very much hope to progress.

IN WHICH I CANN ALWAYS LISTEN TO JOHN

Having turned up for an 11am eye inspection at a local branch of Boots, only to be told that they had no record of my booking, I stormed out in a huff, and spotted an H11 bus at the nearby stop, so on impulse decided to catch it and go to a different inspection – that of the records for sale in Estamira jewellers in Northwood. As you walk in, there is always a tempting array of interesting

LPs, realistically, if not over temptingly priced – but the boss will always listen to offers. Downstairs is the basement I've mentioned before – but I didn't have time to nip down there today.

However, I did learn a couple of things about the shop I'd not previously known, such as, in January 2018 it hosted a musical evening – as four local musicians, including Virgil Vaitkusa on accordion, Michael Serota on bass guitar, and Philip Bridle on lead guitar, played jazz, rock and pop for two hours as passers-by were invited in to enjoy free refreshments.

And that on drums was shop owner, Amir Katz. At long last I now know Amir's name!

I found several possibles in the shop but as I was in a hurry, I just opted to acquire Hard Stuff's 1973 LP, *Bolex Dementia*, purely because of the presence in the group of ace guitarist John Cann, aka John Du Cann. Alongside him in this group was former Merseybeat, John Gustafson on bass, keyboards and vocals. The pair also wrote all the songs – albeit always as individuals. But the clinching reason for needing to have this record is – where else would I find an album dedicated to a hospital?

The Ziekenhuis Henri Serruys hospital in Belgium's Ostend – 'where John Cann passed a week, Paul Hammond (drummer) stayed a month and the Zodiac (no idea, I'm afraid) became both dear and late'. The band apparently suffered a car accident in the area which caused their compulsory medical incarceration. The record was marked at 35 quid. I was offered and accepted a fiver discount and our conversation turned to Norway – where Amir had been a recent visitor, discovering plenty of vinyl to buy. I asked him how many records he'd bought, wondering whether there was any question of an excess baggage charge. 'Oh, about 100,' he told me. 'But I put them in my luggage.' He'd also recently done a record shop trip down to Devon – 'Bideford, Barnstaple – some good shops.'

I've visited the record shops there, as well – no, not the Devon ones – those in Oslo! Once again I'm wondering whether Amir buys to sell, as there are always fresh selections available when I come in, but I have never seen anyone selling records to him. Perhaps he plays them once and then moves them on. I don't really know, but nor do I know where the core of his own collection

lives. Upstairs, over the shop maybe? I enjoy the mystery of not
knowing so probably won't ever ask.

As it transpired, the Hard Stuff LP was not the best indicator
of the talents of John Cann. It is ok and may grow on me. Two
days later I was in the covered area of Camden Market where
there always seem to be little vinyl sections I haven't seen before,
and I soon located one which seemed to have much the kind of
stuff I'd expected to find at my first stop, Camden Lock Vinyl
but hadn't. I was now very happy to find my recent John Cann
experience repeated, as I picked up an Andromeda LP – the group
in which (Du) Cann seemed most at home during his career –
featuring live broadcasts and various different takes on some of
their original material. I didn't even try to bargain as 18 pounds
was undoubtedly a very fair price. The Andromeda record was so
good I listened to it twice that evening.

John (William) Cann was born in 1946 and first came to notice
in commercially unsuccessful psych groups The Attack – with
whom he recorded the first version of 'Hi Ho Silver Lining', even
before Jeff Beck – Five Day Week Straw People, and then, more
significantly, Andromeda. He scored commercial success as part
of Atomic Rooster, alongside keyboardist Vincent Crane, leaving
– reportedly at the behest of Crane – despite, or perhaps because,
of writing half a dozen of the tracks on their LPs, *Death Walks
Behind You* and *In Hearing Of*. Du Cann then formed Daemon,
Bullet and Hard Stuff.

In 1977, he teamed up with Francis Rossi for the album *The
World's Not Big Enough* which didn't see the light of day until 1992.
But before that, in 1979, he had a minor hit with a single, 'Don't
Be A Dummy', helped by its usage in a jeans TV ad, boosting the
record to my waist measurement position – 33 – in the charts. In the
same year, he also rejoined a reformed Atomic Rooster with Crane.
For me, though, definitely his best work was done in Andromeda.

John died on 21 September 2011, (some accounts say 22
September) reportedly of a heart attack, and is buried in Norwich
under a headstone said to be inscribed with the first line of 'Devil's
Answer', which is: 'People are looking but they don't know what to
do'. However, I'd have thought the first line of 'Tomorrow Night',

their other big hit, which begins: 'When I wake up in your bed, I can still hear what you said' might have been more striking! In an effort to determine for sure which of the songs features on the gravestone, I contacted the cemetery. A charming lady told me, 'I'm afraid I'm not allowed to divulge any details of gravestones.' 'Oh well,' I said, 'perhaps I'll come down to have a look, or maybe ask someone to pop in to find out for me.' 'I'm afraid I can't tell you where the grave is...'

IN WHICH JOHN TALKS BUDDY, BEATLES AND STONES

John Henwood became a friend after we met on the Channel Island of Jersey and initially discussed horse racing, but it soon transpired this Jerseyman had some fascinating record-related memories to share:

'The first 45s that I bought myself were Buddy Holly singles on the Coral label. I eventually had every recording he ever made, including some demos. Various house moves, one coinciding with my turntable packing up ended my vinyl buying days. In more recent years I regretted the loss of my collection and tried to replicate it on CDs with some success.

Moya's [John's partner] dad was a jazz enthusiast and on holidays we would look for some of the obscure stuff we knew he liked. I recall spending hours in a little shop we found at Daytona Beach of all places, an Aladdin's Cave. But the biggest and best is the one in San Francisco at the corner of Haight and Ashbury. I swear it still has that lingering smell of weed!' John reflected on how his record collection shrank:

'I lent some (never returned), lost some and, as I recall, gave many away. The albums went to a charity shop. How short-sighted can one be?! Many of the 45s had my name inscribed on the label in white chinagraph pencil. On the black Coral label it was very clear, but that didn't stop people from nicking them!

I saw the Beatles on one of their early tours. They played Springfield in Jersey in the early 60s to a full house of about 600. Later, working in TV, I was the sound recordist when we interviewed them at EMI's HQ in Manchester Square. Sadly, that interview no longer exists, it being thought not worth keeping when film storage capacity was short. For reasons that I don't understand, one or two of a series of interviews recorded for our pop programme *Now Look Hear* survived. I believe the archive includes an interview with Freddie and the Dreamers! I didn't see the Rolling Stones – when they played in Jersey, I was working. But the next night they were at a popular night club called The Deep (long gone) having a few quiet drinks and I met them there. Mick Jagger wanted to know where he should go to buy some nice jewellery and I offered one or two suggestions. Nice guy, very unaffected.'

IN WHICH I PRUNE MY COLLECTION

In early June 2023, thanks to a rail strike, a Cup Final and the Derby, there wasn't much point trying to battle with traffic to attend a record fair or make a shop visit on that day.

So, I began pondering who I would nominate as my favourite psychedelic group? Of course, the Beatles did it better than anyone else, via 'Strawberry Fields Forever' and the 'Magical Mystery' era, but their focus on that style didn't last long. There were many fantastic one-off psych singles and groups with a short-lived interest in the style – the Pretty Things, for example, but giving this question properly serious thought I began to believe that my nomination for this self-invented title should be the Electric Prunes, the LA band, formed in 1965, who appeared in public in

1966 with the promisingly freaky debut single, 'Ain't It Hard' and then unleashed a string of amazing records, matched by few, if any, operating in the same area.

'I Had Too Much To Dream (Last Night)/Luvin" was their next offering, also in 1966, followed by 1967's 'The Great Banana Hoax' backed by the spooky 'Wind Up Toys'. 'Get Me to the World on Time' was possibly peak Prunes in 1967, with 'Are You Lovin' Me More (But Enjoying It Less)' on the B side. Then came the powerful 'Hideaway', also in 1967 but oddly as a B side to 'Dr Do-Good' – maybe their powers-that-be felt that the psych era was fading, I don't know. 'Long Day's Flight' was another 1967 ace effort. 1968's 'Everybody Knows You're Not In Love' suggested the band was somewhat running out of 'psych psteam'. It was little more than a straightforward commercial pop song. The other side, 'You Never Had It Better' was much rockier, much better, much freakier guitar break.

They were also involved in *Mass in F Minor*, ostensibly their third LP, albeit the actual involvement of most genuine Prunes is unclear, and although the record certainly offered many psychedelic moments, the religious element of it muddies the waters somewhat. There are some coruscating psych guitar outbreaks along the way, but they sit uncomfortably within the mass-like sections of this bizarre record.

If you prefer LPs to singles, their 1967 *Underground* and *The Electric Prunes* will cover most of the bases, albeit they do contain some ignorable dross along the way! Add in *Mass in F Minor* and *Release of an Oath* if you're a glutton for it, as well, while *Stockholm '67* is a live set worth acquiring. However, *Just Good Old Rock and Roll*, from 1969, seems to have very little, if anything, to do with the earlier version of the band. A number of albums under the name Electric Prunes have appeared since the turn of this century, but how much similarity they have to the earlier incarnation is unclear.

IN WHICH GROCER DAVE
IS REMEMBERED

There is a website devoted to people who lived, as I did, in Wealdstone many years back. I decide to put a question on the site to see whether I can solve a query dating back to those days. There was a father and son who, it seemed to me – and others at the time – were cut from the same cloth as old man Steptoe and his trendy son. The older of the two ran a greengrocers in Wealdstone, while Dave, the son, sold records from the back, before branching out to run a record shop – a large proportion being second-hand – next door to a pub in Wealdstone High Street.

But I could never remember their surname, so put the query out there, and the initial most popular answers seemed to be 'Russell' or 'Russet', neither of which rang a bell. However, a much more definite response from one Mick Nelson seemed to nail the answer: 'Definitely Dave Russon, with gramps. Dave's E-type Jag was often parked around the corner. His eldest son Andrew Russon is a long-time friend of mine. It was a great shop fronted by the fruit and veg with records, 8 tracks, videos, action comics (Marvel D.C. etc.) and "gentleman's" magazines out the back. Spent a lot of time in there in the mid-90s when Andy reopened it as The Vinyl Frontier. We spent ages sorting through dozens of orange boxes full of porn in order to value it correctly 😂😂 Great memories spending time there with Andy, his sisters and friends.'

Emma Bourke recalled one particular part of this memory: 'Haha yes! I used to hang out with Peter (his younger brother) around 1991/92 and remember having to leave when certain customers came in to browse the magazines😂'

Other locals had stories of buying records from Dave. This one from Richard Tague: 'I bought a couple of records at the greengrocers in Harrow. I managed to pick up Led Zep 4 in limited edition coloured vinyl for a fiver. That was a lot of money to teenaged me in about 1981. Still have it. Wonder what it's worth today?'

And Sarah Smith: 'My Dad always used to take me in there! He got my sister and I a 45rpm of "Blue is the Colour" by Chelsea FC!!'

Mick Nelson recalled his Mum's celebrity-spotting moment at the greengrocers-cum-record shop: 'Mum used to buy fruit and veg there as well. In fact she was walking home from there, laden down with shopping when Ronnie Barker offered her a lift home (which she gratefully accepted) in his Roller.'

Eddie Slavin: 'Bought quite a few albums there throughout the 70s, couple each of the Stones, Beefheart, Humble Pie and others. Always a good deal.'

Jon Hampstead: 'I bought loads of records, mainly singles, late 80s, very early 90s. Best purchase was Urchin 'She's a Roller', which I am pretty sure I scored for 80p.' That Urchin record is a three-figure seller these days.

Jill Hudson declared: 'Yes I bought records from him. If you weren't sure about an LP he'd let you borrow it to play at home before deciding whether to buy it!!'

Although I'm not quite sure which member of the Russon family she is talking about here!

Then Dave's son, Andrew popped up: 'Wow thanks. This has brought back some fond memories. Dad also had a shop on Kenton Bridge. Three shops in total at that time. Running around all the record label suppliers with Dad in his E-type. Being able to listen to so much variety in music was a dream. One lucky boy growing up.'

Sadly, it appears that Dave died in the mid-90s, probably '94 or '95. I will never forget buying an early Van der Graaf Generator LP from him, taking it home, playing it, hating it, taking it back and swapping it for something which I don't even remember now, and over the years watching with horror as that VDGG record, think it was their first, has become worth up to some 400 quid.

IN WHICH I MARVEL AT HUGE SINGLE PRICES

I am taking a look, as I often do, at a John Manship records auction – this one in June 2023 online auction (https://www.raresoulman. co.uk/auction.html). Here you'll find unusual, rare, bizarre singles up for sale via auction bidding. I've seen records here with current offers of well into four figures and I am astonished at how many people out there seem prepared to shell out that amount of money, and whether they are more likely to be buying to keep, buying to sell on, buying to use? This evening I look through the rules for bidding and immediately see an instruction which can be taken in one of two ways. At least, I think it can. Judge for yourself: 'Please do not leave phone bids until the last few minutes, lines get very busy and time is short.' Does this mean wait until the last few minutes before you leave your bids, or please DO NOT wait until the last few minutes to leave your bids?

The sentence can definitely be read in two different ways, but I reckon it probably means the latter. What might I be interested in if I were to bid, I wonder? Looking down the list, I come across a copy of The Thirteenth Floor Elevators' 'Livin' On/Scarlet and Gold' for which the highest bid thus far is, er, £0.00. I'm guessing it won't still be that when the hammer goes down. The same bid has, or hasn't, thus far, been made for Harry H Corbett with the 'Unidentified Flower Objects' on the Decca label, 'singing', 'Flower Power Fred' with 'Saving All My Love'. Surely this, which must be a 'micky take', is not going to find any serious bidders although I note that the RRPG rates it at £15.

I see Timebox's 'Beggin' – a promo copy, I think – is already up to a £66 bid, exactly £6 more than the amount it is valued at in the book. I look at the in-house blurb, and it urges: 'to own it as a flawless 1968 DEMO is the ultimate prize to "beg for".

When it comes to "Beggin" the gorgeous demo is certainly a very challenging 45 to acquire; what is very tough as well, is owning a copy in immaculate condition! Our data reveals this is the only copy we have had in recent times.'

The highest bid for any record at the moment is for Jean Carter's 'Like One' on a pink Decca label, for which someone has pledged £348. Not a record I am familiar with, I admit, and it doesn't seem to figure anywhere in the RRPG, so I have a look on Discogs, and can't find it there, either.

A Marvin Gaye 1966 Tamla record, 'Little Darlin' (I Need You)', here as a 'DJ copy' is rated at £120 in top condition in the RRPG – here the bidding is already at £275. Interestingly, to me, anyway, RRPG list two versions of this, both as TMG 574, both from 1966, but one of them called 'Little Darling' and the other, the far more expensive one, 'Little Darlin'.

Fascinating stuff.

Twenty-four hours later, I went back for another look, and found that Marvin Gaye was up to £314; Jean Carter was still ahead, at £348. My eye was drawn to the apparently neglected copy of the Thirteenth Floor Elevators' 'Livin' On' at an affordable £12 – could have a go at that! There had also been a spurt of interest in The Who's 'Legal Matter/Instant Party' which was now trading at £172.

PP Arnold was attracting £240 for a picture sleeve copy of 'The First Cut Is The Deepest' while an act of which I had no knowledge, Sheppard Bros, with perhaps the longest titled record on the list, 'If She Don't Want You To Have It You Can't Get It' suddenly leaped to the head of the charts with a £352 bid.

And it could well be that a great many of these records will end up sold to DJs looking to stand out from the crowd by having records others do not have or are even unaware of.

I'd just come in from our weekly trip to Sainsburys, clutching the one CD I'd bought after trawling through the three local charity shops – a CD and DVD, Beach Boys' 'Sounds Of Summer' collection which I thought might make me a profit at the next record fair I attend as a seller, when Planet Rock DJ Wyatt – whose show on the station I frequently listen to, as he plays the kind of music both Sheila and I enjoy – broke off for a bulletin, containing the sad news that Tony (T.S.) McPhee had died at the age of 79, officially of 'complications as a result of a fall last year'.

Sheila says, and I agree, that this news, whilst unwanted, is not a shock, as we knew that he had been unwell for some years. We saw some fantastic gigs in which he displayed his marvellous guitar playing and song-writing ability. But on the final occasion we went to see him it was not a pleasant experience. He was clearly an ill man, and I think most of the audience were very unhappy to see him in such a reduced condition. After this, we had no expectation that he would recover.

There is a nice story behind Tony's acquisition of those two initials, which explains how they were bestowed upon him by his producer, Mike Vernon, who suggested that having them would add authenticity to his blues credibility when he released a single – 'Get Your Head Happy!' alongside authentic blues-man, Champion Jack Dupree in 1966. The initials stood for: 'Tough Shit'!

In memory of Tony, I played several of my favourite tracks, including a couple from the LP he made with blues legend, Billy Boy Arnold, in which the mutual respect of two men tackling the same song from different perspectives is positively thrilling as they both go about their business complementing rather than competing with each other. And of course I rounded off with 'Thank Christ for the Bomb', really his breakthrough record.

Philip, who runs the local 'Tropic' live music club posted: 'I was saddened to learn of the death of Tony McPhee. The first album I ever bought when I was 13 was by his band, The Groundhogs. I went on to get many more. Back in 2011 they actually played at Tropic and to have Tony there (with Dave Anderson on bass, ex-Hawkwind and Amon Duul II) was for me a bit special.' I recalled being at the Tropic for that Groundhogs gig, although, even at that point, it was evident the light was fading for this fine musician. Then, later this same evening, we were watching the spectacularly off-the-wall 'Gallows Pole' three-part series on BBC2, when suddenly, almost spookily, The Groundhogs' 'Cherry Red' began blasting out – what a fitting, if unintended, tribute to T.S.

I heard from fellow vinyl adventurer Dave Lewis who had been to a fascinating function in London last night: 'It was a real thrill to meet the legendary producer Joe Boyd at the excellent Nick Drake book launch event at Rough Trade East. Joe discovered and signed Nick Drake and produced his first two albums *Five Leaves Left* and *Bryter Later*. His stories of working with Nick were incredibly enlightening.' Dave sent me a photo of him and Mr Boyd together, and I must admit I envied him that experience. Joe's book, *White Bicycles* from, I think, 2005, which I read some years ago, is worth seeking out.

Great date-fact highlighted from Morgan Howell, aka @SuperSizeArt, today: 'On 3 June in 1970, Ray Davies was forced to make a 6,000 mile round trip from New York to London to record one word in a song. Davies had to change the word "Coca-Cola" to "Cherry Cola" on the band's forthcoming single "Lola" due to an advertising ban at BBC Radio.'

Reading a 2023 edition of *Record Collector* magazine I agreed with the way in which a reader was becoming exasperated, despite having been 'buying and selling vinyl and CDs since 1978'. His particular concern was with the multiple formats in which so many records now appear – estimating that there are 'would you believe, 25 differing LP versions of *The Dark Side of the Moon*.' That was without foreign variations. The reader then demanded: 'Is this good marketing or ripping off the fans?' I suspect most of us will have the same answer to that.

This links in with my own thoughts on the reissue of records which the vast majority of those interested will already own, but now with the incentive of a few previously unreleased demos, outtakes, alternative versions or whatever. Why can't these incentives be released just by themselves at a lesser price for committed collectors who are surely just irritated by the current practice? Who am I kidding? I know full well most of us are as addicted as any consumer of illegal products, and will do virtually anything to be able to afford the delights dangled before us, even when we know full well we'll only play these nicely gift-wrapped items once or twice before salivating for the next one.

IN WHICH I THROW BACK A TROUT

I decide to take advantage of the very good weather we've been having, to trek out to visit shops in Walthamstow for the first time in several years. Having picked up a copy of the *Metro* daily paper to read on the train I notice that this date, 8 June 2023, seems to be the birthday of several notable record-making figures, most of which I own vinyl by – albeit not the youngest of them, now 46-year-old Kanye West, who is now, I learn, known as Ye.

But I do have a Nancy Sinatra (now 83) LP made with Lee Hazlewood, a couple of Julie Driscoll records (76 today), likewise Bonnie Tyler (72) also Nick Rhodes, he of Duran Duran, (61). The surprise to me is that American blues/rock man, Derek Trucks, by whom I have quite a few albums, is just 44.

Emerging into bright sunlight at Walthamstow Central, I have no idea how to find Wood Street Market, but am told by a helpful lady at the Bus Station that the 230 bus will get me there. Immediately, on hearing that number I am transported (sorry) back to a chilly evening in Wealdstone in the late 60s, after I have been, along with several close chums of the day, to the Kodak Recreational Society (I may be slightly 'out' with that name, but it was a regular haunt) for a pre-Xmas drink or three. We emerged to see a winter wonderland, with a thick carpet of virgin snow, being driven slowly through by a 230 bus, at which we immediately began to hurl a volley of snowballs, hoping to hit conductor, driver or passengers.

There was little chance of snow today as I boarded the bus and asked the driver – who appeared to be a long way from his own original home – whether he was en route to Wood Street. He looked a little baffled but nodded his head, so I took a seat. Several minutes later, with no idea where we were, I asked again whether he was going to Wood Street. He nodded again in a way which made me believe that where we now were was indeed Wood Street, so I disembarked, looked around and, round the corner, saw a sign – Wood Street, down which the bus was disappearing. I set off after it, stopping along the way to ask a couple of females if they knew where the Market was, receiving what proved to be accurate directions.

I wandered into a sequence of narrow corridors, with small rooms on either side, and soon found one packed with records, into which I walked, hearing the strident vocal tones and powerful guitar riffs of Paul Rodgers and Paul Kossoff coming from a Free LP. Only two tracks later, the record finished. The stall owner looked round the door and asked if I was ok. I said, 'Yes, great way to start the day, listening to Free.' He nodded agreement but then disappeared without either repositioning the stylus, or replacing the record, so I was left listening to the gentle sound of the stylus bumping against the run-out groove.

The first potential purchase I spotted was a Walter Trout double LP, attractively priced at £12. There seemed to be about ten or twelve brand new, sealed copies – but as I looked more closely, they all seemed to feature different Trout concerts. At most I would only want one, but reminded myself that although I already had a number of Walter's records I couldn't recall the last time I'd listened to one, and also that when I had first heard him, I'd compared him a little unfavourably with Joe Bonamassa.

Looking through a different section I came across a copy of an LP I'd long been aware of, but couldn't recall hearing. It was by the Flock, an American band I knew to feature a violinist, called *Dinosaur Swamps* – no, the violinist wasn't called Dinosaur Swamps, that's the name of the record. The other attractive feature of the record is its gatefold cover featuring, well, a flock of lethally beaked flying creatures, possibly pterodactyls. The record surface looked little played. At £8, I thought it was a probable purchase, as I was confident it would be rock of the kind I enjoy.

Further searching produced nothing else to encourage me to add it to my pile of one – if, that is, one can ever be a pile on its own. Deciding to buy, I went to hand over the money, and as I did so, I heard a lady, walking past, say: 'I've had a nice séance.' I walked further down the corridors, finding a similar unit, outside of which was a man who, it transpired, was a West Ham supporter – in a very good mood, as they won a European Cup competition the night before. But I was not over-enthused by the owner's continuous presence as I was trying to browse, almost as though he was concerned I might make off with something without paying, although I'd have had to fight a way past him to do so.

The atmosphere was draining my enthusiasm, so I decided to cut my losses and leg it.

I knew there was another record shop in the area, Vinyl Vanguard, but couldn't work out any way of getting there in a straightforward manner. I was wilting a little as it was turning hot, so I decided to get back on a 230 and if I spotted St James Street or worked out how my phone might show me where it was (a clue – I had, and still have, no idea how to do that) then I'd visit the shop. Before any hint of St James appeared, I was back at Walthamstow Central, decided the lure of lunch was too strong to worry about finding Vinyl Vanguard, so boarded a tube train, on which I was shocked to hear the announcement: 'The next station has sex reactors.' Sorry? What? I listened more closely, as the message was repeated: 'The next station has step free access.'

Feeling a little guilty at not visiting Vinyl Vanguard, I checked out the shop's website and learned that proprietor, Mike, a lifelong vinyl collector, had started out by flogging records from a kitchen table at a local summer market – 'Every casual browse turned into a conversation, a memory relived of a gig or a club or a holiday or a parent.' Mike loved it and it resulted eventually, in 2019, in the shop in St James Street, via Hoe Street and Wood Street Market versions. He doesn't pretend to connect with every genre personally – his formative music was 60s rock and pop, and he got into jazz, blues, old school R&B, soul, reggae, folk, Cajun, Zydeco, Latin, African, country, and classical. Might have been quicker to list the stuff he doesn't like! In 2017 Simon joined Mike – a good friend, who had been wheeling and dealing in vinyl for many years. His favourite music styles are jazz, singer-songwriters, country, soul, reggae, ska and folk.

IN WHICH I GO FROM BRIGHTON
TO PACIFIC

A trip down to Brighton saw us arriving in the city to check in to the Mercure Hotel, on the seafront. Sheila was meeting up with a friend in early afternoon, leaving myself and pal Mike H to have a wander round the record shops, the first of which was one whose name I didn't really catch, but which hadn't been there last time I was here. It was a neat and tidy little place with much modern music of which neither of us had any knowledge, so there were no purchases made.

We wandered past a pub with vinyl on shelves inside but weren't yet ready for alcohol, so continued our search for the Wax Factor shop which we both remembered, but somehow couldn't find in the first two streets where we looked, but finally it turned up on our radar and in we went, noticing differences since we'd last been in. The man in charge was sitting behind the counter chatting to a gentleman of vintage years who was telling him about the 8000 records ('and how many singles as well?') he used to own but had somehow mislaid or otherwise lost track of. As you do.

There seemed to be far more space than there used to be and I eventually twigged it was because the vast number of books which used to be on display, was now reduced to just a few stacked away in a corner. A query to the counter produced the explanation that 'my partner who sold the books has now gone...'

'Gone?' I queried.

'No,' he laughed. 'Not dead – retired.'

The shop stretches out into three or four distinct rooms and eventually I began to find what I was hoping I would. I unearthed an LP by Bubble Puppy, the group whose original single 'Hot Smoke & Sassafrass' I was destined to stumble across in New Zealand. The LP wasn't from that vintage, but from the mid-80s when original members of the band had regrouped, and had another bash at 'Hot Smoke...' – something which doesn't usually work. As the record was new, only a tenner, all but a penny, and the group members were original, I took a chance and was pleased to have done so when I eventually listened to it. No, the manic energy and invention of those earlier times had been reduced – that was always going to be a certainty. But the new version was enjoyable, if subtly different, and most of the other tracks were at least listenable.

I was also tempted by a Flower Pot Men LP, from which I was confident I already owned most, if not all, of the tracks, but this was a Tenth Planet label release, with a low number – most of their records are limited editions each marked with a number. This was number 50.

Had it also been a tenner I'd have bought it, but at £20 I left it.

We now walked down to Across the Tracks with its usual, what I can only really describe as 'shabby yet inviting' frontage – apologies if that offends the occupants. However, the interior is not exactly likely to be a front-runner in any shop layout and design competition. Not that this will concern the knowledgeable and chatty staff, one member of which was still marvelling at a recent visit by a Japanese gentleman apparently obsessed with late 50s/early 60s UK singers such as Billy Fury, John Leyton, and others for which he was happy to pay top whack. I was prepared to pay medium whack for some of the psych CDs which have always been stored to the left of the counter, and as usual flipped through the entire stock. But this time without finding anything to buy.

Next stop was Rarekind, a more logically set out shop, if not quite offering as wide a choice as ATT. However, I did manage to spot and purchase a five track, 10″ Eric Bell Band record from 1981. I remember seeing him when he was in Thin Lizzy, who he left in 1973, and, as these songs were recorded some 40 years back, figured there'd be a good chance that I'd like them. I did like them and did not at all begrudge the nine quid cost.

Mike and I were now en route to Resident records – which, according to a *Guardian* article in August 2021, Nick Cave called the 'best f***ing record shop in Britain' – but we became distracted by the catchall marketish premises of stalls and dealers opposite, where we found a large number of records, very few of which were in any kind of plastic covers to prevent the inevitable thumbing and flipping marks by which they were almost invariably rendered unattractive and often tatty. I was almost tempted by two singles, each available at £1 – The Mojos' 1964, oddly spelled and punctuated hit 'Everything's Al' Right', and an Amen Corner single I'd never knowingly come across before. Even at this bargain price I was put off by the condition and left empty-handed.

An afternoon at Brighton races produced a rare punting profit as my favourite jockey Jamie Spencer booted home a winner to leave me ahead of the game for once. There was little time available next day for record hunting, but I read a fascinating snippet in the latest copy of *The Oldie*, in which Bruce Beresford wrote a piece mourning his friend, Barry Humphries, revealing, seemingly seriously, that in the early 60s the great writer and entertainer 'did odd jobs, including breaking old vinyl discs in a record factory'.

Returning from Brighton, I was nonetheless able to have a chat with David Chappell of The Record Album shop there, in Terminus Road, the town's oldest such establishment, which he and Keith Blackmore purchased from the retiring previous owner George Ginn shortly before the pandemic struck. David passed on the sad news that he had just discovered that George had died, aged 93, just three days previously, on Sunday 11 June 2023.

I have an interest in an online record selling site called elvinyl, inasmuch as I have put a few records up for sale on the site, but in, I think, about two years, not had a nibble at anything at any price, although I have bought a couple of dozen records via it, all pretty much living up to how they have been described and priced. I noticed a seller had a copy of the Nova label Pacific Drift LP, *Feelin' Free* on offer. This is one of those I once owned, but ill-advisedly parted with (albeit keeping a copy of their Deram single from the album, 'Water Woman' for some now forgotten reason), but very much want to own again. I made an offer of £47.50 for the record, offered originally at £60, and did a deal ultimately for £50. I'm happy with the price, and hoped I'd be equally happy with the condition when it arrived.

When postie, Luigi, delivered the record, I was reluctant to open it up in case – despite the very appropriate looking packaging – I might be disappointed by either, or worse, both, the cover and the record... but... no cause for concern. A few marks and bumps on the cover, but it is 50+ years old, and pretty much a noise-free playing surface. A most enjoyable late 60s rock album, by a group with links to Wimple Winch, jazz-rock group, Sponge, and via them to Blodwyn Pig, released in January 1970. It is somewhat odd that there was no follow-up, and must admit the lyrics to 'Plaster Caster's U.S.A' are somewhat intriguing. I think I know what it is about, but possibly not appropriate to speculate here.

IN WHICH DAVE IS MULTIPLYING!

Obviously up and about bright and early, my vinyl mate Dave Lewis was telling Facebook: 'Saturday is a platterday, hoping to spot some interesting ones in Flashback Records in Islington and just about to venture in!' And there was good news later in the day from Dave, as he announced: 'You can never have too many copies of Led Zeppelin's *In Through the Out Door* – a South African pressing – thank you Flashback Records!'

For some artists, it is inevitable to have more than one version of certain tracks, as they appear on different releases and compilations, but I am not so much of a completist that I'd buy multiple copies of the same record – unless, perhaps, I was also gaining the odd different or additional track along the way. I'd rather put that money towards buying different music I haven't yet brought in to my collection. But I remain in awe of those who diligently set out to acquire such multiples, and obviously attain great joy and feelings of achievement by so doing.

I enjoyed a perceptive comment from owner of 1200 records, wine aficionado Neal Martin, in the latest *Record Collector* – 'Collecting fine wine and vinyl are very similar. The real value is all the memories tied up with every record, where you were and who you were with, good times and bad. It's the same for a special bottle of wine.' Cheers! I reached out and randomly grabbed a CD to play – within a few seconds I was listening to 60s duo Chad & Jeremy, on their 1967 LP, *Of Cabbages and Kings*, of which I'd bought an original LP whilst in New Zealand earlier in the year.

Now, I was listening to a track called 'Just Another Day', originally by Neon Pearl, one of subsequent T2 drummer and main man Peter Dunton's always stunningly good, if under-appreciated previous groups – and a song he wrote, performed here by Hanford Flyover.

This is followed by another Dunton track, this time as part of The Flies, 'Gently As You Feel', but here nicely done by LoveyDove. This CD could have been compiled purely for me – it is one of four in a terrific 61-track set of 60s psych covers, *A Band For All Seasons* from Fruit de Mer's Crustacean label. Amazingly, up comes 'Grantchester Meadows', originally a Pink Floyd composition, about one of my friend Martin's – who I'd been speaking to minutes earlier – favourite places, close to where he lives in Cambridge. This version by Crystal Jacqueline Acoustic Band.

It is now as though some psychic intervention is ensuring that every track I'm hearing has a personal connection, particularly as it runs on via further tracks written by the Velvet Underground and Tommy James & The Shondells, before closing with two songs particularly relevant to me – Kaleidoscope's 'The Sky Children' and the late Phil May, fronting the Pretty Things' live rendering of the achingly sad 'Loneliest Person'. I suppose when you've been collecting and listening to music for 60 years there will be many connections to different bands and songs, but to randomly choose from literally thousands of possible selections – or be given several so appropriately relevant at precisely that time just seemed to defy all odds.

Yet another reason not to become a seller of records online – an eBay message that a Deep Purple LP I'd sold for £15 had 'arrived broken in half', with a photo provided. Forgive me, but my immediate reaction was that this could have been a ploy by someone who wanted to buy a new copy to replace their own, already broken, one. This sort of thing has been managing to diminish my enthusiasm for transacting purchases this way.

IN WHICH WE FIND MOP TOP MAGIC

Sheila and I went to see 'Magic of The Beatles', a tribute Mop Tops group, of which we, like you, no doubt, have seen several over the years. I wasn't expecting anything much out of the ordinary, and to start with that's what the show was as the (fairly) lookalike musicians – 'John' was the most credible in that respect, while 'Paul' was rather, er, meatier than the real thing – performed dutifully competent versions of the group's early singles to a probably four-fifths full Eric Morecambe Centre. But the 'magic' part of the show kicked in once the crowd had warmed up, the group likewise, and they changed into Sgt Pepper-era costume, encouraged the audience to sing along if they liked, and then got them standing up and dancing along as the evening slipped into more of a concert performance.

Maybe because of obviously increasing age and nostalgia, some of the songs affected me rather more than when I've previously seen and heard such shows. It really would be absolutely impossible for any new group to have the same impact as the one being portrayed here achieved, so different is the world now. Listening and singing along it was impossible not to reflect on the effect the Beatles genuinely had on me and my contemporaries, even if we didn't admit it at the time and if we so seldom give them credit for it now – which will probably only happen properly when the two remaining members are no longer around.

I also reflected on how rarely we now sit and listen to Beatles' records at home, and on the inevitability that their world-changing role will become ever more forgotten as our generations die off. But we were THERE, and experienced one of the world's more dramatic resetting phases in real time, and should periodically remind ourselves of that – if only by attending gigs like this.

When we arrived home at around 11pm, it was to watch Guns N' Roses' live set at the Glastonbury Festival. Slash, only a couple of years from 60, was in typically brilliant guitar-slinger mode, soloing and fretting away magnificently, well backed up by the bass and drum section. Meanwhile, Axl Rose howled horrifically and untunefully along, his voice clearly ruined, and unrecognisable from earlier days, albeit this did not seem to faze the audience one iota. I should probably add that not everyone seemed to be listening to the same Axl as me to judge by some of the Facebook and X/Twitter comments, while Hamish MacBain wrote in an *Evening Standard* review: 'Too often, Guns N' Roses descended into guitar noodling of the type that time has forgotten. Nobody on planet earth does this kind of thing better than Slash, but part of the reason this is true is that in 2023 it's an obsolete artform.' And, even more controversially: 'Former perpetual latecomer Axl Rose turned up bang on schedule and did what needed to be done reliably.'

Seriously? *The Independent's* review, by Mark Beaumont who, to be fair, clearly does not enjoy hard rock of this type generally, summed up Rose's blooming terrible vocalising more accurately, thus: 'His voice: a creature that, were you to take it to a vet, would come home in a cardboard box. Mumbling vague approximations of English words as if chronically constipated... he flips between a lower register that resembles a clogged lawnmower and a higher one that sounds like Barry Gibb suffering the mother of all wedgies.'

After the Guns N' Roses performance the previous night, the next day's embarrassment at Glastonbury was, for me, Debbie Harry's pretence that she is still in her prime, during Blondie's time on stage. Yes, I suppose, she'd rather be doing that than sitting at home sunbathing or flipping through brochures promoting homes for the elderly – but I'd rather remember her from the peak years and not have to pretend that she's still singing as well as ever. She plainly isn't. I take on board the opinion I saw aired on X/Twitter that as Debbie is now 77 (only four years older than me) it is just marvellous that she is still prepared to go out and perform, and we should all therefore marvel at and applaud her for so doing.

Fair enough.

She is certainly younger than Paul McCartney, Mick Jagger and others who are still active, and no one should deny her the right to do it, but I am genuinely concerned that by so doing she may end up distracting attention from her fantastic back catalogue and leaving behind an image of someone adversely affecting her own impeccable reputation. Rick Astley, born in 1966, seemed to have the right idea. He poked fun at himself and his hair, engaged with the audience and showed that his voice is still in good, strong condition. Elton John's voice appeared to be in positively strident form at 76, although he used up rather too much of it introducing people I'd either never heard of, or had little interest in. (I wasn't alone in wondering why, with no explanation, he called out someone many of us had never heard of, instead of the great Kiki Dee, when he played 'Don't Go Breaking My Heart' – but, hey, it's his gig.) I own a couple of Guns N' Roses records, several Blondie LPs, a dozen or so by Elton, but just one by Rick Astley.

IN WHICH BOB'S A MILLION SELLER AGAIN

A rerecording of Bob Dylan singing his 1963 classic 'Blowin' In The Wind' sold at auction for just under £1.5 million in July 2022. The disc of the song Dylan wrote in 1962 was sold by Christie's in London. Bidding lasted four minutes – about the running time of the song itself.

The name of the bidder was not revealed. Few people are likely to hear it, as the disc was sold as a one-off physical object, meaning 'the buyer has no rights to distribute it'. Dylan, 81, was backed on the track by a small band, including Greg Leisz on mandolin and Don Was on bass. The song was presented on a unique 'Ionic

Original' disc – a patented technology claiming to deliver higher quality audio than normal vinyl, (don't they all?), and made of aluminium, 'treated with a layer of nitrocellulose, coated with a sapphire and quartz gradient', but apparently playable on any regular turntable. It was the brainchild of Grammy-winning musician T Bone Burnett, who also produced and played on it. It is unclear whether the record has a B side.

I began making some subtle amendments to the way in which my records are shelved, stacked and organised around the house by moving them around, in a clearly desperate and doomed-to-fail attempt to make it seem as though there are fewer in the place than there actually are, thus fooling no one, whilst also drawing attention to the pointless process!

Decided just to pick up a CD from one of my shelves and take it out to the car, to listen to while driving over for a haircut. My verdict on it, having listened to three or four tracks en route, recalls my diary, was: 'total rubbish. Can go to charity shop asap!' I suspect it was returning from whence it had come, as I have no memory of acquiring this Pixies album. I will not be acquiring any more of their back catalogue, either. My loss, I'm sure someone, somewhere will tell me.

On X/Twitter, @Phil282 reported that he had 'walked into #Fopp to be confronted by some loud bloke who felt the need to tell me *Flesh and Blood* is Roxy's best album. I didn't feel the need to tell him the 4 reissues he was buying at £38 each (!!) are all readily available online for £27 each'. Phil also mentioned seeing a copy of *Harvest* by Neil Young available in HMV for £54.

IN WHICH I REFLECT ON SAD NEWS

Former Fairport Convention singer Judy Dyble died on 12 July 2022, aged 71. She was succeeded in that group by Sandy Denny, (being in her own words: 'unceremoniously dumped') but went on to create what to my mind is easily her finest work – even allowing for the copious and excellent solo LPs she would later produce. This was the 1970 Trader Horne LP *Morning Way* on which she and Jackie MacAuley, once of Them, teamed up for a commercially unsuccessful, but musically and creatively satisfying and long-lasting LP. Their group/duo name was allegedly taken from John Peel's nanny, Florence, aka Trader Horne – a reference to the explorer of similar nomenclature, Trader Horn. Seeing Judy and Jackie teaming up to play a once-only live gig, in November 2015, featuring the tracks from the album was one of the most moving and memorable live gigs I was ever privileged to attend.

I was *almost* tempted when, in March 2023, I received an email from JustCollecting.com, an online auction site, offering an autograph book to me for what seemed an eminently reasonable price:

'We can't go back in time to the 60s. I wish we could. But we can remember. Reminisce and smile. This autograph album relives the excitement. The bands. The screaming. In fact, it captures everything it was to be a music-obsessed teenager in 1964. The autographs were collected in person at concerts in Brighton and Worthing UK in 1964. By Teresa, teenage journalist for amateur magazine *Teen Topics*.

Here's the full list:
- Gerry and the Pacemakers
- The Hollies
- Manfred Mann
- The Fourmost
- Billy J Kramer and the Dakotas
- Nashville Teens
- Marty Wilde
- Jimmie Nicol (fifth Beatle)
- The Swinging Blue Jeans
- The Echoes
- The Quotations
- The Untamed Four

- Cliff Bennett and the Rebel Rousers
- Tommy Quickly
- Sounds Incorporated
- The Four Pennies
- The Jynxs
- Eden Kane

The autograph album measures 5.75 x 4.25 inches. The autographs are all in very good condition. Many of the pages are detached from the spine. I have personally authenticated all the autographs. They are all genuine. £295 is the price. You'd expect to pay that for Gerry and the Pacemakers' autographs alone at auction. But the vendor is looking for a quick sale on this one, so is happy to offer it for well below market value. And that price includes free global delivery and 28-day returns.'

The price did look very reasonable – surely the Jimmie Nicol alone could be worth that? 'Fifth Beatle' Nicol signed the autograph book on 12 July 1964, just a month after his two-week stint with the Beatles, filling in for Ringo. I pondered for a while, but that amount of money could more usefully be put towards more records, I thought – yes, but one could also purchase the album and then try to sell it on, but that would lead to hassle, and be time-consuming. Consultation with Sheila produced the response: 'If you buy it you won't sell it. You'll leave it hanging around, doing nothing, taking up space, making my cleaning even harder.' Following this advice – probably accurate – I decided against. I still wonder whether that was the right call, though. I suppose it was something of a signature moment for me.

IN WHICH AT LAST I MAKE A HASH OF THINGS

It was 14 August 2021 – a day, if not date, I'd been waiting for, but for such a long time that, when it happened, I'd virtually forgotten all about it. For reasons of which I've also long had no memory, there is a particular LP I've owned for many, many years, pressed on red vinyl, but for which I owned no cover. What's more it is quite an iconic, sought-after 60s record, by Hapshash & the Coloured Coat, *Featuring the Human Host and the Heavy Metal Kids*, on the Minit label and valued at up to £200 by the *Rare Record Price Guide* which, though, would be contingent upon there being a cover with it.

So, I'd kept the record in its own, original, I think, white inner sleeve, for many a long year, ever hopeful that I might one day be able to team it up with a cover. I had given up on this ever happening by the time I entered Sounds Of The Suburbs in Ruislip Manor on this date, and wandered over to flip through its psych section... flip, hm, got that... flip, interesting, a maybe... no, no... got that... er, what's that again? Hapshash Coloured Coat? Yes, apparently, it was. Not only a Hapshash Coloured Coat record, but also including a Hapshash Coloured Coat COVER. This is going to cost me a high double figure price if not more... let's see... er, £10... surely not... no, yes, a tenner is the price.

Okay, careful, look casual... don't rush over to buy it... besides, I've just heard the boss talking to a customer about a gig they'd been to, and that he'd heard other people there with them had since gone down with Covid – that would be a real double whammy, finding such an elusive record but having to endure Covid as a result! I wandered over, passed the time of day and handed over my £10 note, avoiding the reaction I'd expected of 'Oh, sorry, I think you've misread the price tag – it's 100 quid.'

As soon as I returned home I went and found my red record, numbered MLL 40001 on the Minit label in its original plain white inner sleeve, which does have some small tears and creases – plus a handwritten marking of G.S.24, indicating that this was just the two dozenth LP I ever owned. There are some spindle marks on the disc label, so it has had a few plays, but the surface of the record has no major marks that I can make out – as for the cover, it is in at least VG+ condition, I'd say. However, the cover is numbered MLS 40001E, so maybe the purist could argue that cover and record didn't originally belong together. However, having taken record and cover out of frame I realise I have no idea where the record which came with the cover I bought has gone!

I'll now have to have a mooch around to see in which 'safe spot' I left it. I suppose, as I write this I should also be giving the record a spin... just to see whether it has become listenable in the many years since I last played it. I must admit I doubt that so, here we go – it begins with a nice guitar riff and hefty drum beat with keyboards playing around it. Now, some virtually unintelligible lyrics appear, then clear off... this track is called 'H-O-P-P-WHY?' and is more of a jam than an actual song, with some harmonica arriving towards the end. The answer to the 'WHY?' riddle comes there none, as we move on to track two, 'A Mind Blown Is A Mind Shown', and it is a harmonica-driven, bong(o)-bashing-groove, which doesn't last long, before being followed by 'The New Messiah Coming 1985' – yes, well, I think they got THAT wrong, but if the Messiah has actually heard this track, which is basically an over-extended single, dreadfully repetitive groove, I suspect he won't be bothering to put in an appearance for, oh, probably several hundred years, by which time he will no longer be 'New'!

Track four closes side one – it is called 'AOUM' – no, not a clue, but rather a droning drone of a dirge and, I'm not joking, there may be the sound of a whole lot of toking going on, if I'm not mistaken – which, as a non-smoker, I may be... however, that leaves just one track on the whole of side two – 'Empires Of The Sun' – another repetitive groove/riff which goes on and on, taking its time, without actually really getting anywhere identifiable until one of the participants appears to be having an audible orgasm –

or two! All of the tracks are, er, credited to (possibly they meant to print 'blamed on') Guy Stevens, Nigel Waymouth and Michael English.

It is probably fair – very – to say this record actually sounds better when it is hung on the wall in a frame, to be looked at and admired rather than played and heard. A British Council Visual Arts website explains: 'English and Waymouth set up the design collaborative Hapshash and the Coloured Coat in the 60s. English, born in Bicester, studied at Ealing School of Art. Waymouth, born in India, studied Economic History at University College. The pair met in 1966 after Waymouth opened a shop, 'Granny takes a Trip', on the King's Road, Chelsea for which English had painted the shop front.'

A Wikipedia site suggests: 'Their first album of psychedelic music, produced by a collective in early 1967 and including many famous names (those names include bassist Greg Ridley; on drums Mike Kellie; guitar, Luther Grosvenor; and vocals, Mike Harrison, and it does appear that the "Human Host" were, effectively, the band "Art" that became "Spooky Tooth"), is now seen as being influential on the early works of Amon Duul, and other pioneers of German Krautrock, as well as inspiring sections of the Rolling Stones' *Their Satanic Majesties Request* LP.' Okay, please forgive me if I choose to disbelieve that last claim... possibly 'Gomper' apart!

IN WHICH ZEALOUS ZEP AUTHORITY
REVEALS ALL

Dave Lewis is not only a world authority and leading chronicler of Led Zeppelin. He's also a passionate collector of all types of music, and since we met for the first time a few years back, shortly after *Vinyl Countdown* was published, we've become great pals. Dave shared his thoughts on his record collecting passion with me:

'I was lucky enough to be surrounded by music from an early age – that trend has continued for nigh on 60 years. In the early 60s, LPs and singles were in our house – notably soundtracks such as *South Pacific* and *West Side Story*.

My first record was "Fireball" by Don Spencer on HMV, from the local Frasers music shop in 1962 – the theme to TV series, Fireball XL5. Around the age of seven, I was obsessed by the pop scene, and attended my first gig – a package tour featuring The Dave Clark 5, The Hollies and The Kinks at the Granada Cinema in Bedford in 1964. My next gig was Led Zeppelin at the Empire Pool in 1971. My first LPs were the Island sampler, *You Can All Join In*, and Cream's *Fresh Cream*. But when I heard Zeppelin's 'Whole Lotta Love' in late 1969, the effect was lasting.

I built a career out of my enthusiasm for the group, chronicling their work through books, and the magazine I created, edited and produced, *Tight But Loose* (TBL). I amassed a vast collection of Zep-related LPs, CDs, eight tracks, cassettes and singles, memorabilia and paper goods. I have very rare pressings, including the original Led Zeppelin I album, packaged for a brief period with turquoise lettering on the sleeve.

Working in a record shop, jazz came on my radar in the 80s and I collect classic artists such as Miles Davis on the original Columbia label. I also love vintage crooners – Sinatra, Darin, Rod McKuen, and female singers such as Dusty Springfield, Lulu, Sandie Shaw, Marianne Faithful, Joni Mitchell, Laura Nyro. I am a massive late 60s/early 70s singles collector: original pink Island label, Immediate, Vertigo, Apple. I collect the Swan Song label. I have some 60 album pressings on Swan Song, over 100 singles across Led Zep, Bad Company, Pretty Things, Dave Edmunds, Maggie Bell and Detective. I love 60s and 70s sampler compilation albums produced by various labels. With original price sticker on, so much the better.

Then there's Beatles' cover versions – Vera Lynn's version of "Goodnight", Fats Domino's "Everybody's Got Something to Hide Except Me and My Monkey". I have 180+ singles with Beatles cover versions.

Another of my 45rpm quests is promos and demos, singles

sent to radio stations and reviewers ahead of official release. Also, picture-sleeve singles, coloured vinyl pressings, rare labels, foreign issues, alternates, hype stickers on LP sleeves.

I have multi copies of albums – 37 differing Led Zeppelin II pressings. Recently, I came across a pressing of LZ II, issued in Italy with additional writing on the gatefold sleeve and on an unusual red Atlantic Records label. The buzz I got from seeing, negotiating a price and sharing with fellow collectors was intoxicating. I love CDs, am a big cassette collector, and like Stereo Eight-Track Cartridges. I am not much of a buyer online. I prefer the interaction of a shop environment.

Jimmy Page is a visitor at record fairs and shops. Having enjoyed a good relationship with him with my Zep chronicling, we have had many a conversation when he has been at venues. He is a massive collector of his own work.'

I asked him: 'What inspired you to get back to collecting LPs again?'

He told me: 'Probably when my children grew up... because what doesn't mix is children and vinyl! I kept having to shift it up a level. Then it got put away, then there was separation, divorce. I thought "Right, I'm going to get my records out and I'm going to listen to them again." It's like meeting old friends again, it's great. I've got Led Zeppelin white labels and all the stuff you would salivate over.'

Dave enjoyed a 35-year-career in music retail from 1974 to 2009, before being made redundant. Having produced Zep mags and books as a sideline, he went self-employed, self-published Zep books and wrote freelance for *Mojo*, *Classic Rock* and *Record Collector*:

'I love the tangible aspect of records and CDs. Storage is an issue – probably sooner than later I will need to downsize the collection – 4,500 LPs, 3,900 singles, nearly 3,000 CDs plus boxes of cassettes and eight tracks.

My wife Janet has been a saint in accommodating all this, and my archive of books, magazines and 1,000+ back issues of *NME*, *Melody Maker*, *Sounds*, *Record Mirror* and *Disc*.

Music is in my DNA; my record collection instantly re-connects
me with the music I grew up with – that defines who I am, and I
feel a very blessed man for it to do so.'

IN WHICH I HEAR ABOUT
LISTENING BAN

Writer Matt Novak revealed, in an article on website Gizmodo,
that it was once illegal for sighted people to listen to LPs. Wrote
Novak: 'Long before they were used for music, long playing
records were used almost exclusively for audiobooks. These were
distributed to blind Americans in the 1930s and 40s. And, it was
effectively illegal for sighted persons to listen to LP audiobooks
from 1934 until 1948, due to licensing agreements with publishers
and authors' unions.' From 1935 to 1942, the Talking Book
project produced 23,000 record players, costing $1.2 million, and
providing work for about 200 people.

I was in a relatively local record shop in September 2022.
There was only one other person in while I was there, and he was
trying to buy something, but the owner disdainfully rejected his
offer saying: 'But that's barely 40% of the asking price.' Sure, that
may seem a fair enough comment, but there are a large number
of distinctive records I recognise, which he has had for at least a
year plus, for sure, if not longer. And they are still the price they
were back then.

Many people – and I'm one – don't particularly enjoy haggling,
and would definitely just not bother when a record I think/know
is worth, say £25, has been priced at £50 for the last three or four
visits. I really can't usually be bothered to go through the business
of offering £40 for a £50 record worth £25, and being rejected as
though I'm trying to rip him off.

I've also found the owner makes little effort to engage with me,
unless I instigate that process – even though he must recognise me

as I've been many times before and bought from him, yet on this occasion I had to say 'hello' to him when I walked in, and I really think it's his responsibility to engage and encourage wannabe customers when all's said and done.

I discuss this with friend Gordon: 'He will sometimes talk to me for ages but never asks my name or if there is something I am looking for. The difference between him and [the owner of another nearby shop which we both frequent] is so stark. I do wonder if his hearing has something to do with it – or maybe a natural shyness. And yet, surely he wants to shift old stock so why not have a sale or do something that might offload it. Even a record fair! Or sell a job lot to another trader. I don't like bartering either. Mr Platform 1 [another shop owner] always offered me a discount even on one record. I never solicited it. Offering a coffee is another way to get a customer onside.'

I noticed that in my neck of the woods, it was a sunny morning, so why not take a jaunt up to Second Scene? I found both Julian and Helen in residence. I'd brought a little vinyl present for Julian – an LP, of which I'd been given a few copies while on holiday in Jersey – showcasing a number of local bands. Julian duly stuck it on the in-house turntable, where it was playing away nicely when a chap came into the shop and, after a few minutes, asked Julian what the music was, and could he buy it?

I think Julian declined as he thought it would probably be poor form to accept a free gift and immediately flog it for a tenner. But, hey, had I thought more quickly I could have offered to go halves with Julian – and then given him another of the copies I had at home!

I discovered that Harry Manfredini's film score for the movie *Friday the 13th* was released in a limited edition by Waxwork Records. It is one of the few (perhaps the only?) records advertised as being 'blood-filled' and reportedly 'under' 75 copies were released. In 2023, one copy was being offered on Discogs at £4,000 – 'All Original Beautiful Blood Included. Collector condition – Price is firm.' The site suggested that one copy had already been sold for £3,400. Too bloody expensive.

IN WHICH I REVIEW COLOURED
VINYL PRICES

'OVER 50% OFF SELECTED COLOURED VINYL! NOW THAT'S AMAZING VALUE!' shouted the headline over the Rock Review Records online ad on 24.9.22. Maybe.

But didn't it also suggest that either the product was overpriced deliberately in the first place so that it could be eye-catchingly reduced later? Or that not enough people had been buying? To be fair, with most albums now £9.99, and including Grateful Dead, AC/DC, Prince and more, they did indeed seem reasonably priced – but you'd be a bit gutted if you'd paid the original asking price of £19.99.

Rock Review Records had begun to send me emails at about the same time as a company called Coda Records. Oddly enough the two seemed to be offering a very similar style of record – and at time of writing, still are – almost invariably variously coloured LPs by big names, recorded from obscure live shows or broadcasts.

Small print on each of their sites shows a Chichester address.

I was a little wary, so first checked them out by buying a 10" AC/DC double '1977 live' offering of nine tracks from the Bon Scott days, for £9.99, including p&p. It duly arrived, stamped on the back cover of the gatefold set – with voluminous inside sleeve notes – 0710/2000. I played it to my resident AC/DC specialist tester, Sheila, who approved, particularly of the excellent full colour front cover featuring her much-loved and missed Bon Scott.

So I went a little farther next time – ordering three live LPs, all reduced to £5.99 from £10 – by the Rolling Stones, *Loud And Clear*, from 1964-66 on clear vinyl; Neil Young, 8 tracks live from concerts in Brisbane and California, called *Into The Black* on a kind of turquoise-splatter blue vinyl; and a Creedence Clearwater Revival set, on what I'd call royal blue vinyl – this latter purporting to be from the Royal Albert Hall gig the band played back in 1970, at which we were present. All arrived on time, as promised, play perfectly and sound very good indeed. The two companies also offer a selection of CDs, likewise often at extremely competitive prices. I'd have no qualms about buying from either of these outlets again. Except that, of late, they seem to have dropped the cheap live LPs and concentrated on promoting rarer more expensive ones.

I took a visit to London's Lower Marsh market in the Waterloo area, an old haunt from my early days working at William Hill's then headquarters in nearby Blackfriars Road, in the mid to late 70s. What was a vibrant market, known as 'The Cut', with traders shouting their wares à la Del Boy, now appeared to be 100% food outlets for lunching workers. I turned, somewhat sadly, on reaching the end of the street, and began to walk back – only then spotting a board standing on the road, reading: 'JOHNNY SKATES RECORDS. I BUY OLD RECORDS. TUESDAY TO FRIDAY 09.00 TO 04.00. MOB 07846439034'.

Of course, I dived straight into his wares, which, he told me, consisted of his own collection, added to by purchases from others. There was a decent flow of browsers, most much younger than me. I chatted to Johnny, along with another buyer, as he told me, 'Any three for two – the cheapest one is free.'

I had to go for that – coming up with Brian Auger's LP, *Befour* (a tenner), a slightly beaten-up John Paul Young LP with all the songs written by Vanda and Young (reduced from a tenner to a fiver) and, completely off the wall, because I liked the cover and it would be free, a David Weiss LP.

Johnny's other customer at the time, an interestingly tattooed gentleman, was talking about buying and selling records online or via the post. Johnny explained that his method was far less stressful and had fewer hassles than the various problems of selling by mail and online.

IN WHICH I THINK I DETECT
A COLLECTOR

Watching a random episode of the sublime TV show *Detectorists*, which I have now seen several times, I suddenly picked up on Lance asking Andy rhetorically and out of the blue: 'How many women spend time organising their vinyl collections from A to Z?'

This made me wonder whether 'Andy', aka writer of the series, Mackenzie Crook, is himself a record collector. I found this quote from him: 'I once camped outside Wembley Stadium when I was 15 to see Madonna in concert. I had already bought a ticket, but I wanted to be the first in, to get as close to the stage as possible. In the end I was so exhausted from lack of sleep I just hovered at the back in a daze.' In 2010 he appeared in the biopic about Ian Drury, entitled *Sex & Drugs & Rock & Roll*, and then became more focused on television roles. Mackenzie has also appeared in several music videos, including Paul McCartney's 'Dance Tonight'.

On a dismal, dank evening, I drove out to Uxbridge to see old friend Rex, brother of the late former Shakey Vick and Nighthawks guitarist Bruce Langsman. Rex had asked me whether I would like to take his and Bruce's vinyl records off his hands as he no longer wanted them, and naturally I said I would be happy to do so, albeit I had no idea what may be in the collection. It was a gloomy evening. Rex had brought the records into the hall, and I then deposited them into my car boot. It was too chilly to spend time looking through them, and there was little indication that they had been feeling loved and wanted for some while.

Due to their lengthy storage they were a little less than fragrant, so I let them breathe for a while before having a rummage through them.

It was sunny a day or two later, so I decided to 'air' the records. I went through them all and the obvious highlights were two live

Nighthawks LPs, which I don't believe were ever commercially issued. They really should have been, they'd have surely got some coverage if a shrewd publicist had put them in the hands of someone with John Peel-like tastes.

Most of Bruce's records had a strong blues influence, while Rex's were a little more commercial – the likes of 10CC, Genesis, Beatles, McCartney, Wings, Stevie Wonder, Bowie, Simon & Garfunkel. Later, I listened again to the records with Bruce on them, and once again wondered 'what might have been' had he been spotted by the sort of folk who had discovered the Claptons, Pages, Becks and the like, back in those early days of heavy rock and blues.

A few days later, 'Mike', aka @dudeville on X/Twitter, posted: 'A record I have been chasing for 3 (and a half) years just popped up on my Discogs "want list" for a very, very reasonable price, seems too good to be true, so not saying anything else at this moment. Fingers crossed it eventually lands.'

I was wondering whether the record had arrived, and soon, up popped the answer. 'Postie has been; been searching for this for 3 1/2 years. Yeah there's copies available on @Discogs if you're happy to pay £130+ but I won't pay that, f**k the flippers!! Didn't even pay half that for a sealed copy, play the long game, the win feels sweeter.' You might well be asking: 'What record was it?' It was a 'Replica of the 1974 Test Pressing New York version of Bob Dylan's *Blood On The Tracks*'.

Here's another little-known Dylan story, told to Dave Lewis by his mate, Patrick Crowther:

'One morning in 1993 I exited my flat on Camden High Street with a bastard of a hangover (my drinking days). It was really hot, and I was squinting and cursing the night before. Down the street I saw this guy in a long leather coat and a stovepipe hat coming towards me. "That looks like Bob Dylan," I thought to myself. The gent got closer. "F**k me, it *is* Bob Dylan!" I knew that trying to speak to him was not on the agenda, seeing as I wasn't sure I could form words, let alone a coherent sentence. I decided to tag along behind him and his couple of minders. They crossed the road and stopped outside the old "Record and Tape Exchange".

At that moment the door opened and a young kid of about 16 flew out of the shop and literally bumped into Dylan. The kid apologised, looked up and his mouth dropped open like in a cartoon. His hand moved unsteadily to the plastic bag he was holding and he brought out the copy of *Blonde on Blonde* he'd just bought. "Man, isn't that weird?!" said Dylan. "You just bought my OLD record and then you bump INTO me. You must be feelin' really WEIRD!"

The kid nodded. "I guess you'd like me to sign that for you?" Kid nods again. Dylan writes "Isn't that weird, Bob Dylan" on the cover. The kid heads off, in a daze. I later found out that he'd been shooting the cover photograph for *World Gone Wrong* in a French bistro just before the lock bridge. There used to be footage of him walking around Camden Market on YouTube but it's not up anymore.'

IN WHICH HEIR IS A
HUGE COLLECTOR

Interviewed about his career as a 'probate genealogist' in the *Metro* newspaper, 42-year-old 'heir hunter' Philip Turvey recalled, 'We had a case where a man died, and when we visited his property we could barely get in the door. He had over 100,000 vinyl records from floor to ceiling in every room in the house, even up the stairs. It was like a maze getting through it. You had to turn sideways to negotiate these little passageways that had been created by these huge stacks of records. It took removal men over a week to clear the property. The record collection was valued at £425,000. It was purchased by a specialist auction house and the money paid for the vinyl was paid to the estate and distributed to his relatives.'

I was reading *Mojo* magazine, which had a story asking 'Whatever happened to Maxine Nightingale?' Of course, I know she had a couple of big hits with 'Right Back Where We Started

From' and 'Love Hit Me', after all, she was kind of a godsister to me – we're cousins – her Mum, was my late aunt and godmother. Her Dad, Benny, was a nightclub singer. We – Maxine and I – used to share a bed when either of us was staying over for some family get-together at the other's house. Well, we WERE each about six or seven at the time... but, as for where in the USA she may be at this precise time, I don't have the slightest idea. She never calls, having last done so probably in about 1970.

Amazingly, whilst promoting *Vinyl Countdown* when it was published I appeared on Dotun Adebayo's very late night/early morning BBC 5 Live programme, in which he asked people to ring in to request a song – and to my amazement the first caller requested 'Right Back Where...', and when I explained the relationship between the two of us to the broadcaster and the caller, they were a little lost for words. And recently, as I picked up a copy of Max's mega-hit to buy for 50p in a charity shop, bless me if the radio didn't begin playing the song!

People tell you the most unexpected things when you mention you're writing about specific themes. I've known Derek Mowle since we were both of footballing age, playing for, and managing, a local Sunday league side. He knows little, and cares less, about rock music. But his wife, Linda, mentioned to me that she had a story about Paul McCartney from when she was at Uni:

'1970 to 1972 were memorable years at the University of Hull – poet Philip Larkin was Librarian, the Library had a paternoster lift (doesn't stop, just goes round on a loop and you jump on and off) and Jimmy Savile was kidnapped and sold for charity in Freshers' Week.' The latter seems to have been a missed opportunity to save the world much grief.

During that time many groups came and played at the University – Yes, Airforce, Steeleye Span, Moody Blues, Pink Floyd and Deep Purple. I remember these gigs being held at the Lawns Centre, in Cottingham. On 11 February 1972, a scrappy notice went up in the Students' Union that an unknown group called Wings were playing in the West Refectory that evening. Entry price 50p.

It was a very unusual venue as I didn't know of any other gig

held there. Unbeknown to us, and most others, this was Paul
McCartney's University Tour. He wanted to gauge how his new
band would go down without anyone knowing it was him. First
stop Nottingham Uni on 9 February; second, York next day; Hull
Uni on 11ᵗʰ. 10 venues from 9–22 February.

That evening I paid my 50p and went to see Wings. I cannot
remember who I went to see them with. The Refectory was quite
full – about 800 people. The lead guitarist was very lively and
energetic, dressed in bib and brace trousers. I realised he was
playing left-handed, and that in itself was unusual. The keyboard
player was a woman.

There it was, Paul McCartney and Linda in this band called
Wings. It was amazing for so many reasons, and a talking point
for some time, not only between those who were there, but also
those who missed it. I have been searching for an album of those
university gigs. It appears none exist. There were no mobile
phones, so few recordings or photos were taken.

There do seem to be recordings on the internet but most pretty
poor quality. I have searched for a decent recording, and may have
found one in Japan. The next challenge is to buy this CD, locate
old friends and rekindle memories of this particular evening.'

Wings' Play List at Hull: Lucille, Give Ireland Back to the Irish,
Your Wee Tobacco Box, Blue Moon of Kentucky, Seaside Woman,
Help Me Darling, Some People Never Know, The Mess, Bip Bop,
Thank You Darling, Smile Away, My Love, The Grand Old Duke
of York, Henry's Blues, Wild Life.

IN WHICH RAMSAY REMINISCES

My friend, Gavin Ramsay told me this story, sure to reduce
hardened collectors to tears of frustration:

'This is the tale of two very special 45s each with their own background story. In 1964, two members of the church youth club I belonged to, who were children of US GIs stationed here – Elizabeth Mayberry and Alex Ollinger – like myself were lovers of music of that time. In West Ruislip was an American PX, basically a huge store of goods, food and other things, including records imported from the States.

Through my good friends I was able to get many US imported 45s, unique at the time in having pictorial covers, unlike the vast majority of singles issued in the UK. The first was by the Rolling Stones "Time Is on My Side", not issued as a single in this country. To supplement my day job income, in the evenings I worked in the shoe shop at Wembley Bowling Alley, issuing and collecting bowling shoes.

In the adjacent Empire Pool the Stones were playing three nights of gigs. One evening, "Spike", their Road Manager came in. I asked him if I brought down my Stones' single, could he get it signed for me. Next evening, he picked up my record and, next day, returned it, duly signed by all five original members.

The second single, also acquired from the US base was 'Fun, Fun, Fun' by The Beach Boys. In late 1964, they were appearing at BBC studios at Hammersmith, promoting their next single. I got two tickets and with friend Elizabeth, attended the session. We sat down and were suddenly surrounded by none other than the Beach Boys. Fortuitously, I had taken along the "Fun, Fun, Fun" single and they duly signed it.

A friend was having a party and asked me to bring some records. I took half a dozen, including my prized pair. Due to the effects of over-enthusiastic consumption of alcohol, I forgot to take my records when I left. When I returned the next day my friend could not find any trace of the treasured possessions! A CD which I regularly play, by the great Bobby Vinton, sums up my misery not just for those two particular records, but other vinyl subsequently disposed of – the song is "What Did You Do With Your Old 45s".'

Gavin's second story concerns iconic TV programme, *Ready, Steady, Go*, back in the happy, uncomplicated days of 1965:

'Like most teenagers in the 60s, I did not always get along with my parents! Much of that was my fault – I was like a rebel with a cause: pissing them off! In 1965, the company I worked for was in Wembley Park, opposite Rediffusion TV studios. Every Friday, I would walk across to the studios to watch live recordings of *Ready, Steady, Go*, hosted by Keith Fordyce. After a show, as I was making my way out, I was stopped by one of the door attendants, whom I'd got to know during my weekly visits: "Gavin, YOU know Wembley well – if you are not doing anything, could you go with some people to show them the shops?" There was late night shopping on a Friday, then. I agreed, thinking it was better than going home.

The attendant asked me to wait, telling me a car would arrive outside the studios to take us to Wembley. A huge, black limousine arrived and I was ushered towards it. The back door opened. I stepped in, to find three other people sat there. My travelling companions were Sonny and Cher, along with Cher's sister. I was totally dumbstruck, but Sonny broke the silence, saying how appreciative they were that I was taking them to the shops in Wembley. I sat there, babbling away incoherently when we engaged in conversation, mentioning that I had enjoyed "I Got You Babe" at the RSG production.

We parked, and I walked the shops with them in Wembley High Street and Ealing Road, helping with an ever-increasing amount of overfull carrier bags, until we returned to the limousine, driving back to Wembley Park where they thanked me and we parted company. No, they did not give me any tip, or financial recompense – but I would not part with that experience for a bag of silver.'

Gavin's own fleeting moment of fame in the musical limelight completes his hat-trick of 60s stories:

'I belonged to a church youth club, and formed a band, me on vocals, brother Barry on bass, Alex Ollinger harmonica and vocals, Bob Weir drums, guitarists Pete Cain and Colin Bryant. In 1965, there was a national competition to write songs for a Christian Aid concert in Trafalgar Square. I penned one with an anti-apartheid theme. The song won, and was to be performed at the concert. On the big day, the band was ushered to the crypts in St Martin-in-the-Fields to wait to appear, noticing huge crowds were building! The organisers presented me with the latest 45s from the headline groups. We were met with a wall of sound from the 23,000 crowd. After we finished, I was advised that my microphone kept going on and off during the whole of the number, prompting cheers. I was never able to ascertain whether they were cheering when they could hear me or when they couldn't!'

IN WHICH I HAVE A HARVEST FESTIVAL

I bought a £17 mint rerelease vinyl copy of the now very valuable, Harvest label, *Bakerloo* LP while I was at the St Albans street market in October 2022, with Ron. Regrettably, I sold my original copy of this heavy 1969 rock rarity back in the day for £150. This new one came with a CD, featuring five tracks not on the original release. Ron, meanwhile, snapped up LPs by ELO and Michael Bentine – not together!

Next day I received one of his regular listings via email, from record seller, Jon Groocock. He was featuring an original copy of the *Bakerloo* LP, at somewhat higher cost than my repro of the day before. I trust Jon's descriptions of his records, so decided to buy the original, priced at £125. Jon agreed to give me a discount, and a deal was done. When the record arrived, I gave it a spin, and must admit that although visually it looked very acceptable, it had some unfortunate scratchy sounding hissing on one side. Jon offered immediately to take the record back, showing how genuine he really is.

I felt that wasn't necessary, as I had no doubt he hadn't been trying to stitch me up. So he gave me a partial refund, plus a good discount, when I next bought from him. At least now, I can again boast of my original copy of this iconic album.

*

Discussing the recent phenomenon of some of the greats from the prime of rock music's existence selling off the rights to their songs, and pondering who might still be interested in hearing those songs in years to come, to justify the hefty amounts being shelled out to own the rights, Andrew Orlowski wrote in the *Telegraph*: 'Without wishing to sound morbid, in a few years the audience that has Dylan, Springsteen and Young on endless repeat today will have gone. It's unlikely that the crematoria and graveyards will continue to have their Greatest Hits tinkling away day and night.'

Procol Harum lyricist Keith Reid, born in October 1946, whose often baffling yet never less than poetic words were so much a part of the success of Procol Harum, died on 23 March 2023, at the age of 76.

Who amongst us hasn't pondered just what the words of 'Whiter Shade of Pale' really meant, but still have no idea? Yet, isn't it perfectly appropriate that we should never know, despite the fact that, when he passed away, I saw several claims, as one article in the *Daily Mail* put it, that Reid had 'always said that, at the end of his life he would explain what it all meant'.

You'd have to think he'd have told Gary Brooker at some stage, so perhaps he'll spill the beans eventually. I'm pleased, though, to accept that Reid may have left this eternal mystery behind, to be pondered by listeners every time the wonderful record is played.

*

A *Daily Mail* story revealed, in October 2022 that: 'In his memoir, Bono recalls his close shave when a Dublin record shop where he should have been making his regular after-school visit in May 1974 was blown up by a Loyalist car bomb, killing 14.

'He writes in his memoir: "The only reason I wasn't standing in the record store is that a bus strike meant we'd had to cycle to school. We were already home when the streets around Dolphin Discs were blown to bits."'

IN WHICH MANFREDS STILL
ROCKING FOUNDATIONS

On an Eastbourne visit, I teamed up with pals Mike Hush and Roger Plummer to 'do' the local record shops. The first one we remembered, a small one, turned out no longer to be where it had been. However, on the other side of the road was an antique shop – currently being patronised by a man who looked very much as though he was auditioning for the role of a member of the Monster Raving Loony Party standing for Parliament at a by-election. We nipped past him, taking the stairs to the basement. There we found a gentleman sitting behind a Covid-protection counter, with literally thousands of records and CDs surrounding him. No other customers to be seen, we began digging.

Within a few minutes I'd dug out 80 quid's worth of records, for which I was invited to pay £60 – a Groundhogs LP with a fold-out cover, *Who Will Save the World? The Mighty Groundhogs*; another, by Master's Apprentices; and two super-obscure heavy/psych/prog reissue records – oh, plus an Ocean Colour Scene boxed CD.

The main reason for our jaunt down, was to see the Manfreds – with ever-reliable Paul Jones, Mike d'Abo, Tom McGuinness, Mike Hugg, and Georgie Fame guesting. However, Georgie was indisposed, and was replaced by Zoot Money, who added an unexpected but very welcome 'wow factor' for me. Not only did he perform four numbers on his own, which were all the better for being less familiar than the perhaps too well-known Manfreds' offerings – but his personality shone through. He was amusing and engaging, with no hint that he was showing off. I departed determined to collect some more of Zoot's own music, aware, though, that much of that has a more jazzy feel than is generally palatable to me.

After the show, former *Mirror* racing writer Roger explained his love of jukeboxes, particularly his own. He would agree with

the 1970 sentiment expressed by George Harrison who wrote a
letter to EMI, asking for an assurance that 'all future Apple singles
will have jukebox-friendly push-out centres'.

'What sets vinyl apart from tapes, CDs and, God forbid, streaming?'
asks Roger. 'Obviously, there's the authentic sound, but for me it's
the anticipation and excitement of the needle hitting the record
before an old favourite or first-time spin blasts into the room.

Jukeboxes take that experience to a new dimension. The click
of the selection buttons, the whirring of the carousel before it
comes to an abrupt stop, and the disc hitting the turntable to
the accompaniment of the crackle, hiss and associated pops of
the cartridge connecting with the record. Magical. Jukeboxes are
iconic, and, by far the best way to play 45s from the 50s and 60s.
Some just don't get them – "relics from the past, only enjoyed by
ageing rock stars and DJs".

During my teenage years no self-respecting pub, café or youth
club would be without one of these magnificent machines. 6d for
one play or 1/- for three. Radio Luxembourg apart, jukeboxes were
the best means of keeping up with new releases, especially from
the US. Selections were updated every two to three weeks. Singles
were king and LPs a passion yet to come.

The café along the road from Southfields Station, south west
London, was my go-to haunt, and also of rock and roll royalty, in
the shape of Johnny Kidd and the Pirates' guitarist, Mick Green.
The spine-tingling thrill from the intros of numerous 45s during
that period never left me and has not been dulled by time.

But we all move on. Singles replaced by LPs, vinyl by CDs, and
before you know it, the record deck is stored in the loft along with
that precious vinyl collection. A jukebox gives you the opportunity
to relive the past and rekindle those treasured memories. It's an
expensive way to do it, but you can pick up a serviceable machine
for the same price as a high-end deck, amplifier, and speaker
combination.

For my 40th birthday my wonderful wife, Sue, surprised me
with a Rock-Ola 454. Singles were quickly rescued from the loft.
My advice for anyone thinking of owning a jukebox: think before

you fill the machine. In my haste to play the new toy I removed the centres of numerous valuable 45s and, in doing so, devalued them. The machine was a big hit (sorry) whenever we entertained, even with those too young to remember jukeboxes.

Second piece of advice: some of the discs on the Rock-Ola did not register with family and friends and were not getting played. For parties, stock up with hits.

Third piece: I made the mistake of trimming our 45 collection, keeping only records that would be popular on the jukebox. There were several I let go, which I later realised meant a lot to me.

The 454 served me well for over two decades, but being a design from the 70s, I hankered after a model I could relate to from my own formative years. In 2010, the *Daily Mirror* decided I was surplus to requirements and, after 41 years of service, I accepted their kind offer to part ways. Knowing of a jukebox dealer nearby, and with time on my hands, I thought a visit would not go amiss. I got the same kick from entering the shop as when browsing a second-hand record shop.

I explained to owner, Rob, what I was looking for. He suggested an early 60's Rock-Ola Regis, holding 100 singles, recently salvaged from a local youth club. The machine had superficial faults and scratches. I was hooked. Rob gave me an estimate of what restoration would cost. A deal was done. Luckily, Sue was visiting her mother in Canada when the project started. By the time she returned, it was too late to pull out! The rebuild took months – the result was stunning. The Regis took pride of place in our lounge. There was, though, one hairy moment just after completion. It was at the time of riots triggered by the shooting of Mark Duggan on 4 August 2011.

Watching local news coverage on TV, I was alarmed to see Rob's shop, Jukebox City, come into view as the camera panned along a road showing rioters, smashed windows and burning cars. My finished jukebox was out in full view in the front window. I asked Rob to deliver my pride and joy the next day. Maybe the rioters saw the jukeboxes for the works of art they are and let them be!'

Back to the Manfreds – two years later, virtually to the day, in October 2023, Sheila and I were in the audience at the Alban Arena in St Albans to see them again – now shorn of Fame, Hugg and Money but with excellent replacements, again performing a marathon double set of music, virtually all directly associated with the group and/or individual members.

D'Abo, who fronted half a dozen chart hits as lead singer for Manfred Mann (a name they can't now use, as the eponymous owner has not given permission), did one of the songs it isn't commonly known that he wrote with Tony Macaulay – 'Build Me Up Buttercup', a huge hit for The Foundations. He also remarked that his writing royalties – 'Handbags and Gladrags' is another of his mega-selling compositions – come in very useful given that he has three marriages behind him!

Jones demonstrated admirable stamina during the show, always up front, whether singing or backing up the others with his admirably authentic mouth-harp expertise, and his constantly time-and-beat-marking limbs. It was also great to see ultra-modest Tom McGuinness, paying tribute to his 'other' hit-scoring exploits in the lower profile McGuiness Flint.

I do own a copy of the 1976 LP D'Abo and former DC5 man Mike Smith recorded together, *Smith & D'Abo*. I decided not to add to that total the latest Manfreds release, but was pleased to witness a good number of the audience departing after the concert with vinyl copies under their arms, which were also having to be crammed under raincoats as they emerged into an extremely damp Wycombe late evening, heading to the multi-storeys. On a serious note, with their three main men now into their eighties, albeit still of sprightly demeanour, the Manfreds may not continue much longer.

IN WHICH I FIND EARLY VINEGAR JOE

I felt I'd almost discovered a previously unknown Vinegar Joe record – not one with the band's name on the cover, no, this one was ostensibly by Keef Hartley – effectively his only 'solo' album, as the rest he made seem to have been under the Keef Hartley Band title.

Lancashire Hustler, from 1973, features Elkie Brooks, Robert Palmer and Pete Gage, three of the VJ stalwarts. I bought it, along with Family's old fashioned-iconic bakelite radio-shape cover LP, *Bandstand*. I added a large cardboard reproduction of the Stones – as they appeared when promoting 'Have You Seen Your Mother, Baby, Standing In The Shadow?', all wearing various wigs and uniforms, with Bill sitting in a wheelchair. That Stones single was engineered by Dave Hassinger – the man who discovered, signed and then managed another of my favourites from this era, the Electric Prunes. He died in 2007, aged 80.

Another record-hunting day out, with mate GB had begun at 8.30am as he jumped from an H14 bus. We boarded a following H12, to Rayners Lane, then tube to Hillingdon, catching the Oxford Tube bus to that city.

Once there we located Truck Store Records, where Graham bought LPs by Peter Green, and The Nice. Me, the three LP box-set, *Consequences* by Godley-Creme, knowing full well I'll struggle ever to sit down long enough to get through it, but thinking it is a good thing to own.

Reluctantly, I left a £6.50 Nils Lofgren double in the racks, and we left to catch a bus to Witney. Two, as it happens, after a false start when we headed off in the wrong direction, but corrected ourselves, retraced our steps, and discovered the Rapture shop, which just happened to be conveniently close to a pub, into which we adjourned for wine/beer and ham/cheese toasties. Only, though, after I found Graham a Kenneth Williams 'Rambling Sid Rumpo' LP, and myself three CDs – Wishbone Ash, Barclay James Harvest and Blodwyn Pig – a very decent hat trick.

Refreshed, we retraced our steps and buses, arriving home to the news that, ok, I've spent a few quid on records – but I've also sold a book about boxer Kirkland Laing for an amazing £185, which is, of course, a knockout price.

The November 2021 edition of *The Oldie* magazine declared as its POPTASTIC OLDIE OF THE YEAR, 'Whispering' Bob Harris, 75, who, it revealed, 'keeps his records in a well-appointed Portakabin in the garden of his home in Oxfordshire'. The article noted that, when Bob became involved in a court case over debt in the 90s, 'he successfully argued that his records shouldn't be seized because they were the tools of his trade'.

Born in October 1951, so from my own generation, *Mail on Sunday* columnist Peter Hitchens wrote in February 2023 of 'that strange era, which stretched from the mid-50s to the end of the 60s', adding that: 'The disturbing sound of the new music would sweep away almost everything we had known.' Your author was born just under a year earlier – and I have to say thank heavens for that 'disturbing' new music, which, clearly, never infiltrated successfully the auditory organs of Mr H.

IN WHICH I PLUG *VINYL COUNTDOWN*

The promotional merry-go-round surrounding the launch of this book's predecessor *Vinyl Countdown*, in late November 2019, spun me off to Dunstable to appear on Three Counties Radio, and to record a down-the-line interview with BBC Radio Leeds presenter Stephanie Hirst who has a monumental 25,000+ record collection (Jealous? Me? Yup) and is a radio and club DJ and a genuine vinyl freak – we got on like the proverbial domicile conflagration: 'For me, record fairs and charity shops are never about the individually priced items or the rare first pressings, etc. The bargain bins are where all the fun is to be had – dodgy white labels, reggae I've never heard of, that 12″ I couldn't afford when I was 13. It's all in there.'

The book had also now reached Number 13 on the Amazon music-book chart.

Next day, saw an interview with Robert Elms on BBC Radio London – an extremely empathetic interviewer. He's into jazz these days, having been keen on punk back in the day. I mention the Blue Note record label and he tells me of a black-cab driver who collected that label to such an extent that he amassed a full set – until one day a Japanese man climbed into his cab. They began to talk about music, about jazz and about Blue Note.

When the Japanese man heard about the cabbie's collection he made a six figure offer to buy it, lock, stock and barrel – £150,000. The cabbie accepted with alacrity, laughs Robert. I wonder whether he still expected a tip?

Following the interview I headed for Berwick Street. In Sister Ray, I found a most interesting LP for £9.99 by the previously unknown to me, Olivers, described on its cover as a 'psychedelic gem'. Aren't they all, though? It transpired that this one was genuinely good.

Down to Reckless, where I came across two Quicksilver Messenger Service-related records – £7 for a Gary Duncan-fronted 'Quicksilver', named *Peace of Piece* and a Gravenites-Cipollina collaboration, called, unfortunately enough, *Monkey Medicine* at £8, featuring a cover of one of QMS's best tracks, 'Pride of Man'.

And so to Slough for a United WhatsApp interview with Ian Shirley, editor of the *Rare Record Price Guide*. I got to play a dozen favourite tracks during our conversation, from Vinegar Joe to the McCoys and the Pretty Things, via the Pyramids, Bobby Shafto, Simon Scott, John Dowie, Arcadium, and T2.

Quickly home, then off to London Bridge to meet up with Talk Radio's Martin Kelner, another long-standing acquaintance. Arriving at London Bridge, the tube driver announced the station was shut, so I went to the next one, Bank, and up to the street – where I found there was a police action in progress, and heard rumours of stabbings, terrorists and shootings. I abandoned the

journey and went home, contacting Martin, to discover that
his London Bridge offices were locked down, so we recorded a
telephone interview.

The rumours had been well-founded – five people were stabbed,
two fatally. The attacker, Usman Khan, had been released from
prison in 2018 on licence after serving a sentence for terrorist
offences. He was attending an offender rehabilitation conference
at which he threatened to detonate what turned out to be a fake
suicide vest, then started attacking people with two knives taped
to his wrists, killing two conference participants by stabbing.

Several people fought back, some tackling Khan as he fled the
building, emerging on to London Bridge, where he was partially
disarmed by a plainclothes police officer. He was restrained by
members of the public until additional police officers arrived,
pulled away those restraining him, and shot him.

I did an interview with BBC 3CR presenter Justin Dealy in
the 'Second Scene' shop in Bushey – nice publicity for Julian. I
was also very pleased to appear on veteran DJ Johnnie Walker's
Sunday afternoon BBC Radio Two programme – without, this
time, taking any bets from him on motor sport, something he
used to enjoy placing occasionally, back in the day.

IN WHICH, FOR FOX SAKE

Imagine you were keen to break into the pop world, and had found
a band to be in, only to discover that those in charge weren't mad
about your own name, and decided you needed rechristening.
What might you fancy instead? Something glamorous?

But no, the leader of the group decides you should make up
a name – how about doing so by rearranging the letters in your
own name? Thus it was that Aussie singer Susan Traynor was
reinvented as Noosha when she joined Fox – okay, the letters
weren't quite the same, they'd chucked the 'u' out, and brought

in an 'h', oh, and a couple of 'o's, but who was going to complain?

After all, the band had been put together by a man whose songwriting credentials were impeccable – he co-wrote the smash Drifters' hit, 'Under the Boardwalk'. And he'd changed his own name, after all, making rather more changes, as well – to Kenny Young, from Shalom Giskan.

But Noosha and Kenny Young were not the only fox in the forest, because The Fox got there before them – maybe that's why Noosha had to do without a 'The'. The Fox never made it big, sadly – never really made it small, either, but they left behind an excellent body of work, most of which appeared on their Fontana label LP, which came out in Canada and the USA in 1969 but not in the UK until 1970 and was, subtly, titled – go on, then – guess – yes, of course, *For Fox Sake*. Rather later in 2003 it was finally reissued, on both LP and CD. Pop psych fans should really enjoy, in particular, 'Mr Blank', a track which deserved to make it, but didn't.

Kenny Young and Noosha's Fox – yes, they DID make it pretty big. Kenny had written the smash 'Captain of Your Ship' for Reparata and the Delrons in 1968, as well as hits for Herman's Hermits, The Seekers, and Clodagh Rodgers for starters.

'Only You Can' did the trick to get Fox – not to be at all confused with Foxx, whose 1971 LP, *The Revolt of Emily Young*, was often on my turntable, but not many other people's – into the charts in 1975, despite having failed the year before – probably because, possibly to save money, they'd only used two words in the title that time, 'Only You'. Clearly, 'Can' made the crucial difference, as it charged into the Top 10. 'Imagine Me, Imagine You' was a Top 20 follow-up.

In April, 1976 they scored their biggest success – with a s-s-s-song, which might prove controversial if it were to be released now. The song was called 'S-S-S-Single Bed' and had quite an erotic feel to it – or maybe that's just wishful thinking on my part. It definitely suggested that the character whose role Noosha was singing had something of a stutter or speech impediment, possibly even as much as Roger Daltrey's alter ego had had in The Who's 'My Generation' some years earlier, when he hoped he'd die before he got old… he didn't, and he's old now, for sure.

That was about it for Noosha as a member of Fox, and she slowly drifted into obscurity, making various non-hits as she went, but always able to rely on name recognition wherever she went – 'Oh... Noosha? – Weren't you that Foxy singer?'

Then, of course, there was Samantha Fox, who enjoyed a couple of hits, as well as a morning with me, when, as Press Officer for the company, I had to protect her from screaming fans – male, mostly, who turned up to 'see' her open a William Hill betting shop. I met a couple of other Page 3 presences that way, too.

Not wishing to promote fox-hunting, of course, but Fox(x) has often been a successful name for singers – sister and brother, Inez and Charlie Foxx enjoyed a few US hits in the 60s, notably with 'Mockingbird', while John Foxx – real name, Dennis Leigh – 'Foxx is much more intelligent than I am, better looking, better lit' – might have opted for Ultrafox, but instead founded Ultravox! They did pretty well, but even better once they ditched that exclamation mark, which had clearly been holding them back.

Don Fox, who had a string of Decca label singles in the late 50s, may have been the first to bring the name to prominence, but the oddest singing Fox must have been the man whose parents may have completely invented his Christian name, Uffa – he made his name as an English boat designer and sailing enthusiast, but in 1960 ill-advisedly burst into song with an LP called *Uffa Sings*, which inevitably included a version of 'A Life on the Ocean Wave'. Then, fortunately, he went off to do Uffa things...

'A gorilla made from recycled CDs is due to go on display in Durrell Zoo's charity shop,' reported the *Jersey Post* newspaper in December 2022. The artistic animal was made by local carpenter David Carson, from thousands of reused discs. Mr Carson also turns second-hand CDs into furniture, but made the gorilla sculpture to help raise awareness of the wider issue of sustainability: 'Obviously there was no manual on how to build a gorilla out of CDs.' He used a plywood frame to establish the gorilla's general shape and then – with around 7,000 discs – filled in the body. Good to know he wasn't just monkeying about.

Watching an episode of TV's *Would I Lie To You?*, there was a round in which David Mitchell claimed that he had doubled his collection of 'albums' by buying a second one. Phil Collins' 1989 LP, *But Seriously*, was his first, and, at least ten years later, he claimed, one of Susan Boyle's, the title of which he couldn't remember, possibly *The Gift*, was added. It was duly revealed that he was indeed telling the truth.

IN WHICH JULIAN REVEALS WHERE RUBBISH RECORDS END UP

The week before Christmas, I thought I'd pop along to visit Julian at Second Scene. I took a Christmas card and a box of chocolates to say thanks for all the help he and Helen had given me while I was working on *Vinyl Countdown*. Julian was casting around the shop for enough 'rubbish records' which wouldn't be of any interest to his average customers, in order to fulfil orders he had received for literally thousands of such unloved and otherwise unwanted, and unprofitable, discs. He was rootling around in areas of the shop untouched by human hands for years, where unknown tribes of vinyl deniers may well have set up their homes.

Julian had just unearthed a couple of cases full of reggae singles of less than modest value. One such container emitted something of a damp, rather offensive – to his delicate olfactory organs – odour. I told him I'd recently acquired a couple of hundred crap records from a well-meaning acquaintance which would probably have been ideal for his purposes but had felt too embarrassed at the thought of trying to dump them on him. But he explained what he did with them – which involved sending them to artists, sculptors and other such gifted folk, who would repurpose the vinyl to create an income stream for themselves.

If I'd been aware of that I would not have had to slip out of the house, past the midnight hour in order to distribute the unwanted records into local building-work skips. This, of course, these days, runs the risk that one's image may be caught by the lens of householders' various camera-like devices initially designed to deter catalytic-convertor thieves, burglars, opinion pollsters, and other such undesirables.

Helen came in, relieved to have escaped from the local post office where, during the ongoing Christmas rush, she had been attracting disparaging comments from pensioners trying to send off armfuls of late Xmas cards, as Helen had tried to sort out the relevant rates to post packages of vinyl to Japanese customers.

The couple also commented on their recent brush with local fame as a result of an interview on the BBC's Three Counties Radio via their support for *Vinyl Countdown* – Julian admitted, 'I enjoyed it, but thought I sounded a bit odd, not using my natural voice and accent.'

I doubt whether the lady behind the Customer Service desk at Sainsbury's in Pinner had heard a similar query, but I asked her, 'Er, this is a very odd request, but last week I left a vinyl record – yes, they are round, about 12 inches wide, and you put them on a record player and they play music – in the trolley my wife and I had used in here. I don't suppose anyone will have handed it in?' She searched around thoroughly in the little office, and as I prepared myself for inevitable disappointment, she emerged triumphantly with a Wishbone Ash 12″ single and handed it over with a genuine smile.

IN WHICH I'M BUBBLING DOWN UNDER

Even now, in my, what, SEVENTH decade of record-collecting, the eternal hunt for one of those elusive discs you daren't hope to find, so have stopped even thinking about it happening one day, can suddenly materialise, coming to fruition in front of you, at a time when it is genuinely the furthest thought from your mind. On Christmas Eve 2022, we were in Mount Maunganui in New Zealand, a residential, commercial and industrial suburb of the city of Tauranga, staying in a pleasant property, a couple of hundred yards from the stunning sea front.

My family members were engaged in sensible seaside activities such as shell-collecting, paddling, ice cream-eating, wondering when their burdensome parents/in-laws would clear off back to England, that sort of thing. Trying to keep out of everyone's way, and not annoying them by moaning that I had nothing to do, I remembered that when we'd driven into the town I'd spotted a second-hand book shop, on whose window was a notice that they had begun also selling records.

As there were few other – *no other*, really – shops which held any attraction for me, I thought I'd slip out and wander down to see what they may have in stock. They didn't really have much in stock at all, which was probably unsurprising, as they clearly hadn't had time to amass a decent disc haul. They did, though, have a good few customers – mostly wandering around the bookshelves, one or two flipping through the LPs. I joined the latter and patiently endured a steady stream of very familiar, mainstream titles, none of which appealed to me in the slightest. I took a turn around the bookshelves to see what they might offer. Likewise, nothing of any great interest.

Right, suppose I may as well head back – oh, what's in that box over there? Singles, most of them not in sleeves, so likely to be scratched to buggery even if of any interest. Oh well, let's give 'em the once over... Tom Jones... er, The Bachelors... now, some Kiwi group I've never heard of... here's a few which are actually in sleeves... mm, got that... don't want that... WHAT'S THAT!? A mainly white label, with a strip across its middle, on one side white on blue, the other blue on white, both showing the name of the label, Festival – looks unfamiliar and quite attractive. The title of the track, 'LONELY' in capitals, above the Festival name – below it, the name of the group, 'THE BUBBLE PUPPY'.

Wow, Bubble Puppy – they recorded a 60s psych classic, 'Hot Smoke & Sasafrass' – which seems to be what's on the other side of this 7". Crikey, one of my favourite tracks of that genre – I know it was a minor hit in the States, but wasn't sure it was released in the UK. This is a New Zealand label by the looks of things. I have to have this – a few marks on the surface of each side, but looks completely playable.

There's a note on the box of singles – $1 each. Last time I checked, a Kiwi dollar was worth just over 50p. An undoubted bargain. I took it to the counter. 'Sorry, you won't be getting rich on me, but at least I've found one record to take off your hands.' 'Every little helps,' she says, smiling.

I head off, smiling more than her. I started to check on Discogs, but there were no copies of this New Zealand issue listed. Plenty of US ones – 216 of them, to be accurate – £16.55 seems to be the cheapest price for it from a UK seller. But I'd say the rarity of the Kiwi 'Festival' label copy could add maybe a tenner to that price. On Popsike I discover that an Aussie copy looking similar to my Kiwi one, and in a branded Festival sleeve, except its colours are yellow and black, sold for £19 in July 2017.

The record doesn't warrant mention in the 2024 *Rare Record Price Guide* – nor do any releases by the group, which is odd – not even under the name they later assumed – Demian. Yet, nothing under either of these names goes cheap on Discogs. So, a fantastic bargain for ten bob, a scarce one, too – best of all – a great memory of an unexpected Kiwi Christmas buzz.

The group name 'Bubble Puppy' was adapted from 'Centrifugal Bumble-puppy', a fictitious children's game in Aldous Huxley's 1932 novel *Brave New World* and, of course, most of you will already have realised that the title of the single was inspired by a line of dialogue in an episode of 60s US TV show, *The Beverly Hillbillies*, but hearing it was one thing – spelling it correctly, another. The word should actually have read: 'sassafras'. The band were amongst the first to boast two lead guitarists.

Bubble Puppy's LP, *A Gathering of Promises*, is well worth seeking out. It is easy enough to pick up on CD but rather more elusive and expensive on vinyl.

IN WHICH JON SPRINGS OUT
OF NOWHERE

I buy a good number of LPs from Jon Groocock, as you now know. The mail order seller runs 'White Spring Records' in Glastonbury. I asked him how he first got into the business:

'In 1981 buying and selling records was a matter of whether I ate or didn't. I had a job that paid me very little, so whether I sold something or not equalled whether I got any money.

I lived in a very damp basement in Swiss Cottage with my girlfriend and small son. BUT, at the top of the road was one of the very last Marché Ouverts in England, Swiss Cottage Market. Hallelujah.

A Marché Ouvert was where dodgy people were allowed to sell dodgy things and no one could stop them. No pitches, or payments you just turned up, put a blanket on the ground, in this case on the bombsite by the old Winchester Pub and that was it. No one could or would ask where the stuff came from. On a sunny day the good burghers of Hampstead would empty out their lofts and sheds, and come down with their debris – amongst which were... records.

Every Saturday, up we got early doors, small son in buggy, I, with whatever cash we had (usually not much) and pushed up the hill to the Market, to see if we could magically turn a few quid into a week's groceries. Dealers turned up at dawn, with their torches and boxes, and were gone by 8am, entirely missing the point that lazy rich people from Hampstead would rarely turn up before 9.

We stood there, me puffing on a roll-up, waiting for them to roll out the travelling rugs and then, such treasures: Tony Meehan's kids dumped a small pile of Poets' acetates on the ground, four Marc Bolan acetates from a publicist, with a desperate letter from Marc. Wodge after wodge of Vertigo "Swirls", pink Islands, Harvests.

Export Beatles LPs, Demos, 50 copies of The Afex's "She's Got the Time" [1967 organ-led cracker, goes for three figures now] and 25 copies of The Chords Five 45 on Jayboy, 'Some People', now not far off £100 [and the rest, Jon!] for 50p the lot.

Small son once escaped from his buggy and pulled a Leathercoated Minds LP (A *Trip Down the Sunset Strip*, 1967, Fontana. Now a £65+ record) out of a random pile of *Top of the Pops* LPs, much to the annoyance of a hovering scavenger.

And then, bunk the bus down to Vinyl Solution (not simple with a two-year-old in a buggy) at the fag end of Notting Hill with the haul, and Yves Guillemot, the only person in London, then, who would actually give you real money for records, on the nail. and hope that: 1. Some Germans had been in in the previous 48 hours and bought a pile of prog LPs so he was cash rich, 2. That the gay guy who did East Lane and was a doo-wop collector had either not got there first, or had been lured into trading the lot for some weird New York doo-wop 45 and, 3. That Yves was in a good and expansive mood. Last, the most important!

If the price was good, and the haul sufficient to enable us to eat, maybe, just maybe I could afford to trade for a record I actually wanted. I still have a couple of those magical things: A VG Factory's "Path Through the Forest" that was £15, (MGM, 1968, now probably £1,000 at least) and a battered Wheels' "Road Block" (Columbia single, 1966 with "Bad Little Woman" on the other side, now £350+) for 50p. It was all about Psychedelic and Garage 45s for me back then. And eating. Not necessarily in that order.'

I asked Jon whether the baby grew up to like music: 'Yes, he collects Britpop and cool Jazz on original vinyl!' Jon obviously has a large collection – I haven't dared ask just how large, but we did discuss how we keep tabs on what we own. He told me: 'It took me forever but 90% of it is now on a spreadsheet on my iPad. Which means I have stopped buying EX copies of the first Quicksilver LP because I had an ancestral memory of having a scratched one about 20 years ago!'

He's way ahead of my technological capabilities as I have no idea what a spreadsheet is, but do have my own CD/vinyl collections compiled in two large, what I've always referred to as, 'exercise books'.

IN WHICH I LEARN HOW 'OLDIE' CHRIS TAMED HIS SHOP

Chris McGranaghan took a regular advert in *The Oldie* magazine: 'Wanted for cash Vinyl Records' Here he explains why to me:

'I've been advertising in *The Oldie* for about 15 years. It used to be very good but less so these days. I ran a shop – "Those Old Records" in Rugeley for 11 years – but retired from that two years ago. We also have a record label (TOR Records) and have released about 13 different titles. Buying records in the shop was easy, they brought them in and had made the decision to sell. Working from home means you have to put effort in to get good stock. I travel up and down the country and, in all honesty, it is still the best part of what I do. Meeting people, hearing their stories.

Something about me: I have a dislike for Northern Soul, The Who and the Small Faces. In 11 years of my shop being open, I can honestly state that I never played a Who or Small Faces record. I love Spiritual Reggae, Jazz, the darker side of Folk – Lankum, Lisa O'Neill, Luke Kelly. The shop was an accident, Sally and I went in to buy chicken for dinner and left with a small unit, 11' x 11'. I had a career in IT and was made redundant at 50. I was selling online and had run record fairs locally, so I had an audience when the shop opened. Rugeley, an old mining town, was pretty rundown in 2010. Many advised against opening but I persevered, albeit expecting failure after three months.

This was a dream job. I was in and out of record shops on business and in many ways had become the "£50" man in the 80s and 90s. The reality soon hit me – the tedium of dealing with people who wanted the place as a regular haunt to hang out and buy nothing – a drop-in centre for the disaffected. I knocked that on the head by barring several people, much to the annoyance of the locals. I got control after a few weeks of bickering. That's one of the problems with a good record shop – some people can drag it down, impacting upon serious buyers, who stop coming. I wanted a welcoming environment, especially for women and young people, but always understood that record shops were primarily a male domain.

I knew several serious female collectors and music fans, and wanted them in the place, feeling on equal terms with everyone else. I wouldn't tolerate sexist talk, bad language or racism. This was a tough call, even for myself – partial to the odd expletive if pushed.

The racism was difficult. I hadn't bargained for the amount I was to encounter from people I least expected it from. I persevered and won out in the end – by playing Indian music whenever these people came in the shop, by advertising Reggae/Soul albums in the shop windows in any available space. They banned themselves.

Northern Soul – they come in pairs normally, the Alpha male and his number 2. The Alpha male has it all, he has all the records and will pull them out of the rack and tell his number 2 at which car boot sale he bought it and how little he paid for it. They ask to hear something, but rarely buy anything. Outside Northern Soul, the Alpha knows little about anything – he may be in the EDL (English Defence League) as he's in skinhead attire and he may be going to an imagined "all nighter" in Stoke that evening. He supports Birmingham City.

I used to play a trick on them by playing "Drums" by Michael Holliday (the 60s crooner) – a classic track, which I take responsibility for making part of the Northern canon. There are some serious people in this market who are modest about their knowledge and certainly don't try to recreate the Wigan Casino vibe at weekends. I wanted to open people's minds to music that they probably never encountered before. Record shops should be an exchange of ideas and knowledge. I'd make a point of introducing people to each other and good friendships were formed.

One regular was Clive Walker – an ex miner who always looked unshaven, wore either a Hendrix or Iron Maiden t-shirt, track suit bottoms and hobnailed boots. He had mad hair and spoke in the Rugeley vernacular (he pronounced it Rudgley) – a nicer man you have never met, but he could turn on a sixpence. He had a vast record collection, used to bring in an album, hand it to me and say "hold it and weep Chris". It became a standing joke, so much so that I had a divider written up for rare records with that strapline on it.

He looked difficult to approach. However, over time he made good friendships with many in the shop as he could hold his own on any aspect of music. We released an album by a band from Nottingham, The Madeline Rust, fronted by a wonderful singer – Lucy Morrow. There's nothing of her, and she was in the shop one Saturday morning. Clive had bought the album, so I introduced the two of them – Clive says "So how does yow (local dialect) get a voice like that?" – looking her up and down. She smiled and said – "Clive, I gargle turpentine."

I really wanted live music in the shop – especially from bands pushing boundaries. The first gig was by Peter Parker's Rock N Roll Club – they damn near blew the roof off. That led to the start of our TOR Records labels – we released about 13 titles – they are in the British Library – something that I am immensely proud of.

One busy Saturday morning the door swung open, and in strode this cocky wide boy. I was at the counter chatting to a customer. He positioned himself between us and said:

"You have a record label, don't you?" I replied, "Good Morning to you, too. Yes, I have a record label, how can I help you?" "My lad has a Queen tribute band." He lowers his voice. "The thing is – he's better than Freddie Mercury by a mile. So, this is what WE are going to do."

The regulars had stopped looking at records and had turned around to look at this guy. I have a well-known dislike of tribute bands – even refusing to advertise their gigs in the shop. He continued, "We'll get the lad and his band in a local studio, I have it all set up, record 10 Queen tracks and release them on coloured vinyl on your label – what do you think?"

The shop had gone quiet. The pressure was on to sort this out. I responded with:

"Have you ever considered seeing a psychiatrist?" He exploded: "Well if that's your f***ing attitude I'll go elsewhere." He turned around, headed to the door and slammed it after him bellowing

"F*** Off you ****", which was followed by a rousing set of cheers and a round of applause in the shop.'

IN WHICH I EXPERIENCE UNIQUE WASTELAND WATCH

I could hear 'Teenage Wasteland' by The Who playing as I was told to lie on the bed and 'draw your knees up to your chin'. I was at the Clementine Churchill Hospital, for a procedure which involved – and here more sensitive readers may wish to avert their eyes and jump a paragraph or two – having a camera inserted in to my, how shall I phrase this, back passage. No, not for pleasurable reasons, but the medical reasons needn't detain us here – I'm just explaining how the music I listened to whilst watching pictures from my internal organs on a screen proved to be a calming influence during the experience I very much hope you'll never have to go through!

When it was all over, they wheeled me out to the strains of the Carpenters.

Alan Titchmarsh revealed in the *Guardian* in 2022 that the first single he ever bought was 'China Tea' by Russ Conway and that it cost him 4/6d. But he also revealed that he and his first 'proper' girlfriend, 'had "A Groovy Kind of Love" by the Mindbenders as "our song". I was totally besotted for a good six months when I was 15. Years later, I was doing an autobiography signing, looked up, and someone said: "Hello." I hadn't seen her for 40 years. It was a magical moment. I heard a couple of years ago that she died. I hear the song now with such affection, because it reminds me what falling in love is like.'

Attending a 'Duck Pond Fair' – don't ask – in Ruislip I spotted on one lady's stall a 'cake stand' consisting of two singles and an LP – the latter by Rick Astley, all fixed on a metal spike. I declared with a smile to the lady running the stall that she was guilty of committing a crime against vinyl. She laughed and asked rhetorically, 'Who'd want to play a Rick Astley LP, anyway!' I didn't buy it.

I felt an itch – maybe even an urge to head over to Chesham. Once there I went to Collectors Paradise where, as ever, boss Dale, truly a Dickensian-looking character, was holding forth – 'You wait till you see my bathroom; I'll take a photo of the marble wall to show you.' No, he wasn't directing this remark to me – he was on the phone. 'I've had loads of LPs coming in – I'm getting another 120 tomorrow.' He then told whoever was on the other end of the line, 'Tomorrow I'm seeing my friend who is seven feet tall – you've never seen anyone as tall,' to which I said to myself, 'You've never met the publisher of my books!'

Dale spotted me looking at his CDs – 'I've got a lot of CDs, haven't I?' he asked rhetorically, reminding me of a previous visit on which he'd declared to me, 'I've got a lot of LPs, haven't I?' to which I'd also replied, 'Yes. So have I.'

As usual, there was, behind the counter, a much younger female. I went through all Dale's CDs, but could only come up with a £4 Atomic Rooster, which I bought because of the number of tracks written by John Du Cann.

I handed it to Dale. 'Some days you find loads,' I started. 'And others, very little,' Dale finished the line off for me. Then, noticing what I was buying, 'Oh, haven't seen this before, interesting.' I thought he might now refuse to sell it to me, but he didn't.

Explaining the recent upturn in vinyl sales, Kim Bayley, chief executive of the Entertainment Retailers Association, reportedly couldn't resist saying: 'It's a myth that the vinyl boom is all about middle-aged men indulging in nostalgia.' This comment surely overlooked the fact that had we '(late)middle-aged men', probably aka 'saddos' by people of Kim Bayley's kind, not kept vinyl going in the dark years, there would never have been a comeback to be had.

Kim did have the grace to admit: 'While it's true that the initial revival more than a decade ago was driven by older demographics rebuying classic albums, kids have now embraced vinyl as their own.'

IN WHICH NICK IS SINGLES MINDED

Nick Godfrey, horse-racing hack and record company owner muses:

'Blame the Top 20 countdown – and it WAS Top 20 back then, mid-70s, before BBC Radio 1 doubled their coverage later in the decade. Apart from a lifelong antipathy to Queen's never-ending "Bohemian Rhapsody", number one for half a century, this was required listening every Sunday night for an obsessive only child nowhere near double figures.

It started my enduring devotion to singles. That's seven-inch singles, one brought home every Friday (wages day) by my betting shop manager Dad, and purchased at Chalky White's, the newsagent in Roehampton High St that stocked a few singles alongside the sweets, fags and papers. Glam rock entered the household. I still have Mott the Hoople, even if Showaddywaddy was somehow evicted years ago.

When I was old enough for pocket money, it all went on records. First, punk and new wave via an array of picture sleeves from Blondie, The Jam, Elvis Costello; then post-punk and the long-overcoat "alternative" brigade (Altered Images and Strawberry Switchblade, too); then the Smiths and proper independent music. Today, thousands of records later, of all shapes, sizes and genres – even a few LPs here and there – it is beyond me how anyone can live without *Forever Changes* and *The Velvet Underground and Nico*, *Parallel Lines* and *Setting Sons*, *Psychocandy* and *The Queen Is Dead*.

I'm often accused of liking the artefact more than the music. I would say "as much as" because I do love a beautifully produced package. I've always been a fan of record labels with a distinct identity – from Immediate and Elektra in the 60s via Two-Tone, Rough Trade and Postcard, to Creation and Sarah, and indie imprints of much more recent vintage such as Fortuna Pop! and WIAIWYA (Where It's At Is Where You Are). You should see the latter's singles club – seven years of seven-inch singles, all of them highly covetable. Buy one, you'll want all 49.

Rather like Victor Kiam, I liked it so much I... well, didn't buy the company, but started my own, during Covid. While I am a horse-racing journalist by profession, I am also Precious Recordings of London, a label devoted to releasing BBC radio sessions from the likes of the legendary John Peel and Janice Long under licence. Inevitably, these are dedicated to artists I like – mainly "indie", for want of a better phrase, mid-80s until about the turn of the century so far. All never released before on vinyl, and by artists on independent labels most of the time – just try getting the rights to anything from a major for limited runs of about 500 copies.

Precious is a dedicated vinyl-based label. I'm still virtually a one-man band, albeit with a little help from willing family (don't ask the kids) on packing, and professional input on all-important design from a talented former colleague. I still have to write about horses to pay the mortgage, of course – but moreover, to subsidise my little indie label. For the most prized record in my personal collection I'd go back to those lovely 60s singles. If anyone tried to nick my copy of "Tin Soldier" by the Small Faces, there would be serious trouble. Fantastic song, utterly blistering vocals from Steve Marriott and PP Arnold, on Immediate, and it's got a picture sleeve, for heaven's sake!'

IN WHICH JOHN PONDERS POPULAR POP

A friend since early childhood, John Saunders, now a mean string-plucking vocalist, remembers his vinyl awakening:

'It's 1958; I'm 6; I'm in the record department of the Popular Stores on Wealdstone High Street; I'm armed with my pocket money (and my mum).

My first record; a classic of the time – Charlie Drake's 'Splish Splash'. By 1960, my musical taste had become far more sophisticated – so I bought 'My Old man's a Dustman' by Lonnie Donegan.

The first time a pop record made a distinct impact on me was when I heard 'From Me to You' by The Beatles. I had that early stirring of 'I like this' without the slightest inkling of why. For the next few years, I was totally smitten by The Beatles. I recall buying a Beatles EP – 4 tracks from *Beatles For Sale* – from Wymans newsagents/stationers in Wealdstone High Street.

Each Beatles album was pored over and discussed in depth. It's 1967, I'm at Byron Road rec and Les Wilkinson is telling me about how great *Sgt Pepper* is. I staunchly defend the credentials of *Revolver* – and still believe they are equally worthy.

I have strong memories of the great songs of '67 to '69; Kinks, Cream, Small Faces etc. I also remember LPs going up to 32 shillings and 6 pence – outrageous!

Whilst at school, I used to buy most of my albums from Carnes in Wealdstone. This was my first encounter with the phrase "Do you have...?" This question often had the response of "We're waiting for it to come in."

I bought *Days of Future Passed* by the Moody Blues – only to find when I got it home, that it was in stereo! This was way beyond the capabilities of our Dansette and radiogram so I immediately took it back; they had to order me a mono version.

Then I discovered Creedence Clearwater Revival and the rest is history. I go to work and buy a Ferguson stereo system (from Ketts) with TWO speakers. I think Mum and Dad were considerably concerned when 'Whole Lotta Love' and 'Free Form Guitar' (Terry Kath – Chicago Transit Authority) boomed out from the front room.

Just flicking through album covers was a pastime, a cultural experience, a lesson in life (certainly some of the late 60's covers). I paused at the cover of *In the Court of the Crimson King* a thousand times before I bought it.

Vinyl records – endlessly intriguing, taking you down a rabbit hole like Alice. Songs that millions have heard but they are personal to you. God bless 'em.'

IN WHICH CANCER MATE RON EXPLAINS HIMSELF

Good friend and fellow prostate cancer survivor Ron Arnold most certainly has often been asked whether he has collected records all his life? His answer is always: 'Not yet!'

Given a toy which played a brief burst of instrumental music when he was perhaps four, Ron believes, 'it was that toy which shaped my taste, for the rest of my life, for instrumental music, especially guitars, 70-plus years ago'. The first lyrics he recalls are from childhood favourite, 'Nellie the Elephant'! Aged maybe seven, Ron was introduced to a record player, and 78rpm records featuring the likes of Tommy Steele and Lonnie Donegan and Bill Haley.

When Ron's older brother Jim bought an autochange record player and some records, Ron heard, and immediately loved, The Shadows. Aged 13, he was allowed into a local pub where his Dad had arranged with the landlord to bring his autochange record player in. Recalls Ron: 'Muggins got nominated for the job of playing the records.' He brought a mixed bunch of records along: his, his brother's and his Dad's – Duane Eddy, Adam Faith, Connie Francis, Helen Shapiro, and, of course, the Shadows, entertained – and Ron joined – the drinkers.

A little older, on a Devon camping holiday, walking gingerly down a steep cutting in the cliffs to a beach, he heard, coming from a nearby building, 'Johnny Remember Me' by John Leyton – and 'when I hear it I am transported back to that magical place'.

Now doing building work, Ron was sent to board up the windows of an old Victorian building to keep squatters out. In a room, he 'found an old desk with a flip top, almost full of 7″ vinyl singles, albeit with no sleeves'. He took them to the police station – several months on he had a call saying no one had collected the records, so they were his.

'I remember about 135 records – an eclectic mixture of early 60s pop – Beatles, Troggs, Stones; two "I Wanna Be Your Man" singles – one the more valuable at £35 compared with £20, with a B side saying 'Stones', the other, 'Stoned'); a couple of Shadows. Swinging Blue Jeans, Downliners Sect, Kinks, Lulu, Searchers, etc.' He built himself a record cupboard, holding 200 singles and 25 LPs – 'I still have it' – but his collection is now 'approx 1000 LPs, 1000 CDs, 1500 singles, 100 78s'.

Ron recalls doing work building a recording studio for musician Alan Hawkshaw, who also needed to install a 'small grand piano' in the studio, but as the stairs would not permit this, Ron cut a section of them out while the piano was taken up, then replaced it. Alan wrote for, and played with, the Shadows. Ron got him to sign a Hank Marvin album, on which he'd written a track, and the Shadows' *Shades of Rock* LP on which he'd played keyboards. Alan passed away in 2021, aged 84.

Ron's younger brother David saw a local group playing in the mid-60s, who had just issued their first LP, *Begin Here*, which he bought and got them to sign. That record, even without the signatures, is now worth £500 says the *Rare Record Price Guide...* the group, the Zombies.

On one occasion Ron's record player was stolen, together with six LPs inside it – shrewdly, he visited the local second-hand shops and found the record player and the discs – but no sign of wife Jan's jewellery... until, that is, the villain was nicked – with the jewellery in his pocket!

Ron says: 'Over the years my musical taste has become more eclectic. With most artists I hear a track, like it, buy the album – then go on to get more, if not all, of their work, which I've done for the Carpenters, Genesis, Pink Floyd, Led Zeppelin, Jean Michel Jarre, Sky.' Ron 'got into' both Tangerine Dream and Camel after hearing them on a John Peel show. He plays his collection on the Portadyne stereo record player bought from a catalogue half a century ago.

Ron's Shadows obsession resulted in him correcting the prestigious *Rare Record Price Guide* over a Shadows B side which that publication called 'Quartermasters Stores' (on the B side of 'Apache') but which Ron proved is actually spelled 'Quatermassters Stores' on the disc. 'I acquired two copies of said disc, and dear old RRPG have got it wrong.'

Ron accepts that something he and your author have in common is 'issues with our respective wives over our vinyl obsessions. The main problem is how to smuggle our finds into the house without being detected'. Optimistically, Ron hopes, 'Over the years mumbled comments and disapproving looks have diminished – and on the odd occasion I have found records that Jan likes – a Pan Pipes disc by Incantation, and a Boney M.'

IN WHICH I TAKE THE MIKE, THEN ENJOY A PRETTY GOOD NIGHT

Friend and fellow supporter of Wealdstone FC for well over half a century, Michael Pullin is definitely hewn from the same kind of rock as am I, as he proves here:

'I've known Graham going back to the early 60s. In "Byron Rec" park, along with some 30 others of various ages (I'm two years older) we played football, cricket, or tennis, virtually every day.

On wet days it was a case of whose parents allowed a mini mob round to listen to records. One of the older lads, Paul I'Anson, the best local goalie, started me collecting records, when I bought his portable, one-speaker, Philips' record player. You could stack singles, to automatically drop down – how to scratch and damage a record in one easy go!

At 15, I was music mad. The next step was to obtain records. My first, the Animals' "House of the Rising Sun", from the Music Shop, next to Buntings in Masons Avenue, Wealdstone. When I got it home I discovered I had my first little gem. It had a fault, being wrongly labelled with "House of the Rising Sun" on both sides. Mum every week bought me a couple of singles from Tesco, who sold ex-Jukebox hits – I think they were 3/11d when a new single was about 7/6d. Xmas and birthday presents became LPs, 5 in the first year: Small Faces, Kinks, Animals, Manfred Mann, Shadows.

Until now, my live music experience had been going to the Granada Cinema in Harrow along with the author and other friends to see Lulu, Johnny Kidd and the Pirates, and other acts lost in the passing of time. One Radio London Night unveiled a group who had just played The Windsor Blues Festival – Cream at the local Starlight venue.

In 1967, I bought two records banned by the Beeb for drug references: "My Friend Jack" by the Smoke and "Granny Takes A Trip" by the Purple Gang. Then there was "Morning Dew" by Episode Six – popular in Europe, but never charted. Episode Six were formed after meeting at Harrow County School (where the author of this book was educated) and included Ian Gillan and Roger Glover as founding members.

I bought "Kensington High Street" by Dead Sea Fruit, because I was working in Kensington High Street. I became a DJ by chance in the early 70s, joining the Harrow branch of a group of social clubs, "18Plus". I was elected to the Committee. A members' drive was needed, so we could hold a disco. I said: "I have records, can supply a turntable, speakers and amp, so can give it a go."

The night was successful. I spent six years as a part-time mobile DJ. Hard work, gigging every Friday, Saturday and midweek. But I just wasn't enjoying the music I was having to play.

Highlight was a gig at Oxhey Community Centre with Marmalade and Radio 1 DJ Dave Lee Travis. Funniest moment, a wedding disco for a friend who'd married a soldier. His army mates were at the reception. The gig was going well, but more people were in the bar than on the dance floor. Then, in walked a policeman, who ordered me to stop playing.

Turned out there had been a riot while I had been playing – it had all kicked off in the bar, which had been smashed up, between the army lads and some bikers – I heard nothing! I packed up the gear – outside resembled a war zone. Ambulances, police cars, vans everywhere. The downstairs bar had broken furniture. The bride was being loaded into an ambulance, the groom and his mates into a police van, the wounded sitting on the pavement being seen to by ambulance crews. I was paid my full fee.

My singles collection ended up with over 1000 45s and 12″ singles, which I still have. I married in the early 90s. My wife, a Springsteen fanatic, collected his records from around the world – and everything the Bay City Rollers recorded. I prefer CDs as they take up less space, but continue to obtain vinyl.

I like a good browse around record shops. Once, at Borderline in Brighton, I got carried away, and started handing my friend CDs. After 10 mins I turned around – he was stacked high with them, and was flabbergasted when I bought all 30. My main choice of music now is blues.

The quest to fill in gaps led me online. I discovered good sources such as Custard Box and Rarewaves. Dutch company Music On Vinyl also list UK record shops that sell their records and there's an American Label called Speakers Corner. I frequent London pubs which play vinyl in the bar.'

Michael's memories reminded me of something a mutual friend, and my best mate, Graham Brown had told me about the ultimate destination of his prized records: 'I am lucky enough to have been in my teens in the 60s. My record collection started at the time of Hendrix, Cream, Led Zepp etc., and my vinyl reflects this, along with others, including Tull, Mayall, Beck, Airplane.

'I was given a tome containing values of the old stuff, and had my records out to find out their potential worth. I mentioned this to elder son Rob. Brought up correctly, he appreciated the music on show. I once took him and his younger brother Chris to our local park, but didn't allow them out of the car and onto the swings until a Santana track finished playing on the car radio! My son's initial reaction was: "Lovely, these records are our inheritance!"'

I tend to prefer frequenting clubs, rather than one of Michael's pubs, so took the opportunity to see one of my ultra-favourite groups in action when the Pretty Things played London's 100 Club, in late 2010. There were 418 paying spectators, setting a new venue record – previously 407, set just an hour and not much more ago – when Paul McCartney had been in action there!

Macca was duly turfed out and the Pretties were set up and playing by 9pm, reprising their debut LP, followed by a second set consisting of most of their *S F Sorrow*, which either is, or never was, depending on where you stand on the subject of such things, the first concept album. It was a terrific, enjoyable gig in an old-school venue, fully appreciated by an enthusiastic audience, including me and Sheila. In hindsight, the music sounded better while we were in there soaking up the atmosphere than it does in the cold light of day on the live album.

IN WHICH WE TAKE A PITT STOP

Like your author, Chris Pitt is a horse-racing aficionado, also affectionate about his vinyl:

'I've still got my vinyl collection from the 60s/70s. The first LP I bought was Love's *Forever Changes* in 1967. Still an all-time favourite.

I bought Santana's *Abraxas* at a record shop in Blackpool, the only time I ever visited that seaside town. The Isley Brothers' "Highways of My Life" reminds me of Peterborough, and "The Wombling Song" reminds me of Stourbridge – they were forever on the radio when I was working there. *Forever Changes* was certainly the best, although there was some good stuff on *Da Capo* and *Four Sail*. I regret not going to see Love when they appeared at a club in Dudley and played *Forever Changes* in its entirety.

One of the best concerts I went to at Birmingham Town Hall was Roy Harper with Judee Sill as support. She led an extraordinary life even by rock star standards and this was her sole British tour.

She died young but subsequently became a bit of a cult figure. Her *Heart Food* album has always been a particular favourite.

Probably the most spellbinding musical evening I had was in the upstairs room of a small, local Harborne pub called The Junction, circa 1990. They held weekly folk nights. This occasion featured ex-Pentangle members Jacqui McShee and John Renbourn. They were on for two hours and were outstanding. After the show, I smuggled my way into their "dressing room" (little bigger than a broom cupboard) where I spent 20 minutes talking with them. I'd brought along their *Cruel Sister* album cover and they both signed it for me. Great memories.'

Chris and I exchanged a few memories of Judee Sill: '"Jesus Was a Crossmaker" was on her first LP, just called *Judee Sill*. It was released as a single, produced by Graham Nash. It's worth googling Judee – you'll see what I mean about her "extraordinary" life.' Chris also revealed: 'My favourite Roy Harper lyric is contained in "Nobody's Got Any Money in the Summer". I can't tell you the precise words he sings, otherwise I'd end up with a threatening letter from legal types and a bill from a copyright owner. Suffice to say, it concerns the under-garment of a scantily clad fighting fellow from China, which has been doused in a kind of unappetising fatty cooking substance.'

IN WHICH COUSIN KIM COMMITS TO VINYL

The experiences of my several years younger cousin Kim Balouch add weight to my feelings that our extended family incorporates a great deal of musical appreciation:

'Records have always meant a lot to me,' began Kim. 'Being a child of the 60s this was not unusual. If you enjoyed music then, you most probably enjoyed music on vinyl. The amazing thing about a record is that you don't just get the music, there's also the experience of the way the record looks and feels, especially with LPs.

The cover art, the track-listing, the stories about the band, the mentions and the little cryptic messages sometimes scratched into the middle part of the vinyl where the grooves end and the label begins. I always felt I'd discovered something really special when I found one of those. Even the smell of a new record, it is a whole experience for all the senses.

The first "proper" record I ever owned was Alice Cooper's "Schools Out", bought for me by older brother Steve; T-Rex, "Metal Guru" and Sparks, "This Town Ain't Big Enough for Both of Us", followed. Before that, my record collection had consisted of a bright orange vinyl EP of *Jungle Book* and a 7-inch reading of the Ugly Duckling, oh, and the incredibly sad theme to the 1969 film *Ring of Bright Water*, sung by Val Doonican. I still can't listen to that song without getting a lump in my throat.

During senior school I fell in love with films and film soundtracks and have quite a few on vinyl: *Grease, Jaws, Star Wars, Close Encounters of the Third Kind* and all the spaghetti western soundtracks. John Williams and Ennio Morricone are favourite composers of mine. I'd listen to the soundtracks without skipping a track, staring at the cover while the luscious sounds filled the room, and I'd relive my favourite films, transported.

As a young teenager I was into disco, and getting US imports on 12 inch. Playing them at home was not so easy, as Dad put our record player, which was ancient, in the cupboard under the stairs, with the speakers in the lounge. Changing the record was a bit of a palaver. So, I used to load up a carrier bag full of records and head to my best friend's house – they had a modern turntable with an automatic record-changing arm.

My partner is a DJ in his spare time and our house is full of vinyl. When we first met, I somehow ended up becoming his "record-monkey", carrying his record bag after he'd played his set. That's not the main reason we got together, but I think he was suitably impressed.

A vinyl record is still something very special to me and holds a

magic that CDs and MP3s just don't. You have to give a record a
bit of commitment; you make a choice about what to listen to, put
it on the turntable, lower the tone arm and then enjoy, devoting
the next hour to listening, and being in the moment.'

IN WHICH I NAME PSYCH'S
HOLY GUITAR TRINITY

Gary Quackenbush of SRC had perhaps the most piercingly high
pitched, amazing guitar tones and feedback of the late 60s – never
better displayed in full glory than on a number of sustained breaks
during 'Black Sheep', the band's first single, released in the UK in
1969, and included on their amazing debut LP, named after the
group, which I played incessantly on its release. SRC stood for Scott
Richardson Case, the first two initials from the name of their lead
vocalist. The band also included Gary's brother Glenn on organ.

As the sleeve-notes to a compilation of SRC's finest declared,
'"Black Sheep" is in many ways the exemplary SRC track – doomy
organ, Anglicised vocals and searing bursts of Gary Quackenbush
magic.' Precisely. They made three LPs, the next two being
Milestones and *Traveler's Tale* – but Gary had left by the third, and
his style was irreplaceable; the group's magic largely departed with
him. He played sessions with various other musicians but never
returned to the spotlight.

The *Detroit News* reported in June 2015: 'Gary Quackenbush,
who came to rock fame as guitarist for the SRC, one of the biggest
bands to come out of Detroit's rock scene in the 60s, died after a
year-long bout with pulmonary fibrosis.' Gary was 67.

San Franciscan Band Quicksilver Messenger Service were
amongst the most influential of psychedelic bands of the 60s
via their eponymous 1968 debut LP, featuring prominently
guitarist John Cipollina, whose growling, prowling guitar made
a remarkable impact. The record featured the astonishing and

climactic 12 minute 7 seconds of 'The Fool', on which John's guitar was intertwined with fellow band member Gary Duncan's. I well remember the absolute spine-tingling effect of my first listen to 'The Fool' and the build-up to the 'hairs-on-the-back-of-the-neck-standing-up' peak of the track.

Cipollina is right up there as a guitar god in my humble. He died in 1989, aged just 45, by which time he had contributed his unique sound to many bands following his departure from QMS in 1971, after which he formed Copperhead, who lasted until the middle of 1974.

Flipping through some records and noticing that I have two copies of the amazing debut LP by Quicksilver Messenger Service, I took a close look at the pair, and decided to play one of them, as I hadn't listened to this seminal psych album for some while. If you've never heard this record and, in particular, 'The Fool', you really owe it to yourself to do so, and if you have – but not for some while – just make the time and let it amaze and regress you to those sunlit days of 1968. You will be glad to have done so.

Glenn Ross Campbell, not, of course, to be confused with the other, nearly identically named but far more famous guitarist and musician, Glen Campbell, sadly no longer with us, but the 'double n' Glenn is, perhaps a little surprisingly given his history and age, alive and well at the time of writing (spring 2024). Born in California in 1946, he first made an impact in psych rock band The Misunderstood, formed in California in the mid-60s, before moving to London where they became artistically influential, but commercially anonymous. They had started under the name The Blue Notes in late 1963, playing surf music. After a few changes, they completed their line up in 1965, changing their name to The Misunderstood under which moniker they were championed by influential DJ John Peel. The 1966 single 'I Can Take You to the Sun' showed what they were about, with a real psychedelic flourish from Glenn's tremulous steely strings, but it failed to find a large audience. The B side, 'Who Do You Love?' would have been a better choice for the A side as it turned out. The band disintegrated in 1967 when they were in London, leaving Glenn to recruit replacement band members. The line-up change also saw an end of their psychedelic style. This didn't result in success.

Another, more drastic, change saw Glenn bring in different musicians and change their name to Juicy Lucy – and almost immediately they found commercial vindication, with his guitar sound zinging through their rearranged version of, would you believe, The Misunderstood's 'Who Do You Love?' which charged rapidly up the charts via Ray Owen's strident vocals and Glenn's dynamic string-picking. It was a more rocky than psych treatment and it captured the attention of the masses, becoming a big hit.

However, after a couple of LPs, the band split, as they hadn't quite managed to retain the early momentum. The name survived through a series of personnel changes, and they continued to produce albums before stopping prior to a later, 90s revival of the name. But Campbell departed early on.

In 1982, Campbell reformed with original Misunderstood singer Rick Brown as The Influence and they recorded a single, 'No Survivors/Queen of Madness'.

The Lost Acetates 1965–67 appeared in 2004, showing again the vigour of the early Misunderstood, but by now too late for commercial acclaim. Campbell's guitar was the highlight of the album but Glenn's name didn't figure amongst the composers of the material and he played on only five of fourteen tracks. Eventually, Campbell moved to New Zealand where, it seems, he remains to this day. Not that I've spotted him on my frequent visits there.

IN WHICH I MAKE ANOTHER
MAGICAL PURCHASE

In Jersey in the second half of 2023, I visited a second-hand emporium in St Helier, R&L Music and Memorabilia Exchange, specialising in LPs and CDs, but on this day with a large selection of singles on display. I flipped through them without spotting

much of interest, until I saw a copy of *Magical Mystery Tour*, the
Beatles' double EP from 1967, with its cover and colour booklet in
excellent condition, and both mono records in place, albeit with a
fair amount of wear and tear, as would be expected. No sign of the
blue lyric sheet which was included on release.

Although I already owned a copy of the MMT in its LP
incarnation, I'd never quite got round to acquiring this one, so
I took the plunge and decided to splash out – adding this set to
the *Buddy Guy & Junior Wells Play The Blues* LP I had spotted, plus
the soundtrack LP from the 60s 'coming of age' film, *Here We Go
Round The Mulberry Bush*, which made a big impression on me at
the time. I already had one copy, but this one had a different and
attractive cover.

I knew there was little point trying to bargain down the price
with the gentleman who owns the shop, as he is a consummate
dealer who seldom allows one to get away with a true bargain.
However, I'd spotted a little 'Three for Two' notice on the shop
window as I came in, and was able to take advantage of the offer
– bringing the bill for my purchases down to two pence light of
60 quid.

For some reason, my credit cards wouldn't work on the in-shop
machine so I dug out three 20 quid notes and handed them over.
He said 'Thanks' and sat there. I stood stock still, waiting for my
change, wondering whether a law had recently been passed in
Jersey that all transactions must be paid in full amounts, with
all change banned – seeing as a restaurant where we had dined a
couple of days earlier had produced a bill ending in, if I remember,
84p, which the waitress handed over and declared, 'I'll round it
up.' Finally getting the message, Mr R&L now reached over behind
the counter, rummaged around and finally produced a coin which
he reluctantly handed over. 'Waste not, want not – that's almost a
tanner in real money,' I said. He was unamused.

A day or so later, I was reading a column by Craig Brown in the
Daily Mail in which he referred to one of the *Magical Mystery Tour*
tracks, 'I Am The Walrus', which includes in its surreal lyrics the
phrase 'Semolina Pilchard', of which I was well aware, but he then
went on to explain that this was believed to be a Lennon reference

to one Norman Pilcher, once head of the Metropolitan Police's drugs squad in the 60s, who targeted not only the Beatles, but also the Stones, Donovan, Eric Clapton and Dusty Springfield. Becoming aware of this link, Pilcher, wrote Brown, boasted: 'I do not know if John Lennon was talking about me but I say to you all... I am the Walrus!'

IN WHICH I'M ON HOLLIEDAY

Having already recently seen the Zombies and the Manfreds in concert, I was eager to discover whether The Hollies could produce a display on a par with those two excellent gigs by a pair of the pop-rock world's longest servers, when five of us took our seats in the Congress Theatre in Eastbourne in late October 2023. To cut a long gig short, NO. They fell well short of the standards set by both Zombies and Manfreds.

The biggest downside was the Hollies' lack of founder and long-term vocalist Alan Clarke. Others who have fronted the group include Swede, Mikael Rickfors, who sang on the excellent single 'The Baby', and former Move man, the late Carl Wayne. The current incumbent, Peter Howarth, who was enthusiastic, has been in place for a good few years, and was usually in tune but somehow never felt a natural fit – mea culpa, of course.

I was miffed, too, that their first number was a quite uninspired take of their classic psych track 'King Midas in Reverse' and for me they never really nailed it after that. Not even when they played the same song twice, once with the hit arrangement and again with a different arrangement – which seemed a little pointless as it would surely be better to go the whole hog and make the second version completely different with different tune, lyrics and title.

Originals Tony Hicks and Bobby Elliott both had a couple of brief chats with the audience – the latter telling a story without a punchline which, he told us, could be found in his book, which, surprise, surprise, was available at the merchandise stall where they were also offering, by all accounts, an LP of their best-known material, but without the vocals of their best known lead singer. I neither joined an orderly queue nor had the slightest interest in purchasing a copy. Nor will I be going to any of their future gigs. But, in the interests of fairness, I must report that their performance was given a standing ovation by perhaps three quarters of the audience (those still capable of standing, that is, of course).

Oh, and my friend Di, who was there, said she saw Tony Blackburn in the auditorium.

Being in Eastbourne, which I've always regarded as Brighton's somewhat smaller sister, I was aware of record outlets in the town. Sheila was anxious to do a little early Christmas shopping and for me to accompany her, which did restrict my ability to view vinyl. I managed to persuade her to accompany me into the 'Retro Remake' record section of a shop known as 'Emporium' where I spotted a reissue of the 1968 LP *English Rose* by Fleetwood Mac. I showed Sheila the back cover photo of the group members, including Peter Green, Jeremy Spencer, Mick Fleetwood and John McVie – 'I saw that line up live,' she told me, once again reminding me that, when she was swanning round attending gigs which she can boast about to this day, I was regularly confined to barracks swotting away for O and A Level qualifications which have done me bugger all good during my working life.

Next day, I read an interview with novelist Ian Rankin in City A.M. in which he was asked what questions he would like to be asked, answering: 'Not enough people ask me "what was the last LP you bought?" [revealing it to be by Edinburgh band Broken Records "who are terrific"] and "what was the last gig you went to?" – answer: Lloyd Cole.'

Sent out to do the weekly shop while Sheila waited for the arrival of carpet fitters who, ultimately, failed to turn up, I was waiting to check out, via a human being rather than a machine, when the husband of the lady whom I had invited to go ahead of me when we both arrived at the same time said: 'Where are you from?' 'I'm a Wealdstone boy,' I said, rather than 'And what the

f*** does it have to do with you?' 'Oh,' he said, 'I'm from Yorkshire.
Did you see The Who at the Railway Hotel in Wealdstone?' 'No,
but I did see Screaming Lord Sutch there,' I told him. He appeared
lost for words.

As I packed the shopping in the boot, it occurred to me that
Sheila would be none the wiser if I nipped over to 'Sounds Of
The Suburbs' for a look-see. So, after working out how to get the
£1 deposit for the shopping trolley back, off I nipped. Tony had
only just opened when I arrived. I explained how I had seized
this small window of opportunity and began flipping through the
vinyl sections I generally investigate. I found a £15 Ten Years After
'unofficial' LP, then glanced down to see an unusual 'Half Price
Sale' note and spotted two very appealing offerings, a Byzantium
LP and another by The Mandrake Memorial – a different one
from the one I recently purchased from Julian at Second Scene
and had to return as I already owned it. They were both formerly
20 quid, but now a mere tenner a throw.

'How do you intend to smuggle them into the house?' probed
Tony.

'Ah, you've spotted the perennial problem. Something will
turn up.'

As I write this, the records are still in the car as I await an
opportunity to sneak them in.

I have just read this online story: 'A small New Zealand city
is the site of a "civil war" over who can play Celine Dion's music
loudest. In the city of Porirua, people drive to a particular spot
and, using siren-type speakers, attempt to play music as loud as
possible.'

EPILOGUE

I was talking to a man who sells music memorabilia, who was explaining to me what it meant to him, and how he felt when he managed to acquire a piece of memorabilia relating directly to his late teens. It suddenly struck me that he was actually expressing exactly what I felt about collecting records from the most crucial and influential part of my life.

In my case, it was about accepting that part of the reason, initially, may well have been to disguise the fact that I often felt awkward, had a lack of confidence, was not convinced that I belonged in certain places. So, to convince myself and others, I decided to create a collection to hide behind. Record-collecting is, and doubtless always will be, a changing practice.

Not, though, for me – nor for the majority of those circa my age. We're hardly likely to change our habits now. But we're the ones who now have a few quid of disposable income, having worked hard for many a long year to accumulate it, and deciding now that if we don't start buying those things we've always fancied but never previously quite been able to afford, or justify doing so – we never will.

Record-collectors of my vintage tend to be patient types. We know we almost certainly won't find that elusive psychedelic single from 1967 today, but are prepared to keep searching (sorry, Del Shannon reference) in the hope that one day...

But while I'm still scouring the racks for late 60s/early 70s treasure, I'm well aware that time is running out to find it – not that I don't already have more than I could probably manage to listen to before I expire, even if I started now and kept going for years, without ever repeating a record.

However, I do now see other, often much younger record shop browsers successfully locating what they're looking for, even though I may not recognise the records they depart clutching, or the artistes performing on them.

Whether the gradual dying out of my generation will ultimately result in records currently valued in the high three-figure brackets by *Rare Record Price Guides* losing their value dramatically remains to be seen. But their equivalents from the days when vinyl went almost fatally out of fashion, and possibly in danger of going the way of the twist, the video recorder and many other technological flashes in the pan, will, I'm sure, emerge as desirable purchases in their own right.

So, I for one genuinely hope, the vinyl circle which sparked record-collecting initially will have gone FULLY round and begun to spin yet again for yet more generations.

*

AND A FINAL KING GREAT FOOTNOTE

It was revealed in September 2023 that horror writer Stephen King's wife Tabitha had threatened to leave him – not for writing too many scary stories, but for playing the song, 'Mambo No 5' too frequently.

'Oh yeah, big time,' 75-year-old Mr King told *Rolling Stone* magazine. 'My wife threatened to divorce me. I had the dance mix. I loved those extended-play things, and I played both sides of it. And one of them was just total instrumental. I played that thing until my wife just said:

"One more time, and I'm going to f*****g leave you.'"

We've all been there, Stephen... we really have!

AFTERWORD

IN WHICH I CREATE A COMPILATION
OF DISC-USSIONS

JONATHAN CHARLES – Former news presenter for BBC World News:

'A magical moment... the sound of needle hitting grooves of a 7 or 12 inch record. Those first few scratchy seconds before the music begins symbolise why I love vinyl – imperfect but beautiful... like life.'

ROBERT COOPER – Bob's your vinyl uncle:

TV racing broadcaster Bob Cooper is a true vinyl man, with a collection satisfyingly into three figures. Robert told me, 'Not a vast collection, but my most important possession – not including children. I've loved records since my brother, seven years older, produced a Dansette and a stack of singles – Elvis, Anka, Donegan, Cliff, Chubby, Buddy. I was a huge Bobby Darin fan. My most embarrassing moment was going to James Dace record shop in Chelmsford, with Dad. He'd forgotten the title and started singing, "Jack", not '"Mac(k)" the Knife'. Now I like Chris Thile, a US mandolin player (solo, Nickel Creek and The Punch Brothers), Gillian Welch and Dave Rawlings, The Delines (fronted by Willy Vlautin), also top notch (Lean on Pete).' Robert announced his retirement from his TV racing role in June 2024 – quite possibly in order to spend more time with his vinyl!

GEOFF COX – Tulls me about it:

'My love affair with Jethro Tull's music began at Dunstable Grammar School in the late 60s,' reveals Geoff Cox. 'Lunchtimes accompanied by the sounds of Hendrix, Cream, The Who, Fleetwood Mac. One of the boys played the first album by bluesy band Tull – I was hooked. I became a junior reporter on the *Luton News* and discovered that the group were launched in the town. Ian Anderson and Glenn Cornick were joined by local lads Mick Abrahams (guitar) and Clive Bunker (drums). I wrote about Tull for the paper, buying all their albums.

In the 60s, Anderson lived in a grotty bedsit in Studley Road, Luton. He was upstairs, Cornick down. So poor, they shared a can of Irish stew every day. Anderson walked around town with a lampshade on his head and worked as a cleaner at the ABC Cinema, albeit often sitting, writing songs, rather than cleaning. One of his jobs was cleaning the toilets. When he quit, he took an old, chipped urinal from the storeroom and kept it.'

JOE CRILLY – Worked for me in the William Hill Press Office:

'Music was a formative part of my early life. My uncle took me for a spin in his vintage MG, top down, blasting Green Day's "Dookie". I was eight, and transformed! When I was 16, an album was released that changed my life – Thrice's *The Artist in the Ambulance*. I was bought the original edition by a girlfriend. We spent the summer listening to that album on repeat before seeing them. At university in Leicester, there was a rock night at the bar, Fanclub, frequented by the weird and wonderful – including myself. I entered with a friend. Thrice's "Staring at the Sun" came on, and it is one of my most vivid memories. I was so excited.

I don't seek out new stuff because I have all the memories and truth of what helped to shape me.'

JOHN DARWELL – Photographer (www.johndarwell.com):

'I bought a new copy of Pink Fairies' *Kings of Oblivion* to replace a clapped-out original, but after an hour trying to get the record and poster out of the sleeve, where someone had managed to glue them in, in a fit of pique I tore the sleeve in half... I'll probably never play it ever again as I feel so guilty.

My first record was "Cracklin' Rosie" by Neil Diamond, in 1970. I was 14. The second, "Black Night", by Deep Purple, completely changed how I thought about music. I started to delve into albums; spent weekends haunting local record shops, one run by Janice. I would spend hours there. Janice became a friend and mentor, and would discount the records.

I bought *On the Road* by Traffic. I took it back, stating I hated the music. Janice refused to accept it, unless I promised to listen to it again at least three times to understand the subtleties of the music. I still have it.'

BILLY EDWARDS – Billy's bug (@biiilyedwards):

'I caught the vinyl bug four years ago, as a secondary-school student', Billy confesses. 'Second-hand records are ten times more curious than something just off the factory line. Each with a personal history. My most ruminated question: who was the previous owner? What joy it is to clean, and care for, a record. These criteria bring an elation that returns each time you put that record on. I'm pleased to look after them, a mere custodian of such treasured artefacts.'

CHRIS GIBBS – Chris-is:

'Things have changed somewhat' admits Chris Gibbs, ruefully. His bijou second-hand record shop in South Harrow closed in 2019, due to 'needing a regular income. I had a relationship with records akin to one with drugs or alcohol. I kept so much that came through the doors that I wasn't making the best living. I now have a more zen-like attitude to my collection. Only want what means something to me or will be useful if playing out. I miss the customers'.

MARC HENSHALL – Of 'Sound Matters', 'a vinyl record website for the digital age':

'Vinyl records are arguably more beautiful than CDs, offering more opportunities for artistic expression. The successful resurgence of vinyl is an analogue revolution many didn't see coming. Why do generations who never grew up with vinyl now part with their money in exchange for music they can source for almost nothing? Quite simply, they are desirable items – beautiful and artistic. The great tradition of creative and artistic expression through the vinyl medium continues, and complements the digital age. A prime example, art-driven record club releases from Vinyl Moon. By viewing the cover through a smartphone app, an entire cover comes to life with live animation, neatly uniting analogue and digital realms.'

LAYNE PATTERSON – Fellow Wealdstone supporter:

'Sometime in 1981, a mate called to see if I fancied going to watch a film, *Quadrophenia*. I hot-footed it to "Our Price" to seek out the musical version of this masterpiece. There were two versions – the original 1973 LP, and a soundtrack.

I bought both. The soundtrack got the most play. That first £4.99 cost me a lot more over the years! I have a large Who collection, various copies of *Quadrophenia*, umpteen rereleases on various vinyl colours, and a mint condition promo-copy gifted to me years ago by the author of this book – even one my son rescued from a skip.'

@Primarily_Prog – aka Phil, has his say:

'Outside family, the most important thing in my life is prog rock. It's been ever-present in my life, and never let me down. If I had to select one performer I rate live above any other, it would be the irreplaceable Keith Emerson. He was electrifying to watch. I find it so sad that his often-troubled mind couldn't appreciate how much he meant to those who loved the genre, no matter how much his ageing hands would eventually affect his ability to play fast and fluently.'

BARRY SHARPE – Author's several-years younger little brother:

'Growing up, I had to walk across my older brother's bedroom to get to mine. At a certain age, I noticed a collection of vinyl beneath the window in his room. Curiosity got the better of me. I would stop and flick through the growing collection. Although the memory is hazy, I MAY have taken one or two to my parents' "stereogram".

As I started working, I bought a hi-fi, went to gigs, clubs and discos. The Isley Brothers, Johnny Guitar Watson joined my collection. Once, hearing "Bridge of Sighs", Mum asked who the singer was? "James Dewar." She grudgingly admitted enjoying hearing his singing voice. I look out for record and charity shops. I recently visited my nearest shop, told him what I was looking for. He searched Discogs. "Plenty of copies here," he said. "Yes, but that wouldn't give me the same elation as finding it myself."'

SIMON TONGUE – The case for CDs:

'I'm an avid music collector. Without meaning to offend Graham, a man of a few fewer years, which enabled me to befriend his son at school and for 30 years since, share a love of music that started in the grubby world of heavy metal and expanded into many genres. Vinyl has seen a comeback, but the CD is left in the wilderness. Seems unfair. In a "proper" record shop, you will often see rows of records proudly displayed, yet have to hunt in a dark corner for CDs. For my generation (90s kids), CD was the go-to music format. It sounded great in a different way to vinyl, lasted forever, you could skip tracks (amazingly some bands couldn't write 14 killer songs!).

CD was the last format people bought before the internet changed everything and deserves a place in every record store. It saddens me to see them unloved at five for 50p in charity shops when vinyl by the same artist fetches big money.

The CD generation still enjoy collecting music. Some progressed to vinyl, some to getting everything for free, but a fair few stuck to what got us here in the first place. The CD deserves its place in the hearts of even the most vinyl of vinyl readers.'

MARK WOODHAMS – Mark my words... the former keeper in a football team your author once managed:

'I used to love the Steve Gibbons Band. I was in a record shop in Northampton. I picked out one of his albums, and turned to tell my mate how good it was – when the bloke next to me giggled. My mate said, "This gentleman doesn't think so." I did a double take and said – "I think he should, he wrote the songs... Hello, Mr Gibbons!"

I already had the LP, so didn't buy it again. But I went for a few beers with him. Really cool bloke.'

RECORD SHOP ROUND-UP

I sent a questionnaire to a number of randomly chosen record shops, with the first question to all of them – are you a Record Shop or Record Store?

CASBAH RECORDS, Liverpool

Thoughts of boss, Tony Davis: Record Shop, ('store too American').

'I've run the shop since it opened in Feb 2008. Started buying and selling records on Greenwich market back in the mid-80s. Neutral about the future, because of rising price of wholesale vinyl – already pricing some sections of society out of the market. I blame the "majors". Late picking up on the revival, now block-book pressing plants, charge the earth. Seem intent on destroying their own business.

Business is 60–65% male.

One of my oddest customers once butted into a conversation in the shop about ancestors and announced he was related to King George III.

A customer aged 13–14 came in with her dad. She was so excited. Only had £15, but spent time talking to me about the music she liked, carefully selected some bargains, and was genuinely ecstatic at what she found.

I believe in encouraging women into the shop. We've always employed girls to work with us. Female customers feel at ease.

They're not going to have things "mansplained" by a middle-aged music snob.

One of my favourite customers was 15 when she started buying records. Got a job with us, went to college, came back to work for us for another couple of years – before landing a job as a radio producer.

Said she liked us because we took her seriously and had other women working here. That was rewarding.'

DD MUSIC GEEK, Lowestoft, Suffolk

Dave Dangerfield: 'DD Music Geek started in 2019 from humble beginnings. Took the leap, armed with my small savings; put it into stock, selling at local markets, on eBay and Discogs. Took premises at Oulton Broad after Covid.

"Record SHOP", "store" tends to be more American.

Vinyl is popular. I'm sure it will continue to be so for foreseeable future. Cost of living crisis having major impact on where sales would normally be.

Noticed increase in CD sales around November 2022. Not sure will reach heights of vinyl.

Enthusiasts continue to buy preloved records, although they are, naturally, harder to cater to as they are often after rarer titles. "Younger generations" coming in for vinyl – they will buy both preowned and reissued. Had more requests for new releases and current albums – something I am now growing.'

DERRICKS MUSIC, Swansea
WWW.DERRICKSMUSIC.CO.UK

'I am Christos Stylianou. We began trading in Port Talbot in 1956 (closed in the 80s), and in Swansea since 1968. Original shop opened by uncle, Derrick Evans. Upon passing of grandfather, who also had a shop in Port Talbot, mother opened a second record shop in Port Talbot in 1961. Mother decided to open in Swansea in 1968 on the present site.

Then had shops in Swansea and Port Talbot, till Derrick

passed away in early 80s – fell to me to carry on the business to this day, in Swansea.

There are people who have never stopped collecting CDs with us and have never made the change to vinyl – room for both.

Older customers tend to buy new on CD or vinyl for quality of new product, younger market buy new.

I would say about 60/40% male.

Have had people with us for a long time to the point we have customers' children, who have had children, still coming in.

We think we are the oldest record shop in the UK that is still in the same family.

Final plea – "buy new", as this will keep the record companies willing to keep the whole thing going.'

586 RECORDS, Gateshead

'Open for nine years, seven in Newcastle and two in Gateshead. Optimistic about future of record shops! That's what keeps you out in all weathers and locations, looking for records to share with others. We sell records only. Price of new releases becoming obscene. Financially, younger WhatsApp and record collectors are what keeps shop ticking over. Around 80% of customers male.'

[Lack of communication with customer meant he was repeating where he was from when I asked him – like a Two Ronnies sketch. (He was from Surrey.) "Where are you from?" "Surrey" "I asked where you were from" "Surrey"... You get the idea.]

'My personal collection is about 5,000 records.

Record shops are vital part of community. I believe more should be done to support them with better options on rent and grants.'

FUTTLE, Fife

Stephen Marshall runs the place with partner Lucy Hine.

They sell 'mainly collectible old records and new material either from folk that we know or bands that drop by to play, or things we really want to stock'.

Only open at weekends, don't sell online, look askance at Record Store Day.

Records are sold in same space as their brewery, in which they 'make a small range of seasonal, organic beers in former stable block outside St Monans, in beautiful East Neuk of Fife. Opened in May 2019, somehow still going. I think record shops are essential to the human race. I've been in a lot of record shops, and they perform the same role everywhere – they're a place for the disenfranchised to feel safe and inspired'.

Started collecting records in 1989, aged 13. Don't stock any new reissues, only old pressings and new releases by independent artists. Probably 90% of customers male.

Don't put any records online. 'I love when someone comes from one of the cities and gets something like Judee Sill which they wouldn't find because city shops put good stuff online.'

GIBERT DISC, Paris
Philippe Marie:

'I am optimistic about the future of record shops, and of vinyl – have been running shop for 35 years. I think CDs have mounted a comeback in a similar way to vinyl. Vinyl revival has been driven by established enthusiasts continuing to buy "preloved" record and "new" reissues; and by younger audience buying contemporary vinyl. 70% of customers male.

A guy buying an Elton John Japanese CD asked me whether Elton was singing in Japanese on it...!'

NOTHING VENTURED VINYL, SOUTHSEA

Alex Cave owns and runs record shop and website: 'Have always been a vinyl collector. Vinyl records have unique sound quality that's unparalleled, warmer, more organic compared to digital music. Sound richer, more detailed, and with depth that can't be replicated with the digital format. When you hold a vinyl record, you are holding a piece of history, sometimes a very small run of a pressing which is never recreated.

I love the record shop experience. Place where like-minded music lovers can connect with other music lovers. When I visit a record shop, I know I am among individuals sharing my passion for music.

Made redundant from long-term job. Used redundancy money to buy large collection of records and started selling online from 2015. Started to take it more seriously when I bought huge collection in 2019. Quit job, opened shop called Nothing Ventured Vinyl in March 2019. Stock niche collection of genres as well as record and music-related books, record bags, and "merch". Best thing about Nothing Ventured Vinyl is friendships I've made and growing relationships as by-product of meeting many new lovers of vinyl.'

PHOENIX SOUNDS, Newton Abbot, Devon

Answers from Roger Cox, assisted by Lisa Scattergood:

'We prefer description "Music Store" as this incorporates all formats. Have been part of Newton Abbot Community for 20 years. Owned Phoenix Sounds since 1 July 2022.

Very optimistic about future of music stores and vinyl records. Although prices of vinyl have risen dramatically, having introduced our second-hand section, we can weather the storm.

CDs and vinyl will always be around. There is still the joy of holding something tangible.

Vinyl revival driven by combination of people buying new and second-hand. Customers come in for a new release, browse second-hand and buy a greater selection.

Mix of male and female in store buying vinyl.

Sunny afternoon in Newton Abbot. Man walks up to counter, puts Building Society book in front of me. Wants to withdraw £50. Jackie points out this is a music store and not the building society. He'd failed to notice music playing despite walking past CDs and vinyl!

Woman came into shop: "I'm looking for something. Not sure of the name, or who sings it, but it sounds like this...La La La, La La La"!!!

Music in all formats should be played, loved, and cherished. Collecting vinyl is good, but to not play it is a real shame.'

RAREKIND RECORDS, Brighton

A real world record shop specialising in Hip Hop, Funk, Soul, Reggae:

'Rarekind has been open in different forms for 20 years. Originally a graffiti gallery and supplies shop that also sold records. In the current building as just record shop for some 15 years.

Independent shops face tough time, and I include record shops in that. State of world economically is major reason. I'm concerned about record and record-collecting too – prices of records have become really expensive – both new, and collectable second-hand. I'm naturally quite pessimistic, but increased interest in records has already gone on longer than I imagined. Think demise of CDs was probably overestimated – at one point they made up almost all music sales. I think CDs will continue to be a format that's of interest.

Some people have got back into buying records or started buying for first time, lots of older people never stopped collecting. We have lots of younger customers, 18–30. Probably a good 75% of customers male. I am trying to keep my collection under control, and have got rid of a lot over the years – still collecting, though. I still feel the need to own music I really like on record... not much beats the experience of looking for records – walking into a shop with no agenda and seeing what you can find, or digging at a record fair, it's exciting!'

RECORD CAFÉ, BRADFORD
@therecordcafe, www.therecordcafe.co.uk

Answers by Keith Wildman:

'Been here since November 2014. Optimistic in long term. Price increases may put people off, but whole new generation excited by buying albums on vinyl. CDs more practical than vinyl, and only real option for anyone who wants their music on a portable physical format.

Vinyl revival initially driven by enthusiasts, but now see more younger people buying, or being bought, vinyl. Business is 50/50 male/female.

I started off on cassettes. Then got a turntable. Was buying albums from late 80s to early 90s. When I started driving, switched back to cassettes to play them in my mum's Nova. Then she got car with CD player, so I switched. Returned to records in the mid-00s when I bought turntable and started DJ-ing.'

THE RECORD DECK BARGE

Answers by Luke Gifford. Check Luke's movements here: https://therecorddeckuk.wordpress.com/

Luke Gifford launched The Record Deck in 2014, feeling he'd had enough of his college librarian job. Not just that – his London rent was rapidly rising. Came up with drastic and daring alternative life, deciding on a watery vinyl journey on The Record Deck barge, travelling around the UK selling vinyl from canals and riversides.

'I get most of my stock from the people I meet. People like the idea of their records being redistributed around the country on a boat. They even mention that they'll come to me because they want their records to end up in other places.

Demand is still there, but perhaps it's a more crowded scene than nine years ago, more shops vying for people's trade and more looking for stock. Unlikely CDs could mount vinyl-style revival. Vinyl revival is total mix, many young collectors really into old stuff and hugely knowledgeable. 80 per cent of customers male.'

Asked Luke about oddest/favourite customer-related stories: 'Those which remain in my mind – sometimes negative things like a customer trying to gazump me by buying a collection that I'm talking to someone about when open, that's actually happened twice, bit rude. Shows how competitive it can be I suppose.

Being on the canal we've had a couple of records go for a swim, some kids chucked a first press Ziggy over the roof and into the canal. Think I'd have preferred a theft to wanton destruction. Social side is important, many regulars have become good friends.

My own collection fluctuates, it'll get a bit big and I'll put a chunk for sale in the shop. Try and keep it small, maybe 500 interesting bits.'

RED WOLF RECORDS

Answers by Russell Potton:

'Got into selling vinyl records following new-found love for the sound of vinyl. Heard friend playing something on vinyl, couldn't believe clarity and depth of sound compared to digital formats, so got my own turntable, amp and speakers and set about building my own collection. After buying records from auctions, I had a number left over not to my taste. After investigation, I found some had value. Started looking at ways to sell them to other music lovers.

Started selling at local car boot sale, progressed to conversation with manager of local market in Leighton Buzzard. Agreed to have a stall one Saturday a month and I loved it!

Decided I wanted more ways of selling, so contacted organiser of Leighton Buzzard Record Fair, booked table at next event. Regular dealers at local fairs are helpful, and supportive.

Good to become part of a community passionate about music. There was always a friendly face that was happy to help out the newbie!

So far, I've sold at Leighton Buzzard, Lincoln and Letchworth Record Fairs.

One of the things I like about fairs is interaction with customers. Good to hear how music sparks memories with them. Also surprising how many tell me they gave away vinyl collection years ago and are now rebuying!'

SKELETON RECORDS, Birkenhead

Ben Savage explains why his customers are far from being middle-aged and bearded:

'Customer named Tim once wrote of the shop:

Skeleton Records has a long history, opened by John Weaver in 1971 – as a patchouli-scented 'Head' shop that specialised in rare imports, underground press and hippy paraphernalia. The name of the shop was apparently taken from the lyrics of a Syd Barrett song, 'Skeleton Kissed to the Steel Rail'.

We're definitely a "shop," "store" sounds too transatlantic. Trading for over 50 years, having been founded in August 1972 by two blokes called John. Until he recently passed away, local legend John Weaver ran the shop from the beginning, through five decades of trading. Having worked under John since a disastrous attempt to be a teacher ended in me fleeing the county of Northumberland, the burden of keeping the place open fell to me.

Reasonably neutral about the future – there has been a fair amount of bandwagon-jumping of late, as vinyl is currently en vogue. These will leave as soon as trends change. Record industry has been trying as hard as possible to price buyers out of purchasing new vinyl by jacking the prices up at every opportunity. The price of a new LP from Warner/Universal has gone up by an average of £10 since 2020 and that's especially difficult when your shop is in an income-deprived area.

I foresee shops which only deal in new vinyl struggling in not-too-distant future. We fortunately still do most of our business in second-hand vinyl and CDs!

I'm in my late mid twenties. Started buying vinyl in 2008 because it was cheap and I couldn't afford CDs. You could walk into local second-hand record shop (mine being this one) and walk away with an armful of LPs for ten quid – nobody wanted them. The physical experience of playing vinyl is very immersive. No other format can match the joy of flicking through a pile of LPs, enjoying the cover art, sitting through the crackles and turning it over halfway through. There's plenty of rare, interesting music on CD that's yet to make it to vinyl. To begin with, the vinyl revival was down to young people, who got into vinyl because it was cheap. Without that interest, the record companies wouldn't have bothered to reissue anything at all!

That moved on to it being a bit of a fad, and the days of it being the cheap option are long gone. Many older people have got back into vinyl. We have a large number of regular customers who have been coming to us for a very long time. Their tastes haven't changed; they just want good music at a decent price.

John's (Weaver) personal favourite story was attempting to serve another customer while being repeatedly nagged by a small gentleman, asking did he want some jazz. He went almost apocalyptic when it turned out he was selling Jazz aftershave! My own record collection is well into the thousands, I have no idea exactly how many. I need a bigger house. John's final words on the subject: "If hipsters and small children would stop using the word 'vinyls', I'd be forever indebted!'"

SOUNDS OF THE SUBURBS, Ruislip Manor

Tony Smith, carpenter-turned record shop owner, who held his 60th birthday bash at London's 100 Club – his favourite live music venue, in 2022. Asked 'What do you dislike?' in an interview, in which he named his musical influences as the John Peel radio show, *Record Mirror*, and *Sounds*, Tony spoke for many of us from the, er, senior generations when he answered: 'The new generation calling records vinyls is one that springs to mind.' Had run shop for seven years in June 2023.

'Neutral on the future, although there is a so-called vinyl revival. I've been selling right through the CD years, did record fairs for 25 years, and I think there will always be a market for it, with some of the newer converts dropping off. CDs will always be saleable, but will not make as high a comeback as vinyl.

Probably 70% male customers.

Recently, a youngster returned a 12″ copy of 'World in Motion' by New Order, complaining that it sounded funny. I played it in the shop, sounded fine. Apparently, he had tried to play it at 33rpm, and had no idea at all that there were different speeds. There is no greater job in the world, I also put on bands in the shop to promote new releases; this helps encouraging new people into the shop.'

SOUNDS ORIGINAL, South Ealing (closed down in June 2024)

Demonstrating music's powerful healing qualities in South Ealing, explains Paul Green:

'I suppose I prefer record "shop" to "store", simply because that's the English terminology, but store is OK too. Not too keen on the word "vinyls", though, when referring to records. I always think of those lino tiles that were fashionable in the 60s and 70s. My shop is in its fortieth year, but second location.

I feel it is likely that the resurgence in people buying reissues, which in many cases cost more than the originals, will decrease, but shops selling only second-hand records will always be around. As for CDs making a comeback, I think it is already happening, but not to the same extent of the so-called vinyl revival. I don't believe in a compact cassette revival, though, but if there is one I'll blow the dust off those I've had stored at the back for years.

About 85 per cent of my customers are male, but a few years ago it was 100 per cent. I would say the biggest noticeable change in record-collecting over the last few years has been the increase in female collectors. My own record collection is small, but select. Mostly rock 'n' roll, R&B LPs and EPs.'

Paul flattered me by saying: 'Good taste, btw, with your first 45 being Duane Eddy. My first 45 was Elvis's "It's Now or Never", but I always preferred the B side.' [Editor's note: I had a look at Discogs, which indicated that the 1960 UK B side to this track was 'Make Me Know It' but that the US version had 'A Mess of the Blues' as a B side.]

Paul also recalled: 'Queuing to get in The Railway Hotel, Wealdstone, on my one and only visit, to see Joe Tex who was my favourite soul singer at the time. However, he had a previous gig the same evening at the Cue Club in Paddington, which he apparently liked so much that he stayed there all night. I never saw Joe, but at least I can say I went to the famous Railway Hotel, even if it was just to hear records.'

Paul was planning to close his shop in mid 2024, but told me he was intending to sell online from home.

VINYLUCKY, Singapore

I'm very grateful to Idris, who responded to my queries from 'Singapore's premier location for fine quality, hard-to-find LPs, 12" singles. The shop is at No 1, Coleman St, The Adelphi, Unit #B1-42, Singapore.'

'The shop has been in existence since September 2009. I am optimistic about the future. More young people are getting into vinyl as a "curiosity", "cool factor" and following trends.

I think CDs will always be around. It's cheap. Convenient and high quality.

The vinyl revival's been driven by a combination of established enthusiasts continuing to buy "preloved" records, also buying "new" reissues and by a younger crowd who tend to buy newer music. 95 per cent of our customers are male – a guy came in and thought we were selling Laser Discs. Probably just woke up from a long sleep from the 80s.

I have about 8000 LPs in my personal collection.

This is the best time to be collecting vinyl records as there are way too many choices and selections to get lost in. With the convenience of the internet, finding a particular title or rarity has become ever so much easier.'

VINYL & VINTAGE, Wolverhampton

Claire Howell with the answers:

'Mine is a Record Shop and definitely not a Vinyl shop or even Vinyls!!! I hate that!

I have owned Vinyl and Vintage for 11 plus years, but also traded as It's For You Music.

In Wolverhampton, the city is undergoing major road works and redevelopment, so trade has been a challenge. When the Councillor for Wolverhampton states that he doesn't want "Retail" in Wolverhampton, your heart sinks just a little bit further! So... more coffee shops and restaurants but nowhere else to go? Madness!

I love what I do, if you own a record shop you should have

some affiliation with collecting, or at least music, to relate to your customers.

Whilst we do have new vinyl, I get a bigger "kick" out of selling second-hand records and memorabilia.

Going back to old-school shops, for me, is where it's at, with wonderful picture discs, limited editions and original pressings. I will stay until it becomes financially unviable, and my "want" would be that I sell the shop on to another aspiring record shop owner, once I retire.

I don't stock new CDs, unless requested by customers, but second-hand CDs do ok. People do like a physical item and, if it only costs a few pounds, why download if you can own?

Old vinyl junkies like me still like originals, but plenty out there are seduced by the 15 different versions of, say, the latest Ozzy LP. I'm not into that.

Youngsters love to rummage in our shop for old records as well as new. Whether it be an 80s Led Zepp pressing or a £1 single, there is still something for everyone, small or larger budget.

75 per cent, I should say, are male customers; a good percentage of male customers collect one genre, or even just one artist.

Daily there are extraordinary happenings in the shop – most of which I just can't repeat!

Biggest bugbear is the smell – please, please shower and wash your clothes. I have a lot of great customers, even some kind enough to bring me in treats.

I buy records I like not just for investment, although it's nice when they do increase in value. I have some records that are no longer popular, and worth a fraction of what I paid for them... that's life – you get enjoyment out of them.

I do RSD for my customers, but the cost of the records has increased so much that I debate about continuing; I am disillusioned with pressings released on the day that have been out multiple times before, now a different colour or sleeve.

Seeing some customers just once a year does not help our business in the long term and not being able to save items for those customers that support us weekly is frustrating.

Please don't play valuable records on a £30 suitcase-style new record player – they are just about OK for very cheap records, and mostly 45s. When I sold an original Metallica record, costing £50, only to be told "it doesn't play" on his £30 record player – what do you expect?! It had a 5 inch platter, allowing the vinyl to bend and stylus to skip and skate across the vinyl. Told him to stop buying records for a month or two and save up for a "Rega" or "Project" – not good for short-term business, but I hope he'll be back, and when he makes further purchases will actually enjoy listening to them.'

WHITELABEL RECORDS, Jersey

As I like to do when I visit the island, I'd been buying vinyl records in Jersey – Mal White came to our hotel to deliver the items I'd chosen. He also updated me on his vinyl background:

'I started working in record shops in Jersey back in 1991, at a shop called The Compact Disc Centre.

They had 2 music shops, CDC and Lady Jayne records. Punks, skins, mods, teds, rockers would congregate there. Never much trouble, although it would kick off every now and again. After a few years at CDC an opportunity arose to go and work at Seedee Jons, the best record shop in the islands, John knew his stuff – customer service was second to none.

This is when my love of dance music started. No one catered for local DJs so we dipped our toes in that market and it went from strength to strength. HMV moved to the island. To fight fire with fire, we moved premises and went toe to toe. We stood our ground, but other shops didn't fare as well. The island lost great shops and wonderful, knowledgeable staff.

In 2002, I opened Whitelabel Records. A shop dedicated to local DJs. Fourteen years later, I moved online. Those 14 years were some of the best times. Business was booming, but as technology reared its head, DJs moved from vinyl to CDs then from CD to midi controller. Dance sales on vinyl began to slow down. I knocked the dance vinyl on the head and went down the LP route. Whitelabel Records was no more. I did try and open a shop in my garage – equipment and vinyl – but it didn't work so I went online, opened up a Discogs shop.

Now, I buy back the 12″s I sold then. It's what I know, and I'm happy the way things ended up. Would I do it again? Too bloody right I would, but slightly differently...' Mal handed me a few copies of a sampler record of up-and-coming Jersey-based bands to take to the mainland to distribute. Some good stuff on it, too.

(Record shops I recommend in Jersey, are See Dee Jons, Music Scene and R&L... all worth visiting in St Helier.)

POSTSCRIPT

Springtime, 2024. At a loose end, I spot an H12 bus coming along the road. I jump on, and travel up to Harrow to check out the charity shops. Slim pickings. I'm never going to pay ten pounds for a grubby New Seekers' LP, for sure – and as for compilation CDs at a fiver a throw, when elsewhere outlets are selling them at ten for a quid – no chance.

On a whim, I enter the local 'tube' station and note that a train to Chesham is due in three minutes. I board, and half an hour later disembark there, and walk down to Collectors Paradise in the High Street, a quirky shop run by a quirky gent. As ever, the smallish space is packed with collectables of many kinds – 'early Action Men', 'oriental and unusual items', 'model railways', 'Transformers', 'Toy Planes and Buses', amongst them.

As I enter, the male half of an elderly couple (a little older than myself) is buying an example of the latter, and explaining his potentially fatal ailments to the always upbeat and friendly boss, probably a few years younger than us, who is dispensing medical wisdom to him, answering his phone, directing a delivery man where to leave his packages, whilst chatting with anyone and everyone else, including the glamorous young lady behind the counter, who has a streaming cold.

I move past the large stock of LPs, after a quick flip reveals no immediate must-buys. Today, I'm more interested in his enormous stock of CDs, and quickly spot a box-set compilation of four live CDs of performances by one of my genuinely favourite bands – Quicksilver Messenger Service. The box they are in is slightly creased but the CDs and booklet are spotless.

It bears a price sticker – £12. Fair. But I wonder whether he'll be open to an offer, so I show him, and ask: 'Would you take a tenner?'

He looks sternly at me. 'No...'

That's me put in my place, then.

'... because it is £2.50 – all of the CDs in that section are!'

I'd have happily paid a tenner but am so impressed by his honesty and lack of greed that I then spend another tenner on CDs I wouldn't otherwise have bought.

My faith in human nature – and people who run record shops – has been fully restored.

ACKNOWLEDGEMENTS

Virtually everyone I dealt with, spoke with, overheard, emailed, wrote to, telephoned, listened to, watched, bought from or sold to seemed to be happily involved in record-based matters, and to be very happy for me to be of a like-minded persuasion.

With the possible exception of one objectionable male dealer at a regular, well-known London Record Fair, who dismissed what I thought was a perfectly reasonable offer for a record he owned by The Pretty Things, which had a scruffy, shabby cover. He was abruptly rather rude to me, and completely dismissed my initial bid, leaving me with absolutely no incentive to make a second offer. He was a notable outlier with no apparent empathy – a pure prat amongst overwhelmingly agreeable, friendly folk.

I have to single (double?) out Julian and Helen at Second Scene, the one for refusing to contribute to this book – which didn't stop me recording and recalling a number of his stories – and the other for her regular good humour, and for giving me a profitable evening at Windsor racecourse by telling me which horses to back.

I've regularly made a nuisance – albeit a paying one – of myself in the other record shops closest to my home – Sounds Of The Suburbs, The LP Cafe and the Northwood Jeweller – but always been given a friendly greeting on arrival. They (and, to be fair, the vast majority of others I've visited) have happily provided a welcome 'safe space' for the duration of my visit.

To anyone thinking 'why hasn't he thanked ME?', please feel free to abuse me on my next visit. I obviously deserve it.

This is the follow-up to my gratifyingly well-received *Vinyl Countdown*, whose positive response convinced me that there are very many fellow vinyl addicts out there. I hope you will feel all the better for knowing that you are far from alone in enjoying the envinylment (sorry), which you share with so many like-minded and happily entrapped fellow record collectors.

Keep checking the 'b' sides.

Also available from Oldcastle Books

OLDCASTLEBOOKS.CO.UK/VINYL-COUNTDOWN

●LDCASTLE BOOKS

POSSIBLY THE UK'S SMALLEST
INDEPENDENT PUBLISHING GROUP

Oldcastle Books is an independent publishing company formed in 1985 dedicated to providing an eclectic range of titles with a nod to the popular culture of the day.

Imprints include our lists about the film industry, KAMERA BOOKS & CREATIVE ESSENTIALS. We have dabbled in the classics, with PULP! THE CLASSICS, taken a punt on gambling books with HIGH STAKES, provided in-depth overviews with POCKET ESSENTIALS and covered a wide range in the eponymous OLDCASTLE BOOKS list. Most recently we have welcomed two new sister imprints with THE CRIME & MYSTERY CLUB and VERVE, home to great, original, page-turning fiction.

oldcastlebooks.com

| OLDCASTLE BOOKS	| CREATIVE ESSENTIALS	| THE CRIME & MYSTERY CLUB
| POCKET ESSENTIALS	| PULP! THE CLASSICS	| VERVE BOOKS
| KAMERA BOOKS	| HIGHSTAKES PUBLISHING